The Best
AMERICAN
ESSAYS
2006

The Best
AMERICAN
ESSAYS®
2006

Edited and with an Introduction
by LAUREN SLATER

Robert Atwan, Series Editor

HOUGHTON MIFFLIN COMPANY

BOSTON • NEW YORK   2006

Visit our Web site: www.houghtonmifflinbooks.com.

ISSN: 0888-3742
ISBN-13: 978-0-618-70531-3   ISBN-10: 0-618-70531-7
ISBN-13: 978-0-618-70529-0 (pbk.)   ISBN-10: 0-618-70529-5 (pbk.)

Printed in the United States of America

MP 10 9 8 7 6 5 4 3 2 1

"Kinsey and Me" by Laurie Abraham. First published in *Elle*, January 2005. Copyright © 2005 by Laurie Abraham. Reprinted by permission of the author and *Elle*
magazine. Letters reprinted by permission of the Kinsey Institute for Research in
Sex, Gender, and Reproduction.

"501 Minutes to Christ" by Poe Ballantine. First published in *The Sun*, August
2005. Copyright © 2005 by Poe Ballantine. Reprinted by permission of the author.

"Teaching the N-Word" by Emily Bernard. First published in *The American
Scholar*, Autumn 2005. Copyright © 2005 by Emily Bernard. Reprinted by permis-
sion of the author. "Incident" by Countee Cullen reprinted by permission of GRM
Associates, Inc., agents for the Estate of Ida M. Cullen. From the book *Color* by
Countee Cullen. Copyright 1925 by Harper & Brothers; copyright renewed 1953 by
Ida M. Cullen.

"City Out of Breath" by Ken Chen. First published in *Mānoa*, Summer 2005.
Copyright © 2005 by Ken Chen. Reprinted by permission of the author.

"Beginning Dialogues" by Toi Derricotte. First published in *Creative Nonfiction*,
no. 26. Copyright © 2005 by the Creative Nonfiction Foundation. Reprinted by permission of the Creative Nonfiction Foundation.

"The Culture of Celebrity" by Joseph Epstein. First published in *The Weekly Standard*, October 17, 2005. Copyright © 2005 by Joseph Epstein. Reprinted by permission of the author.

"Whistling in the Dark" by Eugene Goodheart. First published in *The Sewanee Review*, Fall 2005. Copyright © 2005 by Eugene Goodheart. Reprinted by permission
of the author. Lines from "Aubade," "I Have Started to Say," "Sad Steps," "Vers de

Contents

Foreword

I RECENTLY REREAD a novel that made an enormous impression on me when I was eighteen going on nineteen — W. Somerset Maugham's *The Razor's Edge*. I decided to read it again to see why I was so infatuated with the book. Why, after nearly a half-century of being afflicted with what Alice W. Flaherty in her brilliant study *The Midnight Disease* calls "compulsive reading," did I still recall the powerful impact of Maugham's novel? To be sure, I didn't recall many of the details or most of the characters. I remembered only the vaguest plot outline. What stayed with me over the years was the intensity of mood, the way the book had riveted my late-adolescent attention.

Like most impressionable teenagers, I read entirely for content, for moral advice, for a gripping story, for emotional identification. When I learned that Maugham's protagonist, Larry Darrell, spent hour after hour at the library fixated on William James's *The Principles of Psychology*, I had to find that book and read it next. Reading is like that — one book leads to another. The sturdy Dover edition of James, which I still own, turned out to be two hefty and surprisingly inexpensive volumes. I'm sure I didn't read it all at that time, but I got far enough along to see why Larry Darrell was himself engrossed.

In that first encounter with *The Razor's Edge*, I was fascinated by Larry Darrell. Just a year or two older than I, a handsome war hero with a charming manner, an enviable future, and a beautiful fiancée (everything I wasn't and didn't have), he nevertheless renounces all as he pursues an apparently endless quest throughout the world to find truth and meaning. I was fascinated, too, by the power Larry had over others, a power that seemed to derive from an attitude of powerlessness. One moment in the novel astonished me: while sitting in the back seat of the car her husband is driving, the selfish and spoiled Isabel Maturin, now Larry's ex-fiancée, who remains passionately in love with him but whom he's abandoned in favor of his quest, manages to reach a powerful orgasm while staring hypnotically at Larry's wrist and hand stretched along the front seat. And she does this while perfectly immobile, without moving so much as a finger. After reading Laurie Abraham's fascinating essay that opens this collection, I wondered if Alfred Kinsey investigated this phenomenon.

On second reading, I found Larry far less appealing — a total bore, in fact — and I instead enjoyed all the peripheral characters, even those I'd entirely forgotten. One of these, the one that surprised me most on rereading, is the novel's narrator. This person is none other than Somerset Maugham himself, the famous writer, identified as such, complete with references to his previous novels and many biographical details. It's as though instead of bothering to invent Nick Carraway to do the storytelling, F. Scott Fitzgerald claimed himself to be Gatsby's obliging next-door neighbor and narrated the story as if all the events actually occurred during his time on Long Island and all the characters — Daisy, Jordan, Tom, and Jay — spoke directly to the author of the novel. So careful is Maugham about recounting Larry's spiritual journey to the best of his knowledge that he makes it his business always to report the specific sources of his information, lest we think he's making something up or filling narrative gaps with speculative information.

What I never noticed in my first reading is that *The Razor's Edge* is composed entirely as memoir. In the book's opening sentences, Maugham hesitatingly calls it a novel only because he doesn't "know what else to call it." Yet on rereading this book in what we could appropriately term "the age of memoir," I was forced to wonder whether Maugham had met the real Larry and Isabel — as he says he did — at a party in Chicago in 1919. "I have invented nothing," Maugham says at the outset. "To save embarrassment to people still living I have given to the persons who play a part in this story names of my own contriving, and I have in other ways taken pains to make sure that no one should recognize them."

The book's opening section is written in an essayistic fashion, with Maugham carefully explaining his diligent technique and his method of verisimilitude.

By identifying himself in this manner, Maugham invited his numerous readers (*The Razor's Edge* was a spectacular publishing success) to track down the true identities of the book's characters. But though resemblances to actual people can be found here and there, it appears that Maugham did what most novelists do: he constructed his characters out of bits and pieces of many individuals he had encountered or heard about over decades of an active social life.

If we are today concerned about memoirs that may be fictionalized, here is pure fiction in the guise of memoir, fiction that fooled thousands of readers and quite a few reviewers into believing it was based on the true stories of real individuals. That the novel focuses on a young man's search for truth adds a special twist to a narrative technique grounded in deliberate deception. Many novels, of course, are composed as first-person memoirs — the working title of Mark Twain's greatest novel was "The Autobiography of Huck Finn." But Twain did not insert Samuel Clemens directly into the book in order to insinuate that we are reading the memoir of an actual adolescent boy, who happens to be obsessed by lying.

The Razor's Edge wonderfully commingles two popular genres, the novel and the memoir. By doing this, Maugham, who is apparently having fun in the process, makes us aware of how indistinct the boundaries between the two can be. It's nearly impossible to establish internal standards — such as voice, tone, or stylistic features — that help us to easily distinguish one genre from the other. Therefore, if we are curious about the degree of fabrication, we usually need to rely on verifiable external factors — facts, events, people, places and institutions, dates, and so forth. Once the writer begins to disclose concrete or factual information, then other issues come quickly into play. The reader, if so inclined, can use those details to test the writer's veracity or can begin to make inferences that may damage authorial credibility. Records can be discovered that prove someone didn't spend nearly as much time in the Peace Corps as claimed, or was never admitted to a certain psychiatric hospital, or hadn't served as much prison time as reported. According to many accounts, the publishing sensation of 2005, James Frey's *A Million Little Pieces,* was originally widely submitted (and widely rejected) as a novel. It was only when re-purposed as a memoir that publishers jumped.

So anyone writing a memoir (or an autobiographical essay) needs to be careful when recounting verifiable details, or risks being called a liar, a phony, or an opportunist. Take an example: my reference earlier to Isabel Maturin's remarkable orgasm is verifiable (*Razor's Edge,* part one, chapter five), but my account of reading Maugham's novel at eighteen is not. You may accept my word that I actually did read the novel (I'm sure you had no reason to doubt me), but there's not a shred of evidence that could prove I did, and so no one except myself knows whether or not it's true. What would be the point of fabricating such a detail? you might ask. My motive could have simply been to construct a satisfying argument for this foreword. Or perhaps I didn't want to admit that I'd never read a famous book until just recently. (I've frequently heard people say that they were *re*reading *War and Peace, Middlemarch,* or *Moby-Dick.*) Whatever the motive, there's no way to establish whether I am telling the truth or not.

The unverifiable world is vast and accommodating. The classic memoir, in which a celebrated individual offers an account of his or her public life and adventures, along with profiles of the important people encountered along the way, usually depended on verifiable details — at least it is possible to confirm, for instance, whether Benjamin Franklin ever met the famous Methodist preacher George Whitefield or lived for a time in London. But the modern memoir is different, as it so often focuses on the private life of a not well-known or even obscure person. Who's to say if X ever really took a life-transforming midnight swim all alone in Buzzards Bay when she was fifteen? And unless a description is biologically or physically implausible, who would bother to question it? Perhaps a question to ask of a memoir is something the pragmatist William James might have asked: If a report of something is wholly unverifiable, should we even concern ourselves with the issue of truth?

We have thousands of studies dealing with the art of fiction, but very little exists on the art of the memoir, aside from a growing number of "how-to" books. One reason for this is that, despite its present popularity, the memoir has not yet become a fully accredited genre in our universities. Most educated readers are still uncertain about how best to evaluate a memoir or an autobiographical essay. What makes one memoir or essay outstanding and another forgettable? Does it largely depend on the quality of prose? Will the particulars of an author's life bias our aesthetic responses either positively or negatively? Why is it that the first question readers ask of a memoir is "Is it true?" Is it a critical error to apply modern journalistic fact-checking standards to memoirs and essays intended as works of literature? If a personal essay turns out to have some fictional elements and details, does that automatically turn it into a short story? Or does it become something else — a fictive essay? a fable? an outright lie? Does applying the term "creative nonfiction" solve anything?

In the past, writers like Joseph Addison and Richard Steele and Washington Irving could invent characters and situations for their nonfiction works (many of these published in the newspapers of their day) and readers found their essays and sketches delightful. Is that no longer permitted in the world of publishing? Every year this series invites its readers to confront these and related questions, as we attempt to come to terms with both the literal and literary aspects of these exciting and elusive genres.

The Best American Essays features a selection of the year's outstanding essays, essays of literary achievement that show an awareness of craft and forcefulness of thought. Hundreds of essays are gathered annually from a wide assortment of national and regional publications. These essays are then screened, and approximately one hundred are turned over to a distinguished guest editor, who may add a few personal discoveries and who makes the final selections. The list of notable essays appearing in the back of the book is drawn from a final comprehensive list that includes not only all of the essays submitted to the guest editor but also many that were not submitted.

To qualify for the volume, the essay must be a work of respectable literary quality, intended as a fully developed, independent essay on a subject of general interest (not specialized scholarship), originally written in English (or translated by the author) for publication in an American periodical during the calendar year. Today's essay is a highly flexible and shifting form, however, so these criteria are not carved in stone.

Magazine editors who want to be sure their contributors will be considered each year should submit issues or subscriptions to: Robert Atwan, Series Editor, The Best American Essays, P.O. Box 220, Readville, MA 02137. Writers and editors are welcome to submit published essays from any American periodical for consideration; unpublished work does not qualify for the series and cannot be reviewed or evaluated. Please note: all submissions must be directly from the publication and not in manuscript or printout format.

For this edition — the twenty-first of the series — I would like to thank two friends and colleagues from the Blue Hills Writing Institute at Curry College, Allan Hunter and Sandy Kaye. I learn an enormous amount from them each year as we conduct our summer seminars in Life Writing; they are two of the most dedicated and exciting teachers of writing I've ever met. I'm deeply appreciative of all the assistance I receive from Houghton Mifflin: without the help of Deanne Urmy, Nicole Angeloro, and Larry Cooper, this volume would appear perhaps every five years. It was an intellectually gratifying experience to collaborate with Lauren Slater on this volume. I was delighted to include one of her early essays, "Striptease," in the 1994 volume (edited by Tracy Kidder) and was even more delighted when she agreed to move full circle and serve as this year's guest editor. She is someone — as this edition clearly demonstrates — who has brought a new perspective, energy, and edge to the contemporary American essay.

R.A.

Introduction

EARLY ON IN MY writing career I traveled to the Bread Loaf Writers' Conference. I dutifully lugged several short stories carefully typed on onionskin, the watermark visible when held to the slanting sunlight. I don't recall the stories' titles, but something about their spirit stays with me — fiction told in the voices of people on the periphery, a serial killer speaking from the shower, a foster child somewhere on a snowy road in Utah. At Bread Loaf, I expected a Published Writer would critique my work, a man with a gold pen and a pipe, a man who hunted geese, perhaps, drank ocher-colored alcohol from a crystal decanter, and knew something about how to sail.

Bread Loaf was a beautiful place filled, it seemed to me, with beautiful people, parties, poetry, and dances held in haylofts. I felt awkward there, put off in part by the nature of the pursuit — writing fiction — and in part by the culture that sprang from the pursuit. The famous writers at Bread Loaf knew they were celebrities in this small space, and after dinner they congregated in a special lounge reserved for them, a lounge we Little Leaguers could only peek inside, standing at the windows in the field, Queen Anne's lace blowing hip-high and fragrant. Editors milled about the grounds, the smoky smell of their wood-paneled New York offices still clinging to their clothes.

I, of course, was determined to succeed, and spent my Bread Loaf days and many days thereafter laboring away on my Smith Corona, and then my first computer, words blinking up on the black screen and then daisy-wheeled into pale print. But whatever I wrote seemed wrong, seemed strained, seemed more intent on flashing its cleverness and gaining entry to the country club than on truly transcribing the content inside my admittedly mediocre head. My earliest attempts at fiction were rather tortured "show, don't tell" affairs, all thought and feeling crammed into action and gesture, so my characters were constantly wringing their hands or tilting their heads, as though they had a chronic case of swimmer's ear. The number one rule in those Bread Loaf days was to never, ever directly say what a character felt or thought. That was the stuff of expository writing, of college essays, the stuff of the middling masses who could hope to do not much more than pass their course in freshman comp.

The "show, don't tell" rule that dominated the pedagogy of fiction back then, and perhaps still does, has given rise to some fantastic work, and it remains a useful guide to writing a certain kind of story. For me, as a fledgling writer, it was a bit of a disaster. I longed to be able just to *say something straight,* to be able to ask on paper the sorts of questions that consumed me then and still do today, questions such as: What is a moral stance? Can despair be redemptive? Is the urge to make meaning a misguided human coping mechanism that gives a false shape to our existence? How best to live? To die?

Eventually I gave up on fiction, gave up in frank despair because I simply could not find a way to explore these questions through character. This was years after Bread Loaf; I was twenty-five then, and when I set down my pen a silence entered my room, a silence in which I was forced to sit, and sweat, and wait, and watch. A year went by. I worked as a literacy instructor and spent my free time in the library of the Harvard Divinity School, a place that would be soothing even to the most troubled soul, the stacks crammed with books whose titles promised revelation. In those days I was reading William James, Thomas Merton, and Paul Tillich, drinking down the pages, propelled by an intellectual thirst that I have never felt quite so keenly again.

And it was during this long, slow slake that I found, one afternoon in 1988, walking home from the library, my first volume of *The Best American Essays.* I was peering in the window of Words-Worth Books on Brattle Street, and there it was, propped up in the window, a gray book, the color of weather-beaten wood, modest and unadorned. Essays. What was an essay? A long time ago I had read Virginia Woolf's essays — *The Death of the Moth, Three Guineas* — and had been delighted by their thoughtful combination of imagery and exposition. One of my earliest writing memories, in fact, comes from the eighth grade, when I decided I would try to write a Woolfian type of composition. I don't recall its particulars, only that it seemed incredible to me that one might write a piece, a polemic, that had all the strangeness of a story but was not a story.

Now, twenty-five years old, I sat down to read *The Best American Essays* and I was transported. The first piece I read was Elizabeth Hardwick's "The Heart of the Seasons," its language rapturous and vivid. The essay evoked time, heat, indolence, and grief through the sheer force of its imagery and voice. The essay was an artery connecting the mind of the reader with the writer, the writer bare and unpretentious, the writer without the veil of character, without the rouge and foundation that compose fiction, which is, when all is said and done, a game of dress-up. Hardwick's essay, when I first read it, was the literary equivalent of skinny-dipping — *I see you* — and it made me feel found.

So it was that I picked up my pen again and began to write, began to write directly, honestly, began to converse, showing, telling, pausing, contradicting, setting the frayed contents of my mind down on plain paper to be plainly seen by anyone who cared to look. That doesn't mean there isn't art and artifice involved in the writing of an essay. But it does mean that the art is in revealing the voice of the writer, as opposed to trying to transform it to suit the requirements of a fictional character or narrator. Essay writing is not about facts, although the essay may contain facts. Essay writing is about transcribing the often convoluted process of thought, leaving your own brand of breadcrumbs in the forest so that those who want to can find their way to your door.

Essays, therefore, confuse people. They occupy a quirky place in the general genre of nonfiction, a place many people seem not to understand. It has been my experience that people not acquainted with the literary essay expect it to behave like an article or a piece of journalism. Journalism is a broad category unto itself, but it is probably finally defined by its mission to report to readers clear facts that have been thoroughly investigated and digested by the journalist. One does not expect to read a piece of journalism filled with tentative reflections or outright contradictions. However, essays thrive on these, because contradiction, paradox, and questioning best reflect the moving, morphing human mind, which is what the essayist wants to capture.

In 2004 I published a nonfiction book called *Opening Skinner's Box: Great Psychological Experiments of the Twentieth Century*. I thought of each chapter as an essay, an inquiry into a psychological experiment and what it might mean for me during the brief time I came into contact with it. The first essay was about B. F. Skinner, who, I believed at first, had lost a daughter to suicide. I eventually found out that this was a myth: Deborah Skinner Buzan is alive, and the chapter reports this by quoting her sister to that effect. But the essay does not begin with this fact; rather, it traces my struggle to figure out the status of Deborah Skinner in body and in soul, and it emphasizes my doubts and questions along the way. If Deborah Skinner is indeed alive, I asked, then why has the myth persisted? And what does that say about B. F. Skinner in particular and behaviorism in general? My goal was to tussle with these questions and see what larger meaning might emerge from them.

When the book was published, Deborah Skinner reacted angrily. By my dwelling on the rumor that she had gone mad and killed herself, it seemed to her and others that I had injected the essay with false mystery. Deborah Skinner initiated a lawsuit, and soon thereafter I was cited in the press for negligent reporting. If I were a reporter, of course, my job would have been to contact and quote from my main source. But as an essayist, my interest was not in establishing the facts of a life but in mining the meaning, for me, of the questions that life had spawned. An essayist celebrates questions, loves the liminal, and feels that life is best lived between the *may* and the *be* of maybe.

So there was controversy surrounding the publication of *Opening Skinner's Box*. Upon hearing of it, several people said, "There's no such thing as bad publicity." If you are an essayist, then you are probably not primarily interested in publicity, because no one who truly wants to be famous chooses this little genre. However, I found myself in the strange position of being quite suddenly famous. My friend and fellow writer Pagan Kennedy grumbled that there were more pieces in the *New York Times* on my book than there were on Iraq's purported weapons of mass destruction.

Opening Skinner's Box angered people in ways too numerous and too complex to mention here. Suffice it to say that Deborah Skinner Buzan's complaint was not the only one; it was simply the first. Soon after, hundreds of psychologists and psychiatrists in universities from coast to coast wrote comments on a listserve called Slater-Hater, the aim of which was to discredit a book they saw as highly inaccurate, full of fabrications and mistakes, and that smeared the science they had worked so hard to establish. As one contributor to the forum wrote: "Slater's *Skinner's Box* was perhaps the first attempt to fuse the pseudo-memoir with the ordinary nonfiction science book for the general reader. I was about as happy to see that as I would be to see the first human-to-human transmission of the H_5N_1 bird flu virus!"

If the personal reflections that make up the essay/memoir, pseudo or otherwise, are like bird flu viruses, then essay writers are a dangerous breed indeed. I don't think of essays as viruses, although some part of me appreciates the power of that designation. In any case, the rage these academics displayed and continue to display toward *Opening Skinner's Box* made me curious about the workings of their minds and about the psychological dynamics that fuel scandals. So two years ago I joined the Slater-Hater listserve so I could observe what the issues were. Soon I was flooded with e-mails with such subject lines as "Slater Redux," "More Slater Caper," and "Slater, Mean Malicious Liar or Just Mentally Ill?" The discussion on the listserve was more barbed than I was prepared for. So was the accompanying behavior outside the listserve.

Being the object of such predation over an extended period of time has led me to think a lot about the critical role of kindness in writing and in life. It has led me to see that I, like the academics of whom I speak, have in the past written pieces with too much tooth, something the press generally rewards. I no longer write this way. I cannot abide ill will in my own work, and I dislike it when I see it in the work of others. I now believe that good writing, and good living, must have a core of gentleness.

Most of the postings on Slater-Hater were not malicious, however. More common were missives that had about them the veneer of intellect, and perhaps these troubled me even more. One professor, writing about a knotty ethical question, the type that is best explored as plainly as possible, wrote: "More broadly, the logical error we're discussing in this case is what logicians term the genetic fallacy: the error of evaluating an argument on the basis of its origins . . . Admittedly it may be a matter of debate as to whether this fallacy is always a fallacy. From a Bayesian perspective, it may well sometimes make sense to consider the motives, training and group membership of the proponent of the view if such background characteristics have an r>0 correlation with the verisimilitude of the argument(s) in question."

From my membership on the listserve I have learned a few things at least. One is that academia, and the discourse it gives rise to — a discourse potentially relevant for the essayist, since it can and often does inform his material — can be venomous, its culture darkly narcissistic. This was a surprise to me, as I thought professors in general were a little like essayists, who are narcissistic, to be sure, but in a harmless way. I also learned a lot about the language of academia, and this has helped me clarify principles I believe are relevant to the writing of good essays. Academia, at least the part I saw, thrives on jargon. For instance, it is not uncommon, on the Slater-Hater listserve, which has thankfully moved on to other discussions, to read this sort of thing: "We identified the same correlates for MMPI-2point codes types in VA men as Gilberstadt and Duker did for the same MMPI two point code types 40 years earlier." Or, "Self-esteem as a construct has a validity rating of .02% when compared to a two tailed t-test reliability rating of 4."

The sociologist Gerald Rosen, in his study of cosmetic surgery, commented that the less secure a field of study is, the more intense is its use of jargon. This puts essayists in a tough position, because they seem to be a troubled lot, constantly picking at their own imperfections, claiming embarrassment and humility while simultaneously showcasing the scars. The essayist often brings to the writing table an odd mix of shame and showmanship, and it may well be that the tension therein is what propels the work. Joseph Epstein, in his essay "The Culture of Celebrity," included in this volume, frets about his lack of celebrity status, and by doing so he amusingly attempts to seek the spotlight. Such narcissism is redeemed in part by the essayist's awareness of it, and in part by his absolute avoidance of jargon, which seems to me to be an attempt to inflate an idea or co-opt language so it becomes gilded and private. Unlike academic writing, the essay can be defined by its insistence on, and celebration of, the vernacular, a lyrical way of speaking that aims always at inclusion. The academic learns to hide his insecurity behind bloated verbiage. The essayist cannot hide his uncertainty, and by admitting it, he can hope to transform it.

The essays in this volume have made this transformation beautifully. They all speak plainly, the sentences scraped clean of verbal detritus, the result of which is writing that shines on the stumblings of its authors.

A few of the essays here are written by academics about academia. Given my experience as a member of the Slater-Hater listserve, and as the recipient of much professor-perpetrated vengefulness, I came to these essays suspiciously, if not defensively. I was, however, more than pleasantly surprised. Professor Emily Bernard's "Teaching the N-Word" redeems, for me, the patent primitivism of many in the academy. It is itself proof that writing from within the ivy walls, writing that springs from the soil of educational institutions, can be at once inclusive, artful, nuanced, complex, and frank.

The other essays in this collection cover a range of topics. Poe Ballantine reminds us that it is still possible, in the new millennium, to live a Kerouac kind of on-the-road existence, but to do so in a surprisingly thoughtful and sober — if not untroubled — state. Ballantine's writing is secure insecurity at its best, muscular and minimal, self-deprecating on the one hand, full of the self's soul on the other.

Marjorie Williams's devastating essay, "A Matter of Life and Death," chilled me for days after reading it, and chills me still. Such memoirs of catastrophic illness are hard to bring off, precisely because the story is so distressingly common. There is the good life lived by the smart but unsuspecting writer; there is the lump one finds with one's fingers in an idle moment; there are the tests, the diagnoses, the descent into despair, the struggle for hope. The fact that Williams is able to bring her own struggle with cancer to life in such brutally plain and elegant language is proof that any cliché can be conquered, and when that happens, it is always amazing. "A Matter of Life and Death" is, among other things, a fierce refusal of the jargoned life and death, an insistence on finding a language that lasts longer than any human fashion or fad.

Many of the essays deal with loss, with death. This may in part reflect my own concerns as I journey around the sun for the forty-third time, but it may also reflect a growing demographic group that is coming to define this country: aging baby boomers, articulate and insured. The essays on health and illness that I read throw light on certain economic strata; they tell the story of what it is like to grow old, to grow sick, to die, health plan in hand. Thus I read dozens of essays that describe operating rooms, MRI machines, and surgeons' waiting rooms, enough medically inspired writing to confirm what I have always thought: sickness is the natural state in which we humans reside. We occasionally fall into brief brackets of health, only to return to our fevers, our infections, our rapid, minute mutations, which take us toward death even as they evolve us, as a species, into some ill-defined future.

The essays in this volume are powerful, plainspoken meditations on birthing, dying, and all the business in between. They reflect the best of what we, as a singular species, have to offer, which is reflection in a context of kindness. The essays tell hard-won tales wrestled sometimes from great pain.

Some of the writers or their subjects have died since penning their pieces. One of the deaths this collection describes is of a humble, generous hound named George. Soon after I read about George's demise, my own beloved hound became deathly ill and spent some time in the hospital. She is old, my hound, arthritic, temperamental, gentle in soul, coarse to the touch. My daughter, who is six, wanted to know where our dog, Lila, would go when she died. Given that I'm not a big believer in the afterlife, I wasn't sure what to say. It seemed terrible to say, "She'll go into the ground," or "We'll burn her body." It also seemed wrong to fall back on jargon or its close cousin, verbal sweeteners. But then I remembered George, and all the other essays I have been honored to read as guest editor, and it occurred to me then where Lila, where we all, might go. Like the essayists or their subjects who have died since their pieces were written, we too will live inside plain language — if we should be so lucky — language wrung from kindness, from questions, from the deep desire to talk across space and time; language that celebrates the liminal even as it tethers us to each other; language that inspires, expires, the sentence more solid than skin.

LAUREN SLATER

The Best
AMERICAN
ESSAYS
2006

LAURIE ABRAHAM

Kinsey and Me

FROM ELLE

PAGE AFTER PAGE, line after narrow line it goes, the Record of
Marital Contact Frequency of Mr. and Mrs. R. C. Young* from a
small town in the Midwest, so that by the time it abruptly ends with
*Monday, December 31, 1951: 1 male orgasm, 1 female (manual); female
superior,* you've imagined a life — a love life and the other, everyday
kind. And you're bereft that it's over, for them and for you. Because from this terse diary — which includes only the date of each
"contact," the number of orgasms per spouse, whether hers was
through intercourse or by hand, and the position (missionary unless otherwise noted) — you know that he's gone. Mr. Young has
died. Why else would this couple end twenty-one years, from 1930
to 1951, of astonishingly regular intercourse and lovemaking and
wild grappling — some of each, surely — except that one of them
has left this mortal coil? How did Mrs. Young cope without her husband, without his body? How did she go on?

You know Mr. Young is the one who became sick and died because though the log reveals that they discovered the "female superior" position when she was pregnant with their second child, born
October 17, 1937 ("Woman delivered of a baby" is all the diary
says; no gender, no exclamation point — no child would dampen
the Youngs' ardor), Mrs. Young was on top only sporadically until
the spring of 1949. From then on they always use that position; he
must be too weak to do otherwise. Indeed, Mr. Young's pain and
fear recede only, I think, when he's looking up at her, his wife of so

---

* An asterisk indicates that names and identifying details have been changed.

many years, and then afterward when he watches her get out of bed, fish the Champion Line notebook from the drawer where it's hidden beneath a stack of handkerchiefs, and make the usual entry. *How did I get so lucky?* he thinks, watching. *At least I have this, her.*

I found the Youngs in the vast archive of sexual documents, art, and film at the Kinsey Institute at Indiana University (IU) in Bloomington. When I visited in September, all I knew was that I was fascinated by the sex researcher Alfred Kinsey — whose two books, *Sexual Behavior in the Human Male* in 1948, then five years later *Sexual Behavior in the Human Female,* made him one of the most famous Americans of his time — and that I was curious about what was still going on in the place that bears his name. Kinsey was the first to announce loudly and authoritatively — based on more than seventeen thousand highly detailed, in-person interviews — that U.S. men and, yes, women were having sex, and lots of it: with themselves, before marriage, extramarital, oral, with animals occasionally, and so on. As Jonathan Gathorne-Hardy notes in his superb 1998 biography, *Sex the Measure of All Things,* press coverage of the male book alone fills six shelves' worth of bound volumes; loose clippings take up six more.

I'd gone on a bit of a Kinsey binge over the summer in anticipation of the release of the writer-director Bill Condon's (*Gods and Monsters, Chicago*) biopic about the man, called simply *Kinsey,* as well as of a T. C. Boyle novel based on his life. (It's hard to understand the need to fictionalize a life as full and outrageous as Kinsey's, and Boyle's effort does prove pale, or at least superfluous. To give one example, near the end of *The Inner Circle,* prostitutes line the block waiting for Kinsey and a colleague to measure their ejaculation distance. I'd assumed the scene was invented until I read the biography and learned that, indeed, male prostitutes had queued up outside a Manhattan apartment building in November 1948, earning $3 a pop to confirm for Kinsey that the distance is not far.)

Today the most controversial aspects of Kinsey's life — unknown to the public at the time — are that he encouraged his staff to have open marriages, filmed colleagues and other volunteers having sex in his attic, pierced his foreskin during sexual experimentation, and used a sex diary given to him by a pedophile for a chart on orgasms in preadolescent boys. This last item should have been apparent to the earliest readers of the male volume but it inspired not a murmur of protest back then, when the culture was not so attuned to the sexual abuse of children.

The Kinsey Institute of 2004 is in one sense full of secrets. By its namesake's order, the home movies are locked up here ad infinitum, and you can't get into the library without being buzzed in. When I visited in the fall the staff was visibly on edge, worrying about the public's reception to the November movie, starring Liam Neeson. All the fretting, the furtiveness, can seem excessive — until you remember the attacks that Kinsey and his progeny have regularly endured, the latest of which being a congressional attempt in July 2003 to strip nearly $500,000 worth of National Institutes of Health funding from an ongoing study of sexual arousal. The project survived, barely.

In another sense, the modern Kinsey Institute seems the opposite of mysterious: a warren of offices where a handful of researchers toil away at projects that inevitably seem banal compared with Kinsey's planet-rocking work — and vaguely depressing. To satisfy funders, modern sex research is always framed in terms of disease or dysfunction. So the study of sexual arousal is called "Mechanisms Influencing Sexual Risk Taking," the goal being to stem the spread of HIV and other sexual scourges. Important, of course, but Kinsey — who was sex positive long before "sex positive" was a phrase — must be howling in his grave.

Or maybe not. Erick Janssen, the lead investigator on the arousal study, says he's not "ashamed" of the sexual-danger spin, and Kinsey probably would have admired his pragmatic willingness to work within the constraints of his time. "If you're creative, you combine basic things with the applied," says the Dutch native. "The project was almost defunded anyway, so if we had focused on the pleasure, God knows what would've happened."

And despite its sobering title, the arousal study *is* about pleasure. It's yielding basic information about what sparks and extinguishes arousal in all of us, which is one of those subjects that, like the Kinsey Institute itself, is utterly obvious and utterly shrouded, a subject about which we know everything and nothing.

Walking through IU's leafy, rolling campus the morning I volunteer to be a guinea pig in Janssen's lab — for journalistic purposes, and who wouldn't jump at the chance to check out how her sexual systems are operating? — I'm light, swingy: I've been able to run and have breakfast alone with the paper for the first time in a long time. The sun is warm on my skin (come to think of it, on the sex-and-mood survey Janssen had me fill out before coming here, I'd checked AGREE next to "Sometimes just lying in the sun sexually arouses me" — though in truth, I can't remember the last time that happened), and there are fresh-faced girls and boys crisscrossing the paths all around me. Do I look old to them? I think. If only they could see into my heart! I'm as tender and alive as I was at their age. I am, I swear.

When I get inside the Institute, I notice I'm nervous. The explicit art that lines the halls (like a drawing of a woman in foreshortened perspective, her legs spread and her bare feet and genitalia practically jutting off the paper) is one sign that this is not the History department, and it's off-putting, as I'm soon to be attached to a sensor that will measure my physical arousal while I view an erotic film. The nakedness and rampant coupling is taunting me: *That woman, sexy? She's not going to respond at all. Dead as a doornail.* Like many married women I know, I'm capable these days of going long stretches without wanting sex, which is maddening and frustrating and not just a little bewildering. I've had the best sex of my life with my husband — and not in the misty past but recently, in our eighth or ninth year together — so why don't I want it more? I know, I know: I've got two small children and demanding work, I'm getting older, my marriage is getting older. But what about Mrs. Young? She didn't succumb to such exigencies.

Janssen's lab assistant is a pleasant young woman who gives me an overview of what to expect and shows me how to insert the vaginal plethysmograph, which will record my blood flow, or level of excitement. She leaves while I get settled, and then the first movie begins, about the habits of domestic cats. (*Pussycat?* Is there something going on here? I'm paranoid — it's a nature film to gauge my baseline physical responses.) Then I'm shown a series of photos of men of varyingl levels of hotness and asked to rate the likelihood that I'd sleep with them following a few hours of talking in a bar (assuming I were unmarried). This bit is designed to assess my typical risk tolerance, so I'm told each potential paramour's number of previous partners, whether he usually wears a condom, and if one is available for our make-believe dalliance.

From cute boys the video moves to . . . the scene in *Sophie's Choice* where a Nazi soldier orders Meryl Streep to choose which of her two children to keep! If she refuses, presumably both will be sent to the gas chamber. Janssen is specifically examining how emotions — anxiety, depression, happiness — impact sexual arousal (which could help predict when someone is more likely to, say, lose her head and have unprotected sex with a stranger). He told me beforehand that so far he's found that contrary to the usual expectation, up to 20 percent of men and women are *more* aroused when they're blue or fearful. The theory behind this is that some people use sex to escape ugly moods, like a vet who told Janssen in a focus group that he got an erection when his helicopter lost power and went into free fall in Vietnam, to his lasting shame.

Through my tears — *How in the world did she choose?* — I'm next forced to imbibe three minutes of soft porn. Afterward, as I sit there punching through questions on the computer, I'm a little pissed. *No, I don't feel aroused! It would be a sin to get aroused after watching a mother give up her child!*

You can guess the end of this story. Later, handing me what look like electrocardiogram results, Janssen points to spiky red lines indicating that though I was still roiling from Meryl's suffering, my vaginal blood flow rose as I watched a Barbie blonde get it on in a gazebo (though I'm not among the one fifth of the population who's especially stoked by sadness). The disjunction between my reading on the plethysmograph and my so-called subjective arousal isn't unusual for women. One study showed that while women report preferring "female-centered" porn clips to male-, our nether regions respond equally vigorously to both (which is not as vigorously as men respond to either male or female erotica).

So my body may have something to tell me — if I'd let it. Because another piece of information I picked up from Janssen suggests that my mind is not my friend in the bedroom. In addition to excitability, he measures two types of inhibition on the written survey. My first score — gauging the chill factor of unwanted pregnancy, disease, and the like — confirmed what I already knew about myself: I'm not a poster girl for safe sex. But while I'm less inhibited than average in this regard, I'm more so when it comes to factors such as distractibility and preoccupation with things going well sexually. It's a "compensation" pattern Janssen says he's seen before. Once in the flow, distractible people like me are loath to mess with success — so, hey, who needs condoms?

I have been with the same man for nearly a decade, so my irrational tendencies no longer threaten my health or happiness. Still relevant, however, are the damned intrusive thoughts. If I'm to notice my body's signals — and Janssen believes that, contrary to the conventional sexual-response model, before one has thoughts of desire, "something has to happen first in your brain; some automatic trigger you could call arousal" — I have to hack through a thicket of anxieties and obligations. I've got to clear the mental brush. But then, am I trying too hard?

A common opinion in research circles is that sex surveys, like the one the University of Chicago published in 1999, inflate the extent of female sexual unhappiness. The poll concluded that 43 percent of American women were suffering from a "sexual dysfunction," based on the following question: In the past year, have there ever been several months or more when you: lacked interest in sex; couldn't have an orgasm or had one too quickly; had physical pain during intercourse; didn't find sex pleasurable; felt anxious about your performance; had trouble lubricating?

The respondents weren't asked whether they perceived such "problems" as, well, problematic, but in trying to tease out the difference, former Kinsey Institute director John Bancroft reported in 2003 in *Archives of Sexual Behavior* that the portion of women who say they're distressed about their sexual functioning is roughly half the number that the Chicago team counted. "Central to this conceptual debate," Bancroft writes, "is the question of whether absence or reduction of sexual interest or response is necessarily . . . maladaptive." Not being into sex, he goes on, may be "an appropriate or at least understandable reaction to . . . states of fatigue or depression or the presence of adverse circumstances."

So perhaps I'm admirably adapted and only need to gracefully accept the lot of an exhausted working mother. Back at the Institute, Associate Director Stephanie Sanders doesn't seem opposed to this path of least resistance. "It's easier, on average, for men to get in a sexual mood or decide to have sex," she says, her tone kindly. And Janssen adds that even men aren't as uniformly lustful as everyone assumes. All those dudes popping Viagra? He argues that a fair number of them merely have a modest level of desire, but any man who doesn't perpetually want sex believes he must have a medical problem — a notion the drug companies gleefully encourage. "*You* give a guy a stiffy," Janssen says, scowling slightly, "and he's supposed to be fine."

Wait a minute here. This is the Kinsey Institute; these people are supposed to be frantically copulating maniacs, proselytizers for the glory of sexual fulfillment. All this science, judiciousness — it may be the truth, but it occludes this for *me:* sex feels good and I want more of it. My own body, my husband's — I don't get enough of either.

To this end, my lab work may crack open a few new opportunities. I've tended to conceive of my personal desire-enhancement project as one that depended on steering my thoughts in a more sexual direction, which would in turn rouse my body and then — my husband willing — lead to mutual quadruple orgasms, or something like that. But instead I might think of tuning my ear to my body, not my brain. But there's that word "think" again — and all of this can get pretty circular, not to mention laughably dualistic. In focus groups conducted by Sanders, one woman described the situation this way: "The arousal, the interest, they tend to blur . . . I'm not even sure how to separate one from the other." (The trickiness of female arousal definitely has been a cold shower for the makers of Viagra and its knockoffs — they've basically given up on marketing the drugs to women after trials showed that for most of us, increasing blood flow to the genitals does not translate into arousal or desire.)

Science can take you only so far. The true inspiration at the Kinsey Institute is found in the archives, where, in touching relic after relic, you contemplate how real humans project tenderness and commitment. Over the years, Kinsey received some sixty thousand letters, many from people distraught because sexual pleasure had eluded them or because the sexual pleasure they did experience was somehow "wrong."

Dear Dr. Kinsey:
 I would be grateful if you would advise me where I may find out about curing impotency. I am frigid and my physician has not been able to do anything to correct this condition. One has advised a tonic, but I have heard this is irritating to the kidneys. Is this true?
 Very truly yours, Catherine Flowers*

Dear Dr. Kinsey:

My wife and I cannot pay you a fee. We are poor. But we read your article in *Time* and thought you would be good enough to answer our sex question. Here it is: We cannot take the conventional face-to-face position in bed because the opening to the vagina is almost at the rectum. So we have to [lie] like this: T. I think I get results but my wife gets nothing, only by hand manipulation. And she is very sad about it and asked me to write you.

Sincerely, Mr. and Mrs. J. Meyer*

Dear Dr. Kinsey:

I am writing to ask to be a subject in your research . . . in hopes of understanding why my husband and I are separated. I am 24 years old, have been married eight years, and have two children, ages three and five.

Sincerely, Ann Martin*

For years Kinsey personally responded to each request for help, advising people to find a qualified local psychologist or psychiatrist but also offering comfort in the form of very scientific-sounding advice, like this to the Meyers: "If hand stimulation is satisfactory it is difficult to understand why there can be any objection to such a technique . . . Whatever the technique the husband and wife use, if they secure satisfaction from it, it should bring the two individuals together in a satisfactory emotional relationship."

Reading one after another of these exchanges is transfixing — I can't budge from my hard library chair. The boldness, the earnestness of Kinsey's confidants fills me with grief and respect and love. I'm immersed in the yearning and shame of people who lived just fifty years ago — one scene in the Condon movie shows Kinsey asking a dewy young couple if they'd tried oral sex. "But my brother told me that that causes problems later on with having babies," the husband demurs — and the power of sex is palpable, as is Kinsey's bravery in testifying on its behalf. An entomologist who combed the continent collecting a whopping 300,000 gall wasps before he turned to obsessively amassing human sexual histories, Kinsey hoped that mountains of data would prove what he fervently believed: that sex was the most natural of activities, and if repressed only led to suffering, the kind he'd endured as a young man growing up in a stern, unforgiving religious household.

When Kinsey died in 1956 it was of a broken heart, his friends and family told his biographer. He'd become an object of derision, in large part because of the lies he supposedly told about women: that 62 percent masturbated, that more than two thirds of unmarried women who'd had premarital sex did not regret it, and that "vaginal orgasms" were a myth — Freud and his insistence that the "stubborn" clitoris be trained into quiescence be damned.

Apparently the Youngs didn't hear or heed the "experts" of their time, until Kinsey. Answering his call for the public to send him sexual ephemera of any kind — more proof — they posted their meticulously kept record to Bloomington. It's impossible to know which one had the idea to donate their lovemaking to science, or for that matter who actually made the entries in the diary. Interestingly, I immediately assumed that she'd done it, though men are thought to be the more common keepers of sexual statistics.

But that may be because until recently women weren't permitted to publish such scandalous things. Two years ago, the most talked-about sexual diarist was the Frenchwoman Catherine Millet, and this year it's the former New York ballerina Toni Bentley. In Bentley's memoir about anal sex, she reveals that she kept notes of each encounter (precisely 298, if *you* like to count) so as to make the unreal seem real. It's a kick to imagine how delighted Kinsey would have been by the respectful reception *The Surrender* has received — a full-page (mixed) review in the Sunday *New York Times,* no less. But with reams of clinical detail mixed with clunky paeans to her preferred act, Bentley wasn't nearly as stirring to me as the . . . belt fetishist.

The last treasure I came across in the library was a journal chronicling a middle-aged belt fetishist's courtship of a sad divorcée who, after time and gentle persuasion, agrees to join in with the former's self-described hang-up. The man is also some kind of community-theater director, you deduce as you read, and there are many passages like this (slightly paraphrased) one, from the couple's first date: *The* [South Pacific] *rehearsal was a pleasure for both of us. During the break, I presented her with the gift I had in my jacket pocket. It was the maroon belt. She held it for the remainder of the show. On the way home, she commented that she would have to make an outfit to go with it.*

She held the belt for the remainder of the show; it wasn't red, it was maroon. Does the nearby librarian, who's formidably formal, notice that I'm practically weeping? "A fetish is a story masquerading as an object," the psychiatrist Robert Stoller famously said. Unlike Bentley, who keeps her sex completely cut off from the rest of her life — she never once did anything so deadeningly pedestrian as have dinner out with her cherished "A-man" — the belt fetishist wants to be loved and tied up, and he can't experience the former without the latter. The Youngs, in my fantasy, wanted a version of that too. Sex and love and love and sex, until it was all mixed up in one rich stew. For the first two years, the entries in their diary are virtually identical:

> Thursday, January 30 1930: 1 male orgasm
> Monday, February 3 1930: 1 male orgasm
> Wednesday, February 12, 1930: 1 male orgasm

Then, as the crocuses start to open in the spring of 1932, you read, in script as neat and lovely as my grandmother's: *Wednesday, April 13, 1932: 1 male orgasm, 2 female orgasms.* A banner beginning, and from that day forward Mrs. Young's pleasure is as regular as the seasons.

My plane from Indiana arrives back in New York very late, and when the cab drops me off at home it's almost midnight. I get into bed, still thinking of the Youngs, of the belt fetishist, of the devotion of Alfred Kinsey. I press into my husband. "Is this the Kinsey Institute?" he asks, laughing a little.

"Yeah," I say.

POE BALLANTINE

501 Minutes to Christ

FROM THE SUN

For Kim Hansen

One might also say that an apparition is human vision corrected by
divine love.

— WILLA CATHER

OUTSIDE OF A PSYCHOTIC who attacked me a few months ago
(I stuck his head into a snowbank until he promised to leave me
alone) and a middle-aged fellow who drives around town shouting obscenities from a riding mower, there is not much happening here in Middlebury, Vermont. It's a handsome town, though:
kindly in spirit, smart and well run, home of a fine college with an
extraordinary library. My position as cook at the Café Chatillon
down along scenic Otter Creek is more than tolerable. So too are
my living quarters: usually I'm stuck in a single room near the railroad tracks. Here I live far from the tracks in a small, clean apartment attached to the comfy house of a middle-class family who
spend most of their time watching television. The canned laughter
fluting melancholically through the walls has become as familiar to
me as the sounds of plumbing or forced air from the vents.

I am, unfortunately, watching a lot of TV myself. The cable is
spliced in gratis from the house, and ever since I sobered up, I
don't seem to get out much anymore. Granted, I could screw that
teenage girl who's been coming around, or I could have an affair
with that married woman who eyes me at the gym, but that's all
part of the old life. The old life had no meaning. I have learned,
through my many years of depraved blundering, that men are not

mere flesh, for flesh without spirit cannot move, laugh, drink ab-
sinthe, forgive, or consider the end of time. Flesh without spirit
(see: *meat*) simply goes bad, simply stinks.

But enough about my old life. These days I have whittled my wel-
ter of vices down to gambling (I do love the horses), two beers in
the evening, and an occasional cigarette. I fancy myself an upright
figure, a man of honor, a future novelist of minor distinction (even
if I can't *give* away a story), a weightlifting, monastic hobo of whom
people might say a generation or two hence, in the small likelihood I am remembered, "He was honest."

I don't recommend the writing life — at least not the one in
which you move around a lot, live alone, and work odd jobs. Swing
a gig where you hit the big time quick. Be a prodigy, if your agent
can arrange it, and then get yourself banned in Boston. I arrived at
the discipline late, at the age of twenty-nine, in part because I
needed material, but mostly because I boarded a train called the
Romantic Debauchery in the mistaken assumption that it would
somehow get me to my destination quicker than the ones marked
Hard Work and Paying Attention. Hundreds of wrong trains and
many lost years later, I have learned that, despite the jovial public
legends, inebriation and lucid expression are at odds with each
other. If I am to write with spiritual integrity, I cannot be a drunk-
en butterfly.

All that time I was watching those cocktails and powders glide
down my throat or slide up my nose, I did little in the way of matur-
ing as a writer. I'd felt raw-nerved, out of place, and shy all my life. I
found achieving worthwhile goals difficult, but *talking* about them
was easy, especially with the help of drink and drugs, and in the
company of fellow dreamers. I knew I had to quit the gliding cocktails and the sliding powders, but I did not have the courage or the
know-how. Romantic Debauchery kept pulling up to the station,
doors open, plenty of seats, magic confetti fluttering gaily down. At
thirty-six, my pockets jammed with ripped railway tickets, I'm still
scrambling to recover the lost years, still trying to "find my voice."

But now that I am reformed, a disciplined writer at last, mature
at least in accumulation of years and control of appetite, I feel entitled to my modest deserts: a good night's sleep, esteem from my
neighbors, a humble career in letters, a mate, certainly — and not
one of those slovenly, voracious creatures who always took the win-

dow seat on the train, but a respectful, book-loving brunette who owns cats, enjoys clarinet solos and avocado sandwiches, and has come, like me, the long, hard way to virtue. I'm sure I will meet her soon.

In the meantime, after a few hours of searching for my "voice" and a vigorous workout at the gym, I sit in front of the TV munching on snacks and experiencing great emotions while watching glib characters skillfully solve personal problems with warmth and humor on the half-hour. Human intercourse at last! I am interested in politics, sporting events, unsolved mysteries, comedy of all brands, movies, news, documentaries, debates, interviews, biographies of serial killers and stars — anything to keep me distracted from the fact that I have once again backed out of the human arena, afraid of getting stomped or regressing into the old life, and that I should have left Vermont long ago.

One night, without warning, H. Ross Perot's earnest, nasal rant about the arrogant complacency of the American people triggers the realization of my own arrogant complacency, and self-reproach suddenly gurgles up to my eyelids like storm water in a backed-up sewer. I think to myself: *I'm thirty-six years old and rotting in front of a television set.* The electrons that bomb that cathode-ray tube are crumbling the cartilage of my soul, eating away my youth and the children in my loins. I don't need to see another riot, or plane crash, or evil twin, or clever light-beer commercial, or guy pointing a gun at me, or steroid millionaire swatting a home run. I snap off the tube, and all those emotions that have been sluicing into my veins, all the opinions and ideas I have mistaken for my own, zip dizzily up into the atmosphere, and I am suddenly a man alone on a fold-out couch in the empty darkness of an add-on room.

Without the distraction of television, that life-support system for people with no lives, I sit for a long while, steeping in the sudden revelation of my own stagnancy. The family next door is watching *Murphy Brown*. Why has probity not rewarded me? Why, through the exercise of conscience, am I not a measurably better human? Why, after seven years of dedicated Hard Work and Paying Attention, have I not published a single story or poem? And what will I do, I wonder, to eradicate this monstrous disgust I've amassed for myself? March back into the bar? Walk out the door and just keep walking? Commit suicide?

Instead, I begin punching myself in the head. Having a palpable outlet for my hatred feels good. I'm slamming away like Marvin Hagler on Thomas Hearns in the first round of that famous three-round championship bout when I hit my nose, and blood drips onto my sweatshirt. Then it begins to pour, and I have to stop punching and cup my hand under it. I cry a bit, but it only makes the loathing worse.

After I've cleaned myself up, I take a walk. It's a spectacularly clear spring night. Vermont is one of the prettiest places I've ever lived. I once thought I might stay here. I thought things might be different. I nod at my neighbors, pass my two old friends who always ignore me: the post office and the bookstore. There is still blood on my sweatshirt, which at least is physical proof that I am still alive. When I get home, I feel better. Self-battery has dislodged a few forgotten imperatives. I can't write anything worthwhile about America or its inhabitants if I have withdrawn from them, and no one really wants to hear another criticism of TV. It's time to throw myself back into the fire. In the morning I will give notice at work. My employer will be surprised. My employer is always surprised.

Like most people, I detest moving. Once you get started, though, it isn't so bad. You get into a rhythm, throwing things away. You realize how little you really need, how much of a drain these coffee mugs and dead houseplants and Bic pens and tortilla presses are. It feels good to give away a television set or discard an embarrassing manuscript printed in dot matrix. A day or two before I leave, I usually get sick with diarrhea and worry that I'll have to cancel the trip. But I know it's just my craven way of trying to wriggle out of the duty of waking up and being alive. The diarrhea usually dries up a few hours before I leave.

There is inexpressible satisfaction in leaving my stale and cowardly life behind, in saying goodbye to the room of loneliness with its acre of rejection slips, and to the me I despise so much. Yes, I know I will see that self again soon, but for a while I will be lost, scuffling, distracted. Who knows: maybe something will happen. I will rescue children from a house fire, or a tree will fall on my head, or a famous editor will discover me, or (dare I say it?) I will find the dark-headed girl.

I buy a one-way bus ticket for Louisville, Kentucky. I have always wanted to visit Churchill Downs, home of the Kentucky Derby. They just ran the Derby a couple of weeks ago, so the track should be reasonably quiet, with fewer plastic mint-julep cups to wade through.

As the Greyhound leaves from Burlington, a girlish, yellow-haired German woman of about fifty, wearing box spectacles and a backward white painter's cap, takes the seat next to mine. Her name is Annie, she tells me in a warm cackle of a voice, and she's going to Chicago.

I'm not much for bus conversation. It's a bit like talking to yourself. But I nod along as Annie begins to relate to me, with glittering sobriety, a story about the Death Bays of 1954, when the Indian landlords came with their Polish prostitutes and bought all the YMCAs, and for $50,000 you could sign your own death contract wherein a boy would be assigned to extract the juice from your liver, spleen, and heart, though it usually didn't work. I try not to laugh. Greyhounds have electromagnets in them that attract the disturbed and the desperate. Manic Annie talks for hours and sits with me at all the food stops, where she never eats anything, only pockets crackers and dressing packets, which she snacks upon fastidiously back on the bus while explaining about the substance called Senn (you mean you haven't heard of it?), which melts women into creatures that resemble sheep, or her brother-in-law who nearly became a world-champion boxer but lost the European title bout because his feet suddenly began to stink.

Two states later, God bless her soul, Annie suddenly decides to change seats, though she keeps waving and whistling for me to join her in the back. I return her waves but don't get up. I've heard enough about the Polish whores who exchange their feet with yours while you sleep.

When the bus pulls into Louisville, I think for a moment that Annie might follow me out the door, as she has faithfully at every stop, but when I look back, she's jabbering to the man next to her about the ability of Peruvian (or Tibetan?) people to stare at you through their llamas until you are dead. And the man is in *stitches,* as if she were some sort of highly advanced comedian. Maybe I should have laughed instead of wasting my time being polite. I suddenly realize that if Annie is going to Chicago, she's on the wrong

bus. Oh, well, good luck, Annie. Many laughs to you. I suppose the
joy of finding an appreciative audience is better any day than some
feeble notion of a destination.

The letters across the depot wall in front of me read, TAXIS
GAMES WOMEN — a perfect banner for my entrance into an unknown city. I've managed to strip all my possessions down to two
bags: one contains my cooking tools, screwdriver, scissors, can
opener, and assorted household gear. The other holds mostly
clothes, an alarm clock, a Bible, and a notebook. Because bus de-
pots represent a constant supply of temperature-controlled air, cigarettes, spare change, pinball, restrooms, snack machines, little
televisions, and places to sit, they will always attract lost and marginal (and sometimes dangerous) souls in temporary need. I ad-
just my walk and my bearing accordingly. On the street, as it is in
nature, 99 percent of all confrontations are settled or avoided by
gesture, expression, and appearance, most of it false bluster. To
blend in with the hustlers and their prey, I wear my bloodstained
sweatshirt and crusty high-top cooking shoes. I am unshaven. I
don't smile or talk casually to people. I don't think whatever you
just said was funny. I don't respond to finger-crooking or "Hey,
c'mere for a minute." I don't give money to panhandlers. I have
$1,200 cash in my left front pocket, and if you think you're getting
any part of it, you are sadly mistaken.

Downtown Louisville is a slick-looking city, with green-mirrored
buildings, swanky outdoor bistros, the scent of cherry blossoms,
and the usual dreary sprinkle of chain outlets. I follow the busi-
nesspeople in their suits and wonder how I will find a place to live,
how I will get around. And where is that girl? She must be here
somewhere, staring into her aquarium, slicing bananas into her
Wheat Chex, or studying her ten principal Upanishads. First things
first, though. I need a map.

I duck into what appears to be a college bookstore, massive and
sterile, without a single customer. "Help you, sir?" says a scholarly-
looking young man in a beige turtleneck.

"Map of the city?" I say, setting down my bags.

"No map of the city, sir," the young man says, adjusting his wire-
rims. "Maybe if you tried the gas station across the street."

"Is there a motel close by?"

He mentions the Holiday Inn, the Ramada.

"No, a *cheap* motel," I say. "Something with weekly rates."

"You mean the San Antonio," he says, the hint of a smirk crossing his face. "About a mile," he says, pointing down the street. "It'll be on your left."

A mile later I come upon the San Antonio, a weary-looking motel in a rundown part of town: windows cracked, letters missing on the sign, trash scattered about. Across the street, an old phonebooth leans in the dogwood shade. If there were another motel within a mile, I might keep walking, but I'm hungry, and my arms are tired from carrying my bags.

In the office, the clerk sits behind bulletproof glass and sips grape pop from a foam cup.

"Hello," I say.

"Hi," she replies without a glance.

A yellow sign in the corner of the glass partition reads, COM-PETITIVE HOURLY RATES.

"How much for a week?" I ask.

"A *week?*" she says, as if I have just offered to buy the place.

"Yes, do you have weekly rentals?"

"Most people only stay for a few hours."

I feel flattered to get more than two words from her. "I'm traveling," I say. "I just got into town."

"A hundred and thirty-five," she says with a shrug. Throughout the entire wooden-scoop, no-touch transaction, not once does she meet my eyes.

My room is as dark as a cave, with red, rubbery curtains and a thin, mud-brown carpet. The orange door is constructed of steel. Scrawled in pencil on the smudged walls are the names of prior guests: "Joe + Tanya = Jarrod '92," "David Ratcilff [*sic*] was here." I set my bags on the table and get a glass of water from the sink. A fiendish moaning emanates throughout the building, as if from many rooms. The German cockroaches that hang on the walls seem to be absorbing the vibration, as if deriving nutrition from it. I turn on the television, and a greenish copulating couple swims into focus, twittering tongues entwined.

I sit down on the bed. I really don't need porno right now. I have wasted too much of my life with it already, whacking off and getting nowhere. I am far from sainthood, you understand. I spent many years indulging the flesh while the spirit languished. The bed of fertilizer from which my virtue has purportedly blossomed is sufficiently deep. I change quickly over to the news and watch a segment about gangs of black Louisville teenagers robbing whites apparently at random and then beating them to death with baseball bats. Louisville Sluggers, I imagine. A coin dealer was killed last night, says the cheerful, smooth-eyed newscaster, the third person murdered in the last month in these "wildings."

I turn off the television. Like pornography, the news is a lurid concoction that panders to the basest emotions. *I won't watch either of them,* I think. I have brought French essays. I am going to study my *Racing Form* and read my Bible. I need to check out the job market and the rentals. I'll find the library and continue my investigation into the mysteries of Hinduism. (Note the remarkable similarities between the second members of their trinities: Vishnu and Christ.) The girl is out there too, probably leaning out her garret window at this moment, wondering about my arrival before she returns reluctantly to her tabby cat, her clarinet music, and the painting of her toenails. This time I'm not going to miss her because I'm too busy watching the narcissists preen on a twelve-inch screen or swallowing the myths offered nightly by Ted Koppel. But right now I would like to eat. And because I budget $3 a day for my meals, I head to the Kroger across the street.

The minute I slip out my door, two hookers with extra-sensitive meat thermometers, parasols tilted daintily on shoulders, whirl about and make their way toward me, their hips wagging. I hurry across the lot like a child playing Red Light, Green Light and land triumphantly on the other side of the street without speaking to them. At Kroger I buy radishes, a box of chocolate doughnuts, four bananas, a loaf of white bread, a can of Allen's chopped mixed greens, a small jar of Jif peanut butter, two York Peppermint Patties, two cans of Bush's great northern beans, one can of Goya black beans, one can of Franco-American cheese ravioli on sale, three cans of Brunswick sardines with chilies, and one can of Brunswick sardines in mustard: total, $11.29. Enough for four days.

After successfully running another gauntlet of floozies, I'm back in my motel room, my radishes floating in the sink. I have new neighbors to the east, who shout at each other:

"Retard!"

"Tramp!"

"Hillbilly!"

"Whore!"

Obviously the week with the marriage counselor was a bust. I tie all my groceries except the canned goods into plastic sacks to keep the roaches out. As I organize my cutlery and prepare my meal, I can't resist the television. I am too curious to see what the humans are doing. For supper this late afternoon I have canned fish with chilies, a banana-and-peanut-butter sandwich, and a couple of big, musky radishes while a Japanese girl massages herself with a red rubber relay baton. For dessert I eat two chocolate doughnuts and watch a moaning threesome achieve awkward release on a pool table, all still wearing their sneakers. The roaches wheel merrily around the top of the can of Franco-American cheese ravioli. The couple next door have finally stopped trading insults, and their headboard is banging. I turn on the air conditioner fan to drown them out.

In the evening it begins to rain. I slip out for a couple of beers and a *Racing Form* and run smack into two streetwalkers cruising the front of the motel under a single gold umbrella. I step off the sidewalk to go around them.

"Excuse me," says the more attractive of the two, her lips as shiny as a cherry-frosted doughnut, "but are you staying here at this hotel?"

"Yes, ma'am, I am."

"C'mere for a minute," she says, crooking her finger at me. "I gotta ask you a question."

You know, I hate this finger-crooking, this "c'mere" stuff. I hold up my hand — perhaps too vigorously, for it seems to startle them both — and say, "Whatever it is, I'm not interested."

"Like, how do you know what I was going to say?" she replies indignantly, eyelids flapping, hand on hip.

"I'm not trying to be Moses, honey," I reply. "Just trying to keep my act clean."

"Shee," she replies. "Well, you in the wrong part of town for *that*."

A few blocks down the street at Dick's Liquors, the clerk, enclosed in his crime-resistant conservatory with the wooden transaction scoop, nods a friendly hello.

"*Racing Form?*" I say.

"Track is dark today and tomorrow."

"Dark two days," I say.

"*Form* in tomorrow about three for Wednesday."

"Which way is Churchill? I don't have a car."

"You can ride the bus for a quarter," he says. "Get you pretty close." He draws me a map.

"You play the horses?" I ask him.

"Now and then."

"Nice track?"

He cocks an eyebrow. "Is there better?"

"Santa Anita?" I suggest. "Saratoga?"

"Never been to those," he says.

I buy a couple of tall cans of Stroh's and a newspaper. That's all the money I can spend today.

That night I watch the porno for about seven hours and beat off like a teenager, my Bible and book of Malraux essays unopened on the nightstand; my newspaper, with two jobs and two rentals circled, folded in the headboard compartment. Man may not be mere meat, but flesh makes its demands. Anyway, the brown-haired girl has already turned off her radio with a sigh and gone to bed.

At midnight a party starts up next door. Perfume seeps through the vents. Ice rattles in plastic cups. Boisterous laughter fades as the porno grows louder. Water rushes through pipes in the walls. Every time a toilet flushes, my television seems to dim. The roaches float gracefully over the penciled graffiti: "ASSHOLE." "Bridget loves John L. forever." The murmur of forty televisions tuned to the same channel echoes along the hallways like the groaning of chained demons in an infernal city.

Weak and ashamed from spending my seed, I sleep fitfully while guests bang in and out the steel doors for an hour or two of carnal recreation, lovers scratch the names of conquests on the walls, and roaches skitter through my sheets. I wonder why God doesn't descend to clear us all out with his staff, or break open the clouds and the dams and wash us away like rats to the sea. I wonder about Annie, who must be crossing Nova Scotia by now, maniacally slapping her thighs, every passenger on the bus roaring in appreciation. About five, I finally fall into a sound slumber and dream of a French knight wearing too much armor who goes crashing through the roof of a mansion shouting something about hors d'oeuvres.

In the morning the maid raps on the metal door with her big keyring. "Housekeeping!" she shouts. Groggily I make my way across the room in my underwear and open the door to a large, pepperoni-smelling woman, who looks me up and down critically. By now I must be known by all who work here as the pitiful pud-puller who has come not just for an evening, but has thrown down money for an entire *week.* "You need anything?" she drawls, rolling a wad of gum around her mouth. "Towels? Sheets?"

"No thanks," I say. "Come back on Friday."

She squints at me, takes out a pad, and makes a note. The next morning, and every morning after that, she will come by, rap on the door with her keys, and shout, "Housekeeping!"

On Wednesday morning I go to the library and sit for a while in the carpet-scented peace, reading sacred Hindu writings and wondering where all this sublime order, this fearlessness of truth, has gone. Then I take the bus to the racetrack. Hallelujah! Let's have a little fun, boys.

I've seen Churchill Downs dozens of times on television, but to view it firsthand — water fountains, banners flapping everywhere, all the decks and finery, like a grand sailing vessel built especially for bored, desperate, sexually frustrated men who've come to exercise their futility — is a privilege beyond words. The fresh air feels good. I stand by the rail and watch the horses thunder by, chips flying. Between races, I glance left and right, looking for my imaginary girlfriend.

Though I've studied and circled my *Form* carefully, and though I apply proven methods and empirical principles accumulated over years of experience, I do nothing but lose at Churchill Downs for the next three days. Let's say it's the rain, the unfamiliar track, the consistently uninspiring weekday cards (little but two-year-old fillies, four-year-old maidens, and state-bred nonwinners of two). Admittedly, after the track takes its 17 percent, even the most astute horseplayer has trouble breaking even. Though I've known many gamblers who made their living playing cards or betting football, I've never been acquainted with one who could consistently beat the horses. I have good days, which I no longer mistake for a

change in fortune or proof that I've finally struck upon "the system." But I've never actually won, not over a season.

On Friday night, after losing $16 at the track, I turn in early, feel-
ing desolate, my eyes glazed from staring at blurry images on the
television screen. My brain feels physically changed, hissing and
saturated with tawdry color. My Bible is a prop. The Vedas are forgotten. Malraux is dead. I can't even conjure up my nonexistent
girlfriend without seeing her in pieces, a doll with detachable arms
and stretch-apart lips, her stuffed cats torn to bits on the floor. I lie
in bed for a long while listening to the televisions, feeling severed
from humanity, wondering how the charm of solitude becomes the
curse of isolation. Finally, my self-reproach rising to the Hearns-
Hagler line, I lurch up out of bed, pull on my bloody sweatshirt
and high-top cooking shoes, and stomp out of my groaning, scrib-
bled-on chamber into the night.

Even angry, it isn't smart to walk in this part of town after dark.
There's glass smashed on the sidewalks, a trash can overturned in
the middle of the street, a house entirely covered in graffiti. A
streetlight has been extinguished, shot out or shattered with a
rock. Across the street, a pack of snuffling mutts, noses down, offer
me a collective disinterested glance before shuffling past. Antic figures in comic street poses angle toward me out of the darkness:

"You got a cigarette?"

"You got any quarters?"

Old Spooky rides by on his ten-speed, then circles back around
like a vulture. "Hey, man, what you doing in this part of town?"

In the distance a shriek rises above a wobbling siren. I hear a
gate squeak, then a volley of male laughter and a sound like baseball bats clattering down picket fences. I can't help but picture
Louisville Slugger trademarks embedded in my forehead and the
headline in the next day's paper: "Yankee Pud-Puller Bludgeoned."

"You *lost,* man?"

"Hey, gimme a dollar."

I must not be far from the railroad tracks. Yet within four blocks
I pass four churches. Unlike the surrounding bars, liquor stores,
massage parlors, crack houses, and porno motels, all crumbling in
their definition of man as pork chop, these Roman Catholic,
Gothic First Methodist, Byzantine Baptist, and Greek Orthodox
structures appear built to last, even if their doors are locked, their

mad and destitute turned out into the street. In the doorway of the Greek Orthodox church stands a lone sentry in a filthy robe and a gold Burger King cardboard crown, the smoky stump of a candle burning at his feet. Under his shabbily bearded and thickly lugubrious face he holds a sign that reads, 501 MINUTES TO CHRIST.

I've seen Christ twice in my life: once while stoned and all alone in a flea-ridden Mission Beach bungalow; the other time, not long ago, while praying out of the depths of my despair. On both occasions the darkness parted and my heart was lifted with awe. In clear and sane seasons I understand that Christ is merely a refined cultural label for spirit, an archetype who will not return like Superman to save the world in its final chapter of time. But, the smell of my old life still in my nostrils, I also know that spirit (and all its archetypes and guises) is all that I will ever possess of worth.

When I return to my room, exhilarated by my reckless stroll through the ghetto and my encounter with the mystical wisdom of the insane, I smell perfume. It seems there has been a tussle on my bed. One of my bags is unzipped. I can't tell if anything has been taken. I look in the bathroom. I check behind the shower curtain and under the bed.

Many hours later, keys rattle in the door. *Must be the maid,* I think. Then I glance at the clock: 4:20 A.M. I dredge myself from sleep, heart knocking at the top of my chest. The door creeps open across the carpet. A square of moonlight falls on the foot of the bed. A form moves toward me, then stops suddenly, strands of hair lit by the moon. My bag with the knives sits on the table across the way, open but too far to reach.

"You got the wrong room," I say, straining to keep my voice calm.

"Oh," a feminine voice replies. "I didn't know anyone was here."

"You got the wrong room, baby," I repeat, sitting up.

"You sure?" she croons.

"Get out," I say.

At the depot an hour later, two days still left on the room, I stare at a map a long while before buying a one-way ticket to Waterloo, Iowa. (Strange choice, Waterloo, symbol of a great defeat.) As I stroll about the station, I struggle with the riddle of the madman's sign. I wonder: Does 501 have some numerological significance, the way 666 does? And does the man ever update his sign? If not, there will always be 501 minutes to salvation and no one left on earth to save our wretched souls but us. For a moment I wonder if the man in the doorway was not some sort of personal apparition. I check the travel time from Louisville to Waterloo, thinking: *What if it's eight hours and twenty-one minutes* — 501 minutes — *to my own salvation?*

Now I'm losing *my* mind, seeing magic messages planted everywhere. (Travel time between the two cities is fifteen hours and fifty minutes.) No, nothing has changed. Yet I must believe in something more substantial than longevity through vitamins, or protein globules accidentally evolving into Leonardo da Vinci. Whatever I believe must have the depth and power to repel evil, insanity, loneliness, and despair. It must be built on the observation of what is good and true.

I am a shy person who lives in his head. I seek chemical and dramatic escapes from an unspectacular existence. I will likely finish my life alone in a room. Still, I can only do what I know how to do, these crude pilgrimages of moving, searching, and starting over. I am heartened by the cryptic message of the peculiar prophet in the doorway. If I am indeed spirit, eternal and indestructible, I have nothing to fear. The sun is up now, three hours to go before my bus leaves. I buy a Mr. Goodbar from the machine and sit down to wait.

EMILY BERNARD

Teaching the N-Word

FROM THE AMERICAN SCHOLAR

Once riding in old Baltimore,
Heart-filled, head-filled with glee,
I saw a Baltimorean
Keep looking straight at me.

Now I was eight and very small,
And he was no whit bigger,
And so I smiled, but he poked out
His tongue, and called me, "Nigger."

I saw the whole of Baltimore
From May until December;
Of all the things that happened there
That's all that I remember.

— COUNTEE CULLEN, "Incident" (1925)

October 2004

ERIC IS CRAZY ABOUT queer theory. I think it is safe to say that Eve Sedgwick, Judith Butler, and Lee Edelman have changed his life. Every week, he comes to my office to report on the connections he is making between the works of these writers and the books he is reading for the class he is taking with me, African-American autobiography.

I like Eric. So tonight, even though it is well after six and I am eager to go home, I keep our conversation going. I ask him what he thinks about the word "queer," whether or not he believes, independent of the theorists he admires, that epithets can ever really be reclaimed and reinvented.

" 'Queer' has important connotations for me," he says. "It's daring, political. I embrace it." He folds his arms across his chest, and then unfolds them.

I am suspicious.

"What about 'nigger'?" I ask. "If we're talking about the importance of transforming hateful language, what about that word?" From my bookshelf I pull down Randall Kennedy's book *Nigger: The Strange Career of a Troublesome Word,* and turn it so its cover faces Eric. "Nigger," in stark white type against a black background, is staring at him, staring at anyone who happens to be walking past the open door behind him.

Over the next thirty minutes or so, Eric and I talk about "nigger." He is uncomfortable; every time he says "nigger," he drops his voice and does not meet my eyes. I know that he does not want to say the word; he is following my lead. He does not want to say it because he is white; he does not want to say it because I am black. I feel my power as his professor, the mentor he has so ardently adopted. I feel the power of Randall Kennedy's book in my hands, its title crude and unambiguous. *Say it,* we both instruct this white student. And he does.

It is late. No one moves through the hallway. I think about my colleagues, some of whom still sit at their own desks. At any minute, they might pass my office on their way out of the building. What would they make of this scene? Most of my colleagues are white. What would I think if I walked by an office and saw one of them holding up *Nigger* to a white student's face? A black student's face?

"I think I am going to add 'Who Can Say "Nigger"?' to our reading for next week," I say to Eric. "It's an article by Kennedy that covers some of the ideas in this book." I tap *Nigger* with my finger, and then put it down on my desk.

"I really wish there was a black student in our class," Eric says as he gathers his books to leave.

As usual, I have assigned way too much reading. Even though we begin class discussion with references to three essays required for today, our conversation drifts quickly to "Who Can Say 'Nigger'?" and plants itself there. We talk about the word, who can say it, who won't say it, who wants to say it, and why. There are eleven students in the class. All of them are white.

Our discussion is lively and intense; everyone seems impatient to speak. We talk about language, history, and identity. Most students say "the n-word" instead of "nigger." Only one or two students actually use the word in their comments. When they do, they use the phrase "the word 'nigger,' " as if to cushion it. Sometimes they make quotation marks with their fingers. I notice Lauren looking around. Finally she raises her hand.

"I have a question; it's somewhat personal. I don't want to put you on the spot."

"Go ahead, Lauren," I say with relief.

"Okay, so how does it feel for you to hear us say that word?"

I have an answer ready.

"I don't enjoy hearing it. But I don't think that I feel more offended by it than you do. What I mean is, I don't think I have a special place of pain inside of me that the word touches because I am black." *We are both human beings,* I am trying to say. She nods her head, seemingly satisfied. Even inspired, I hope.

I am lying, of course.

I am grateful to Lauren for acknowledging my humanity in our discussion. But I do not want me — my feelings, my experiences, my humanity — to become the center of classroom discussion. Here at the University of Vermont, I routinely teach classrooms full of white students. I want to educate them, transform them. I want to teach them things about race they will never forget. To achieve this, I believe I must give of myself. I want to give to them — but I want to keep much of myself to myself. How much? I have a new answer to this question every week.

I always give my students a lecture at the beginning of every African-American studies course I teach. I tell them, in essence, not to confuse my body with the body of the text. I tell them that while it would be disingenuous for me to suggest that my own racial identity has nothing to do with my love for African-American literature, my race is only one of the many reasons why I stand before them. "I stand here," I say, "because I have a Ph.D., just like all your other professors." I make sure always to tell them that my Ph.D., like my B.A., comes from Yale.

"In order to get this Ph.D.," I continue, "I studied with some of this country's foremost authorities on African-American literature, and a significant number of these people are white.

"I say this to suggest that if you fail to fully appreciate this material, it is a matter of your intellectual laziness, not your race. If you cannot grasp the significance of Frederick Douglass's plight, for instance, you are not trying hard enough, and I will not accept that."

I have another part of this lecture. It goes: "Conversely, this material is not the exclusive property of students of color. This is literature. While these books will speak to us emotionally according to our different experiences, none of us is especially equipped to appreciate the intellectual and aesthetic complexities that characterize African-American literature. This is American literature, American experience, after all."

Sometimes I give this part of my lecture, but not always. Sometimes I give it and then regret it later.

As soon as Lauren asks me how I feel, it is as if the walls of the room soften and collapse slightly, nudging us a little bit closer together. Suddenly, eleven pairs of eyes are beaming sweet messages at me. I want to laugh. I do. "Look at you all, leaning in," I say. "How close we have all become."

I sit at the end of a long narrow table. Lauren usually sits at the other end. The rest of the students flank us on either side. When I make my joke, a few students, all straight men, I notice, abruptly pull themselves back. They shift their eyes away from me, look instead at their notebooks, the table. I have made them ashamed to show that they care about me, I realize. They are following the cues I have been giving them since the beginning of the semester, cues that they should take this class seriously, that I will be offended if they do not. "African-American studies has had to struggle to exist at all," I have said. "You owe it your respect." *Don't be too familiar* is what I am really saying. *Don't be too familiar with me.*

Immediately, I regret having made a joke of their sincere attempt to offer me their care. They want to know me; they see this moment as an opportunity. But I can't stop. I make more jokes, mostly about them, and what they are saying and not saying. I can't seem to help myself.

Eric, who is sitting near me, does not recoil at my jokes; he does not respond to my not-so-subtle efforts to push him and everyone else back. He continues to lean in, his torso flat against the edge of the table. He looks at me. He raises his hand.

"Emily," he says, "would you tell them what you told me the other day in your office? You were talking about how you dress and what it means to you."

"Yes," I begin slowly. "I was telling Eric about how important it is to me that I come to class dressed up."

"And remember what you said about Todd? You said that Todd exercises his white privilege by dressing so casually for class."

Todd is one of my closest friends in the English department. His office is next door to mine. I don't remember talking about Todd's clothing habits with Eric, but I must have. I struggle to come up with a comfortably vague response to stop Eric's prodding. My face grows hot. Everyone is waiting.

"Well, I don't know if I put it exactly like that, but I do believe that Todd's style of dress reflects his ability to move in the world here — everywhere, really — less self-consciously than I do." As I sit here, I grow increasingly more alarmed at what I am revealing: my personal philosophies; my attitudes about my friend's style of dress; my insecurities; my feelings. I quietly will Eric to stop, even as I am impressed by his determination. I meet his eyes again.

"And you. You were saying that the way you dress, it means something too," Eric says. *On with this tug of war,* I think.

I relent, let go of the rope. "Listen, I will say this. I am aware that you guys, all of my students at UVM, have very few black professors. I am aware, in fact, that I may be the first black teacher many of you have ever had. And the way I dress for class reflects my awareness of that possibility." I look sharply at Eric. *That's it. No more.*

September 2004

On the first day of class, Nate asks me what I want to be called.

"Oh, I don't know," I say, fussing with equipment in the room. I know. But I feel embarrassed, as if I have been found out. "What do you think?" I ask them.

They shuffle around, equally embarrassed. We all know that I have to decide, and that whatever I decide will shape our classroom dynamic in very important ways.

"What does Gennari ask you to call him?" I have inherited several of these students from my husband, John Gennari, another professor of African-American studies. He is white.

"Oh, we call him John," Nate says with confidence. I am immediately envious of the easy warmth he seems to feel for John. I suspect it has to do with the name thing.

"Well, just call me Emily, then. This is an honors class, after all. And I do know several of you already. And then wouldn't it be strange to call the husband John and the wife Professor?" Okay, I have convinced myself.

Nate says, "Well, John and I play basketball in a pickup game on Wednesdays. So, you know, it would be weird for me to be checking him and calling him Professor Gennari."

We all laugh and move on to other topics. But my mind locks onto an image of my husband and Nate on the basketball court, two white men covered in sweat, body to body, heads down, focused on the ball.

October 2004

"It's not that I can't say it, it's that I don't want to. I will not say it," Sarah says. She wears her copper-red hair in a short, smart style that makes her look older than her years. When she smiles I remember how young she is. She is not smiling now. She looks indignant. She is indignant because I am insinuating that there is a problem with the fact that no one in the class will say "nigger." Her indignation pleases me.

Good.

"I'd just like to remind you all that just because a person refuses to say 'nigger,' that doesn't mean that person is not a racist," I say. They seem to consider this.

"And another thing," Sarah continues. "About dressing for class? I dislike it when my professors come to class in shorts, for instance. This is a profession. They should dress professionally."

Later, I tell my husband, John, about our class discussion. When I get to Sarah's comment about professors in shorts, he says, "Good for her."

I hold up *Nigger* and show its cover to the class. I hand it to the person on my left, gesture for him to pass the book around the room.

"Isn't it strange that when we refer to this book, we keep calling it 'the n-word'?"

Lauren comments on the affect of one student who actually said it. "Colin looked like he was being strangled." Of the effect on the other students, she says, "I saw us all collectively cringing."

"Would you be able to say it if I weren't here?" I blurt. A few students shake their heads. Tyler's hand shoots up. He always sits directly to my right.

"That's just bullshit," he says to the class, and I force myself not to raise an eyebrow at "bullshit." "If Emily weren't here, you all would be able to say that word."

I note that he himself has not said it, but I do not make this observation out loud.

"No." Sarah is firm. "I just don't want to be the kind of person who says that word, period."

"Even in this context?" I ask.

"Regardless of context," Sarah says.

"Even when it's the title of a book?"

I tell the students that I often work with a book called *Nigger Heaven*, written in 1926 by a white man, Carl Van Vechten.

"Look, I don't want to give you the impression that I am somehow longing for you guys to say 'nigger,' " I tell them, "but I do think that something is lost when you don't articulate it, especially if the context almost demands its articulation."

"What do you mean? What exactly is lost?" Sarah insists.

"I don't know," I say. I do know. But right here, in this moment, the last thing I want is to win an argument that winds up with Sarah saying "nigger" out loud.

Throughout our discussion, Nate is the only student who will say "nigger" out loud. He sports a shearling coat and a caesar haircut. He quotes Jay-Z. He makes a case for "nigga." He is that kind of white kid; he is down. "He is so down, he's almost up," Todd will say in December, when I show him the title page of Nate's final paper for this class. The page contains one word, "Nigger," in black type against a white background. It is an autobiographical essay. It is a very good paper.

October 1994

Nate reminds me of a student in the very first class I taught all on my own, a senior seminar called "Race and Representation." I was still in graduate school. It was 1994 and *Pulp Fiction* had just come out. I spent an entire three-hour class session arguing with my students over the way race was represented in the movie. One student in particular passionately resisted my attempts to analyze the way Tarantino used "nigger" in the movie.

"What is his investment in this word? What is he, as the white director, getting out of saying 'nigger' over and over again?" I asked.

After some protracted verbal arm wrestling, the student gave in.

"Okay, okay! I want to be the white guy who can say 'nigger' to black guys and get away with it. I want to be the cool white guy who can say 'nigger.' "

"Thank you! Thank you for admitting it!" I said, and everyone laughed.

He was tall. He wore tie-dyed T-shirts and had messy, curly brown hair. I don't remember his name.

After *Pulp Fiction* came out, I wrote my older brother an earnest, academic e-mail. I wanted to "initiate a dialogue" with him about the "cultural and political implications of the various usages of 'nigger' in popular culture."

His one-sentence reply went something like this: "Nigga, niggoo, niggu, negreaux, negrette, niggrum."

"Do you guys ever read *The Source* magazine?" In 1994, my students knew about *The Source;* some of them had read James Bernard's column, "Doin' the Knowledge."

"He's my brother," I said, not bothering to mask my pride with anything like cool indifference. "He's coming to visit class in a couple of weeks, when we discuss hip-hop culture."

The eyes of the tie-dyed student glistened.

"Quentin Tarantino is a cool-ass white boy!" James said on the day he came to visit my class. "He is one cool white boy."

My students clapped and laughed.

"That's what I said," my tie-dyed student sighed.

James looked at me slyly. I narrowed my eyes at him. *Thanks a lot.*

September 2004

On the way to school in the morning, I park my car in the Allen House lot. Todd was the one who told me about the lot. He said, "Everyone thinks the lot at the library is closer, but the lot behind Allen House is so much better. Plus, there are always spaces, in part because everyone rushes for the library."

It is true that the library lot is nearly always full in the morning. It's also true that the Allen House lot is relatively empty, and much closer to my office. But if it were even just slightly possible for me to find a space in the library lot, I would probably try to park there, for one reason. To get to my office from Allen House, I have to cross a busy street. To get to my office from the library, I do not.

Several months ago, I was crossing the same busy street to get to my office after a class. It was late April, near the end of the semester, and it seemed as if everyone was outside. Parents were visiting, and students were yelling to each other, introducing family members from across the street. People smiled at me — wide, grinning smiles. I smiled back. We were all giddy with the promise of spring, which always comes so late in Vermont, if it comes at all.

Traffic was heavy, I noticed as I walked along the sidewalk, calculating the moment when I would attempt to cross. A car was stopped near me; I heard rough voices. Out of the corner of my eye, I looked into the car: all white. I looked away, but I could feel them surveying the small crowd that was carrying me along. As traffic picked up again, one of the male voices yelled out, "Queers! Fags!" There was laughter. Then the car roared off.

I was stunned. I stopped walking and let the words wash over me. *Queer. Fag.* Annihilating, surely. I remembered my role as a teacher, a mentor, in loco parentis, even though there were real parents everywhere. I looked around to check for the wounds caused by those hateful words. I peered down the street: too late for a license plate. All around me, students and parents marched to their destinations as if they hadn't heard. *Didn't you hear that?* I wanted to shout.

All the while I was thinking, *Not nigger. Not yet.*

October 2004

Nate jumps in.

"Don't you grant a word power by not saying it? Aren't we in some way amplifying its ugliness by avoiding it?" he asks.

"I am afraid of how I will be affected by saying it," Lauren says. "I just don't want that word in my mouth."

Tyler remembers a phrase attributed to Farai Chideya in Randall Kennedy's essay. He finds it and reads it to us. "She says that the n-word is the 'trump card, the nuclear bomb of racial epithets.' "

"Do you agree with that?" I ask.

Eleven heads nod vigorously.

"Nuclear bombs annihilate. What do you imagine will be destroyed if you guys use the word in here?"

Shyly, they look at me, all of them, and I understand. Me. It is my annihilation they imagine.

November 2004

Some of My Best Friends, my anthology of essays about interracial friendship, came out in August, and the publicity department has arranged for various interviews and other promotional events. When I did an on-air interview on a New York radio show, one of the hosts, Janice, a black woman, told me that the reason she could not marry a white man was because she believed if things ever got heated between them, the white man would call her a nigger.

I nodded my head. I had heard this argument before. But strangely I had all but forgotten it. The fact that I had forgotten to fear "nigger" coming from the mouth of my white husband was more interesting to me than her fear, alive and ever-present.

"Are you biracial?"

"No."

"Are you married to a white man?"

"Yes."

These were among the first words exchanged between Janice, the radio host, and me. I could tell — by the way she looked at me, and didn't look at me; by the way she kept her body turned away from me; by her tone — that she had made up her mind about me before I entered the room. I could tell that she didn't like what she had decided about me, and that she had decided I was the wrong kind of black person. Maybe it was what I had written in *Some of My Best Friends*. Maybe it was the fact that I had decided to edit a collection about interracial friendships at all. When we met, she said, "I don't trust white people," as decisively and exactly as if she were handing me her business card. I knew she was telling me that I was foolish to trust them, to marry one. I was relieved to look inside myself and see that I was okay, I was still standing. A few years ago, her silent judgment — this silent judgment from any black person — would have crushed me.

When she said she could "tell" I was married to a white man, I asked her how. She said, "Because you are so friendly," and did a little dance with her shoulders. I laughed.

But Janice couldn't help it; she liked me in spite of herself. As the interview progressed, she let the corners of her mouth turn up in a smile. She admitted that she had a few white friends, even if they sometimes drove her crazy. At a commercial break, she said, "Maybe I ought to try a white man." She was teasing me, of course. She hadn't changed her mind about white people, or dating a white man, but she had changed her mind about me. It mattered to me. I took what she was offering. But when the interview was over, I left it behind.

My husband thought my story about the interview was hilarious. When I got home, he listened to the tape they gave me at the station. He said he wanted to use the interview in one of his classes.

A few days later, I told him what Janice had said about dating a white man, that she won't because she is afraid he will call her a nigger. As I told him, I felt an unfamiliar shyness creep up on me.

"That's just so far out of . . . it's not in my head at all." He was having difficulty coming up with the words he wanted, I could tell. But that was okay. I knew what he meant. I looked at him sitting in his chair, the chair his mother gave us. I can usually find him in that chair when I come home. He is John, I told myself. And he is white. No more or less John and no more or less white than he was before the interview, and Janice's reminder of the fear that I had forgotten to feel.

I tell my students in the African-American autobiography class about Janice. I say, "You would not believe the indignities I have suffered in my humble attempts to 'move this product,' as they say in publishing." I say, "I have been surrounded by morons, and now I gratefully return to the land of the intellectually agile." They laugh.

I flatter them, in part because I feel guilty that I have missed so many classes in order to do publicity for my book. But I cringe, thinking of how I have called Janice, another black woman, a "moron" in front of these white students. I do not tell my students she is black.

"Here is a story for your students," John tells me. We are in the car, on our way to Cambridge for the weekend. "The only time I ever heard 'nigger' in my home growing up was when my father's cousin was over for a visit. It was 1988, I remember. Jesse Jackson was running for president. My father's cousin was sitting in the kitchen, talking to my parents about the election. 'I'm going to vote for the nigger,' my father's cousin said. 'He's the only one who cares about the workingman.' "

John laughs. He often laughs when he hears something extraordinary, whether it's good or bad.

"That's fascinating," I say.

The next time class meets, I tell my students this story.

"So what do we care about in this sentence?" I say. "The fact that John's father's cousin used a racial epithet, or the fact that his voting for Jackson conveys a kind of ultimate respect for him? Isn't his voting for Jackson more important for black progress than how his father's cousin *feels?*"

I don't remember what the students said. What I remember is that I tried to project for them a sense that I was untroubled by saying "nigger," by my husband's saying "nigger," by his father's cousin's having said "nigger," by his parents' — my in-laws' — tolerance of "nigger" in their home, years ago, long before I came along. What I remember is that I leaned on the word "feels" with a near sneer in my voice. *It's an intellectual issue,* I beamed at them, and then I directed it back at myself. *It has nothing to do with how it makes me feel.*

After my interview with Janice, I look at the white people around me differently, as if from a distance. I do this, from time to time, almost as an exercise. I even do it to my friends, particularly my friends. Which of them has "nigger" in the back of her throat?

I go out for drinks with David, my senior colleague. It is a ritual. We go on Thursdays after class, always to the same place. I know that he will order, in succession, two draft beers, and that he will ask the waitress to help him choose the second. "What do you have on draft that is interesting tonight?" he will say. I order red wine, and I, too, always ask the waitress's advice. Then we order a selection of cheeses, again soliciting assistance. We have our favorite waitresses. We like the ones who indulge us.

Tonight David orders a cosmopolitan.

We never say it, but I suspect we both like the waitresses who appreciate the odd figure we cut. He is white, sixty-something, male. I am black, thirty-something, female. Not such an odd pairing elsewhere, perhaps, but uncommon in Burlington, insofar as black people are uncommon in Burlington.

Something you can't see is that we are both from the South. Different Souths, perhaps, thirty years apart, black and white. I am often surprised by how much I like his company. *All the way up here,* I sometimes think when I am with him, *and I am sitting with the South, the white South that, all of my childhood, I longed to escape.* I once had a white boyfriend from New Orleans. "A white southerner, Emily?" my mother asked, and sighed with worry. I understood. We broke up.

David and I catch up. We talk about the writing we have been doing. We talk each other out of bad feelings we are harboring against this and that person. (Like most southerners, like the South in general, David and I have long memories.) We talk about classes. I describe to him the conversation I have been having with my students about "nigger." He laughs at my anecdotes.

I am on my second glass of wine. I try to remember to keep my voice down. It's a very nice restaurant. *People in Burlington do not want to hear "nigger" while they are eating a nice dinner,* I say, chastising myself. I am tipsy.

As we leave, I accidentally knock my leg against a chair. *You are drunk,* I tell myself. *You are drunk and black in a restaurant in Burlington. What were you thinking?* I feel eyes on me as I walk out of the restaurant, eyes that may have been focused elsewhere, as far as I know, because I do not allow myself to look.

Later that evening, I am alone. I remember that David recently gave me a poem of his to read, a poem about his racist grand-mother, now dead, whom he remembers using the word "nigger" often and with relish. I lie in bed and reconstruct the scene of Da-vid and me in the restaurant, our conversation about "nigger." Was his grandmother at the table with us all along?

The next day, I see David in his office, which is next to mine, on the other side from Todd. I knock on the door. He invites me in. I sit in a chair, the chair I always sit in when I come to talk to him. He tells me how much he enjoyed our conversation the night before.

"Me too," I say. "But today it's as if I'm looking at you across from something," I say. "It has to do with race." I blame a book I am reading, a book for my African-American autobiography class, Toi Derricotte's *The Black Notebooks.*

"Have you read it?" David is a poet, like Derricotte.

"No, but I know Toi and enjoy her poetry. Everything I know about her and her work would lead me to believe that I would en-joy that book." He is leaning back in his chair, his arms folded be-hind his head.

"Well, it's making me think about things, remember the ways that you and I will always be different," I say abruptly.

David laughs. "I hope not." He looks puzzled.

"It's probably just temporary." I don't ask him my question about his grandmother, whether or not she is always somewhere with him, in him, in the back of his throat.

John is at an African-American studies conference in New York. Usually I am thrilled to have the house to myself for a few days. But this time I mope. I sit at the dining room table, write this essay, gaze out the window.

Today, when John calls, he describes the activity at the conference. He tells me delicious and predictable gossip about people we know, and the divas that we know of. The personalities, the infighting — greedily we sift over details on the phone.

"Did you enjoy your evening with David last night?" he asks.

"I did, very much," I say. "But give me more of the who-said-what." I know he's in a hurry. In fact, he's talking on a cell phone (my cell phone; he refuses to get one of his own) as he walks down a New York street.

"Oh, you know these Negroes." His voice jounces as he walks.

"Yeah," I say, laughing. I wonder who else can hear him.

Todd is married to Hilary, another of my close friends in the department. She is white. Like John, Todd is out of town this weekend. Since their two boys were born, our godsons, John and I see them less frequently than we used to. But Hilary and I are determined to spend some time together this weekend, with our husbands away.

Burlington traffic keeps me from her and the boys for an hour, even though she lives only blocks away from me. When I get there, the boys are ready for their baths, one more feeding, and then bed. Finally they are down, and we settle into grown-up conversation. I tell her about my class, our discussions about "nigger," and my worries about David.

"That's the thing about the South," Hilary says. I agree, but then start to wonder about her grandmother. I decide I do not want to know, not tonight.

I do tell her, however, about the fear I have every day in Burlington, crossing that street to get back and forth from my office, what I do to guard myself against the fear.

"Did you grow up hearing that?" she asks. Even though we are close, and alone, she does not say the word.

I start to tell her a story I have never told anyone. It is a story about the only time I remember being called a nigger to my face.

"I was a teenager, maybe sixteen. I was standing on a sidewalk, trying to cross a busy street after school, to get to the mall and meet my friends. I happened to make eye contact with a white man in a car that was sort of stopped — traffic was heavy. Anyway, he just said it, kind of spit it up at me.

"*Oh, that's why,*" I say, stunned, remembering the daily ritual I have just confessed to her. She looks at me, just as surprised.

December 2004

I am walking down a Burlington street with my friend Anh. My former quilting teacher, Anh is several years younger than I am. She has lived in Vermont her whole life. She is Vietnamese; her parents are white. Early in our friendship, she told me her father was a logger, as were most of the men in her family. *Generations of Vietnamese loggers in Vermont,* I mused. It wasn't until I started to describe her to someone else that I realized she must be adopted.

Anh and I talk about race, about being minorities in Burlington, but we usually do it indirectly. In quilting class, we would give each other looks sometimes that said, *You are not alone,* or *Oh, brother,* when the subject of race came up in our class, which was made up entirely of white women, aside from the two of us.

There was the time, for instance, when a student explained why black men found her so attractive. "I have a black girl's butt," she said. Anh and I looked at each other: *Oh, brother.* We bent our heads back over our sewing machines.

As we walk, I tell Anh about my African-American autobiography class, the discussions my students and I have been having about "nigger." She listens, and then describes to me the latest development in her on-again, off-again relationship with her fifty-year-old boyfriend, another native Vermonter, a blond scuba instructor.

"He says everything has changed," she tells me. "He's going to clean up the messes in his life." She laughs.

Once, Anh introduced me to the boyfriend she had before the scuba instructor when I ran into them at a restaurant. He is also white.

"I've heard a lot about you," I said, and put out my hand.

"I've never slept with a black woman," he said, and shook my hand. There was wonder in his voice. I excused myself and went back to my table. Later, when I looked over at them, they were sitting side by side, not speaking.

Even though Anh and I exchanged our usual glances that night, I doubted that we would be able to recover our growing friendship.

Who could she be, dating someone like that? The next time I heard from her, months later, she had broken up with him.

I am rooting for the scuba instructor.

"He told me he's a new person," she says.

"Well, what did you say?" I ask her.

"In the immortal words of Jay-Z, I told him, 'Nigga, please.' "

I look at her and we laugh.

In lieu of a final class, my students come over for dinner. One by one, they file in. John takes coats while I pretend to look for things in the refrigerator. I can't stop smiling.

"The books of your life" is the topic for tonight. I have asked them to bring a book, a poem, a passage, some art that has affected them. Hazel has brought a children's book. Tyler talks about *Saved by the Bell*. Nate talks about Freud. Dave has a photograph. Eric reads "The Seacoast of Despair" from *Slouching Towards Bethlehem*.

I read from *Annie John* by Jamaica Kincaid. Later I will wonder why I did not read "Incident" by Countee Cullen, the poem that has been circulating in my head ever since we began our discussion about "nigger." *What held me back from bringing "Incident" to class?* The question will stay with me for months.

The night of our dinner is an emotional one. I tell my students that they are the kind of class a professor dreams about. They give me a gift certificate to the restaurant that David and I frequent. I give them copies of *Some of My Best Friends* and inscribe each one. Eric demands a hug, and then they all do; I happily comply. We talk about meeting again as a class, maybe once or twice in the spring. The two students who will be abroad promise to keep in touch through our listserv, which we all agree to keep going until the end of the school year, at least. After they leave, the house is quiet and empty.

Weeks later, I post "Incident" on our listserv and ask them to respond with their reactions. Days go by, then weeks. Silence. After more prodding, finally Lauren posts an analysis of the poem, and then her personal reactions to it. I thank her online and ask for more responses. Silence.

I get e-mails and visits from these students about other matters, some of them race-related. Eric still comes by my office regularly. Once he brings his mother to meet me, a kind and engaging woman who gives me a redolent candle she purchased in France, and tells me her son enjoyed the African-American autobiography class. Eric and I smile at each other.

A few days later, I see Eric outside the campus bookstore.

"What did you think about 'Incident'?"

"I've been meaning to write you about it. I promise I will."

In the meantime, *Nigger* is back in its special place on my book-shelf. It is tucked away so that only I can see the title on its spine, and then only with some effort.

KEN CHEN

City Out of Breath

FROM MĀNOA

SO ALL NIGHT, we walk in one direction: up.

This is really the only direction you can go in Hong Kong, a direction hinted at by skyscrapers and aspired to by the Hong Kong Stock Exchange. By "we," I mean my father, myself, and our guide — my stepgrandmother-to-be — who somehow possesses both our combined age and our combined speed. Trudging up the stairs behind her, my father and I are already panting. We stop and laugh — really only an excuse to catch our breath — but by the top of the stairs we're bent and sagging, our hands on our knees. And there, at the end of the street, she's waving at us to hurry up, almost as if to fan away whatever remains of our quaint Californian version of walking. When we catch up with her, she says, in what seems like an especially Chinese blend of ridicule and public affection, that we walk too slowly.

If an American city at night is film noir, then Hong Kong is just a camera blur. The residents of Kowloon speed around with the same look on their faces, as if they're irked at their bodies for not being cars. You feel that if you stood still, the city would just rotate past you, as if you have no other choice but motion. Hong Kong accelerates as though located on another, faster-spinning earth. Anyone who has been there knows that time and space can flick off their objectivity and instead pulse and jump, symphonic rather than metronomic. In Hong Kong the world stretches time until time — along with space and language — goes elastic. It's like a Chinese painting in which conflicting perspectives soak through the landscape like radiation. A McDonald's sits next to a vegetable cart tended by a woman who looks about five hundred years old. The all-Chinese police band plays bagpipes and marches in kilts for the St. Patrick's Day parade. Street markets are the opposite of flowers: opening up at night and closing at day. In Hong Kong, all times are contiguous. All times are simultaneous. This essay is an attempt to describe a city that is itself already a description — Hong Kong is a description of time. This essay is also an experiment in time travel — an artifact of memory from July 2000. Hong Kong is now the same city but a different place. Prosperity — once the city's one-word gloss — is slowly becoming synonymous with Shanghai. "I hear everyone's real depressed over there," I say at dinner to the mother of a friend of mine from Hong Kong. "That they're jealous, with all the jobs heading over to the mainland and all." She chews on a piece of lettuce and says, "Yes, they are jealous. But they have a right to be."

Five years later, we spend the next half-hour taking elevators that lead to stairs that lead to elevators. I don't have any idea where we're going and just follow my father, an immigrant from Taiwan whose Mandarin, I realize, makes him only a third less lost than I am. He's following our guide, who, like Hong Kong itself, is all energy and no conversation. "We're headed for Victoria Peak today," my dad announced this morning. The touristy lookout could be the only spot where Hong Kong can be made comprehensible.

Suddenly our guide stops. Are we lost? This possibility is not surprising. It feels like we've been going in spirals, victims of some kind of geographic hoax. Our guide decides to ask for directions in Cantonese. She stops a man with a dark complexion who reminds me of the vendors at the Taipei night market. He has short, wiry hair that resembles a scouring pad and is wearing a security guard's uniform. Chinese — I think — obviously. Probably a migrant from the mainland. "Where is Victoria Peak?" she asks him in Cantonese. The security guard looks at her and says, "Do you speak English?"

Dad and I look at each other. He says, "This is a strange city," and I start laughing, relieved that I'm not the only one who thinks so. We seem to be fumbling through different languages, shifting, testing, trying to find one we can all stand in. A bus rocking through the northern hills speaks to its passengers in Miltonic English: *Do not board or alight whilst bus is in motion.* (Lucifer alights.

Buses throttle.) And a week ago in Taiwan, my father had shed the most mundanely engrossing fear of any Chinese immigrant to America: his accent. He became a master of languages, all traces of self-consciousness suddenly gone from his voice. He chatted with taxi drivers and strangers about the drenching humidity or about which restaurants were good, casually code-switching to Taiwanese for jokes, Mandarin for information, and English for translation and one-word exclamations. When we showed up at the desk of the Taipei Hilton, the girls on staff spotted my dad and approached him in nervous English. He paused, got an odd look on his face — the fuzzy expression that Looney Tunes characters have when they're suspended in midair and about to fall — and said in Mandarin: "I'm Chinese!"

Back to searching for Victoria Peak, my father starts to ask the question in English, but someone interrupts. A Hong Kong yuppie standing thirty feet away muffles his cell phone in his blazer lapel and tells us the answer in rushed Cantonese. Some men in black blazers walk by, and some teens with blond spiky hair walk by, and some middle-aged men with grimy white aprons walk by — mostly Chinese, but otherwise unidentifiable. Indian? Polynesian? British? Hong Kong is an intensely international city. Every street in Kowloon is an intersection, not only of wet-walled alleys and futuristic buildings of glass, but also of the more transparent rays of cultures.

Somehow you are supposed to teach yourself how to comprehend Hong Kong's energy and flashy contradictions: Asian and Western; the encroaching Chinese mainland and the remnants of England; the greasy night markets of sticky-rice tamales and knock-off leather boots that slouch right across from Tiffany, Chanel, and Prada. The only things common to these are the offices sending air-conditioned blasts into the street, a kind of longing for money, and, most important, the sense of storytelling that the city seems to require as a visitor's pass. Hong Kong has a way of turning on your internal monologue. Walking becomes an act of silent storytelling, figuring people out. You feel like you are lost in some prelapsarian novel in which the plot has begun but the characters wait for you to name them. In some time, at some place, we step into an underground Cantonese restaurant and I see a gray-suited, red-tied man act like a parody of the States. American, I say, with an American

accent: good-natured smiles, occasionally the slow English dis-
patched on foreigners and children, and a slightly uncomfortable
look, as though he's worried he's outnumbered.

Finally we find Victoria Peak, by which I mean that we find the
gondola to get us there. We buy tickets and step in, waiting to be
hoisted up into the humid nighttime atmosphere. The cab starts
moving. At first, nothing in the windows but the ads on the sides of
the tunnel, and then suddenly the city. Our gondola windows have
become postcards. Hong Kong poses before us, bright, earnestly
capitalist, electric, multiplying. A concrete wall blocks the view, and
then the city is back again. Under us, a small red house sits on the
cuff of the panorama. Light drops out of a pair of shutters, a door
or window is open; someone is home. More stone, more wall. We
hit the crest, reach our destination: Victoria Peak, the highest spot
in Hong Kong and, for a tourist, the best. We have a God's-eye view
of the skyline. The buildings shine yellow, white, orange, blue, all
reflected in the dark bay waters; giant corporate logos shrink, skyscrapers huddle, and the city glows with a brilliant coolness. My eye
seems too small to hold it all in.

We take the bus back. I sit on the top of a double-decker bus, on
the left side, in a city where they drive on the left side of the road.
As we shake downhill, making acute turns, I begin to regret my
seating preference: the wobbly tourists' corner. The bus hits a
few branches, careens over double yellow lines, winds downhill.
Whipped by full-motion vertigo, I grope for the metal railing,
squeezing it as if for juice, and then laugh at my own cowardice. I
gasp, then yawn in a slow, measured sort of panic, a civilized form
of suffocation. Hong Kong — a city out of breath.

After we've been back from Victoria Peak for a few hours, I go to
the front desk of the hotel. A Hong Kong–Chinese woman in her
mid-twenties looks up the Internet rates for me. She reads the per-
minute charges off a small white card, and her voice compresses
Mandarin, English, and Cantonese into a linguistic diamond: the
Chinese-British accent. There's the Merchant-Ivory sound, the lilt
that movies tell us is cultured but that also seems austere and impe-
rial, the way Chinese period films do. Yet the sound is also familiar,
humble, and awkward: a Chinese voice wandering inside the English language. The sound of it reminds me of my parents. I can't
get enough of it.

A few days later, we are ready to leave. Samuel Johnson wrote that when one has tired of London, one has tired of life. But Hong Kong seems denser than any dream an American could have about London. We are suddenly sick of it. Everywhere is crowded: the restaurants at two on a Wednesday afternoon, the train platform every few minutes, the sidewalks wet with people. This is the opposite of loneliness. It is the abundance of people that alienates us.

My father and I step into an underground Cantonese restaurant, the one with the red-tied American, and the other diners fly by us, blurred, the abstract expressionist's version of people. A man sits across from us, the only person at his big round table. I'm guessing he's Indian. He has a sharp lawn mustache and a black satchel. A businessman from Britain? An engineer out for dinner? The other diners speed by us in streaks. I turn around and see the waiters coming by our table — or maybe just one waiter over and over — to set teacups upright, rip open chopsticks from their packaging, bring dishes, bring towels, even bring blankets when we say we are cold, bring the check. I hear another noise drift over the wheel of our table: the TV at the bar. The news is on: a fire yesterday in Tai O burns down homes in one of the few remaining fishing villages in Hong Kong, leaving seven hundred homeless. No, I'm getting it wrong. I'd read about it on the front page. There was no TV in that restaurant, not even a bar. Hong Kong quivers, not out of fear or sadness, but the way something quivers when our idea of it has changed. The waiters push out of the kitchen as if it's on fire, as if they're scrambling to escape it.

But the fire is Hong Kong.

TOI DERRICOTTE

Beginning Dialogues

FROM CREATIVE NONFICTION

ON THE WAY, he said, "When you visit the cemetery, you do it for yourself. They don't know you're there." But maybe some part of me believes she will know, that she's brought many good things to me after her death, that she's taking care. Maybe I visit her grave because she would have visited the grave of her mother, because she taught me to send thank-you notes and be a good girl. Maybe I'm going to find signs of whether she's still there; maybe she hasn't blown open the ground, and we'll find an angel lounging on her gravestone, saying, "She's not here. Go and find her elsewhere."

I don't seem to suffer the pains of anguish that many women whose mothers have died feel. Last night, a group about my age, all in that midlife past midlife, late fifties or early sixties, ate dinner and talked about our mothers' deaths. It's not a new conversation; women whose mothers have died always talk about it. They did even when I was in my twenties. Yet here no one is hearing these stories with expectancy; everyone has faced that which at one time was unthinkable. It's as if we're all in the same club, as if we have all finally arrived, as if we could all look back at those women on the other side and know we are totally new.

One woman talked about that inconsolable stabbing in the heart when she realized she wouldn't buy a Christmas present for her mother again this year. I've wondered about it, about perhaps having grieved the separation between my mother and me in my early childhood, for, in a way, I truly do not miss her like that, do not feel that irreversible moment of no return, as I did when she would go into the bathroom and shut the door, the ache that breaks the heart and has no answer. I felt the goneness of her then, as if the center of me was gone, and I tried to bring it back by peering through the crack at the bottom of the door, trying to see anything, even her feet.

I said this to the women who talked last night about their mothers. One woman, who said that her mother had died a few days after she was born, had always struck me before as cold, contained, and now, as she spoke, I noticed she was squeezing the fleshy part of her cheek, near her mouth, making a little fat bubble of flesh between her ring and baby fingers. I have seen that before, a kind of clumsy, unconscious pinching of the self, and it makes me feel great pity. Her fingers seemed squat, doing an act whose purpose I couldn't imagine — perhaps a partial holding to signify that she could not hold the whole of what she needed held. Now, clumsily, here was her body (was it her clumsy body that had killed her mother, ungracefully slipping out?) — her liveliness covered by a dreary cape, her hair dreary, her face unmade, as if who would care? — speaking about her mother's death (we had never heard of this, though we had known her for years!) without tears, just those two fingers clenching and opening, pinching a clump of cheek, letting go and clenching again, moving slightly, as if she couldn't find the right spot, and since the cheek is larger than what those two fingers can grasp, and since the two fingers form a small vise and take in only a slot of flesh, it seemed she was stopping the flesh from moving, clamping it in place. It seemed inadequate, incomplete, and ill chosen; in literature, the small thing signifies the whole of something we can imagine from the reference to the small thing, but here, the small reference did not convey. It was a clumsy effort, as a child might pinch the breast. Or perhaps it was an effort to make another mouth, to pucker the face, as the lips of the child might pucker for its mother's breast.

At my mother's grave, I tried to imagine what I should do. My partner had taken my picture at the grave and a picture of the inscription. He was sitting in the car. How long should I stay? My mind didn't know what to settle on. No particular feeling or idea carried me. I became lost in nothing. Just me, stuttering over an immensity that I couldn't absorb, the way I used to feel guilty for not feeling enough happiness at Christmas, after my mother's great efforts. I guess I felt that I was incompetent, too broken to hold. I sang her favorite song: "This little light of mine, I'm gonna let it shine." I wanted to give her a promise; I wanted to change my life because of her, just the way I did before.

I am struck by my own inability to feel grief. It feels like a refusal to face an end. I know I have great trouble facing boundaries, my own and others'. So, instead, perhaps there is this magical thinking built on my own inadequacy to face the truth: I say I get messages from my mother, that she is still in my life, and now, perhaps even more, she is reaching me, since her destruction is out of my way.

Once, when I called a friend to say I couldn't go on teaching at the prestigious workshop I was visiting because I could not stand the torturing voices in my head, twenty-four hours a day, saying I was no good, stupid, not as smart as the others, not as respected or loved, that I had no value, that I was there only because I was black, that I had done or said the wrong thing, that I was not really a poet, my friend said, "Why not ask the torturing voices from where they get their information?" I did, and without hesitation they answered, "From your mother."

  Things had changed by then, so I flipped back, "You haven't got the latest information!"

  Just a few months before she died, my mother turned the universe of an unloved daughter around with one sentence. Instead of screaming at me when I asked her not to come to one of my readings because I might read things that would make her uncomfortable, she said, "Oh, dear, would you be uncomfortable? I don't want you to be uncomfortable, so I won't come."

  I've written a lot about messages from her — I won't repeat them here — just to say my conversation with my mother isn't over, and I think it isn't over for her, either.

In the manuscript of my mother's book, I read about the women in her childhood — her mother, aunts, and grandmother — who helped each other beyond the bounds of the imaginable. Because of their hard labor, our family succeeded. I read this manuscript, which she put into my hands to publish only two days before her death, and I think that, although my mother began writing after I did, after I was published, she was a writer before she began writing. Though she is dead, our stories are in dialogue: my writing has been against her writing, as if there was a war between us. It is more than our writing that is in dialogue; it is our lives.

When I was seven, she told me how, when she left the house of the rich white people her mother worked for, the white kids were waiting to beat her up on her way to school, and as soon as she crossed the line to the black part of town, the black kids were there to beat her up too. Why would she tell me that story? Why would a mother tell a seven-year-old such a sad story, such a defeating one? I thought it was her way of saying, "Trust no one but your mother," a way of binding me to her by making me fear.

It's a question — what she said and did that I didn't understand, what she did to hurt me. It is not over; it is still a riddle being solved. I do not need to be held, and so, therefore, isn't my mother free too? Is that why she told me those stories? Was I to be the mother who freed her?

My partner and I have just spent a delightful weekend together, a sunny, windy fall weekend with the trees half shredded, the bright blue sky both miraculous and unavoidable through the nude branches and their silence. On the drive home, my mind comes to how my life has changed since my mother's death: slowly, I have been loosed from those heavy, nearly inconsolable fears like Houdini's chains, lock by lock, as if some magician part of me occasionally appears, from some unseen and undetectable room, with one more chain gone. Finally, I am gloriously undrowned.

Everyone says that I changed for the better, as if, when my mother's slight body, not even one hundred pounds, slipped into the earth, the whole world suddenly belonged to me. The first year I stopped jogging. People said it was grief, but whatever grief felt like — except for the first few days after her death, especially the burial day, heavy lodestar — it was too indistinct for me to grab on to. Two years later, I bought a house and found a man in my life, like a spectacular hat pin in just the right hat. The simple explanation would have been my mother's narcissism — the way she

pushed me toward independence, screaming, "You're weighing
me down," and yet, when I was sixteen and came in late one night,
slamming the door, she was behind it in the shadows, like a bur-
glar, and her hand went around my neck while she screamed, "I'll
kill you!" Who hasn't wanted to kill the one she loved?

But there was so much unaccounted for, so much in my mother's
past that I couldn't fix, not ever, or make up for. Maybe my mother
never had such a weekend of happiness with a man as I have just
had, though a former lover of hers once told me, when I asked
about the affair, how much she had loved to make love to him. Perhaps he told me because he loved me and thought I should know
that aspect of my mother, because knowing might help me put a
necessary piece in the puzzle. Perhaps he had sympathy for me —
in spite of the fact he had loved my mother — and didn't feel the
need to protect her. Perhaps he thought it was better to give a
daughter that important piece than to keep still about a dead
woman. And perhaps he was bragging a bit when he said it.

My mother had slept alone, in another room, in another bed,
for eighteen years of her marriage, until my parents divorced. I
never saw her kiss my father, and the only touch was the time I
heard him smash her against the table. My mother always gave
abundantly with one hand and pushed you away with the other.
The mystery of a beautiful woman. Perhaps in some reciprocal
way, my unhappy, angry, guilt-producing mother had also been a
planter, had been planting the seeds of my happiness with an invisible hand, the hand I didn't see. She left me enough money to buy
a house. She told me all my life she loved me, as if she completely
forgot the hundred slights, humiliations, threats, and insinuations.
Of course she loved me; why would I think otherwise? She loved
me more than anything. Sometimes she'd scream, as if my doubts
were another evil, another proof of my unworthiness. How exas-
perating my complaints must have been when, all along, she was
planting seeds with that invisible hand.

The women of that generation, my mother and aunts, counted
their blessings: Chinese food and beer on Friday nights after work,
and fried chicken breasts, twice-baked potatoes, and broccoli for
early Sunday afternoon dinners. And there were parties with boun-
teous tables; polished glasses and silver, a chandelier, every bauble
ammonia-shiny; and heat's seven coolnesses, the little cups of rice

turned over and decorated, each small, white breast with a nipple of parsley. Polished floors, shopping trips, lunch at Hudson's — these were the good things, the punctuation marks that held back despondency, that danced away despair. No hardship was unredeemable to women who had one endless belief: bread on the water always comes home. It wasn't until I was in my sixties that I realized it did, but not necessarily to the ones who cast it. I am eating bread from hands that are no longer there. I cannot reach back to touch their actual bodies. It is good that they are gone.

My mother helps me. She sends me signs: her African violet bloomed for the first time on my windowsill three years after her death, on the first day of her death month. She says, "Remember me. My miracles are still there for you, still becoming apparent as you have eyes to see." I love my mother now in ways I could not have loved her when she was alive, fierce, terrifying, unpredictable, mad, shame-inducing, self-involved, relentless, and determined by any means necessary. When she was a child, to get what she wanted from her mother, she would hold her breath until she was blue and pass out. Even if she had to inflict the greatest pain — making me see her suffer, making me fear her death and that I had caused it — she would do it without thinking, without hesitation. That worst threat was always between us — that she could take herself away, that she could hurt herself in my eyes — and it was out of my control to stop it. She was the hostage of an insane government, her own body. And so I revoked my love: I took away, as much as I could, the only real currency between us. I would not count on her to save me from her death. And therefore I saved myself by cutting the part of my heart that was in her heart; I cut it off as if snipping a pigtail. It is only now, when I am at a safe distance, that my heart begins to grow again, as if a surgeon has inserted a little gray balloon to open it up to blood. There begins to be an invisible cell, a chamber, a thumping like the thump inside the embryo shell, tissues paper thin, of hardly any substance, except that, somewhere in it, it still knows what it is, what it will grow up to be used for.

JOSEPH EPSTEIN

The Culture of Celebrity

FROM THE WEEKLY STANDARD

CELEBRITY AT THIS MOMENT in America is epidemic, and it's spreading fast, sometimes seeming as if nearly everyone has got it. Television provides celebrity dance contests, celebrities take part in reality shows, perfumes carry the names not merely of designers but of actors and singers. Without celebrities, whole sections of the *New York Times* and the *Washington Post* would have to close down. So pervasive has celebrity become in contemporary American life that one now begins to hear a good deal about a phenomenon known as the Culture of Celebrity.

The word "culture" no longer, I suspect, stands in most people's minds for that whole congeries of institutions, relations, kinship patterns, linguistic forms, and the rest for which the early anthropologists meant it to stand. Words, unlike disciplined soldiers, refuse to remain in place and take orders. They insist on being unruly, and slither and slide around, picking up all sorts of slippery and even goofy meanings. An icon, as we shall see, doesn't stay a small picture of a religious personage but usually turns out nowadays to be someone with spectacular grosses. "The language," as Flaubert once protested in his attempt to tell his mistress Louise Colet how much he loved her, "is inept."

Today, when people glibly refer to "the corporate culture," "the culture of poverty," "the culture of journalism," "the culture of the intelligence community" — and "community" has, of course, itself become another of those hopelessly baggy-pants words, so that one hears talk even of "the homeless community" — what I think is meant by "culture" is the general emotional atmosphere and institutional character surrounding the word to which "culture" is attached. Thus, corporate culture is thought to breed selfishness practiced at the Machiavellian level; the culture of poverty, hopelessness and despair; the culture of journalism, a taste for the sensational combined with a short attention span; the culture of the intelligence community, covering-one's-own-behind viperishness; and so on. Culture used in this way is also brought in to explain unpleasant or at least dreary behavior. "The culture of NASA has to be changed" is a sample of its current usage. The comedian Flip Wilson, after saying something outrageous, would revert to the refrain line "The debbil made me do it." So, today, when admitting to unethical or otherwise wretched behavior, people often say, "The culture made me do it."

As for "celebrity," the standard definition is no longer the dictionary one but rather closer to the one that Daniel Boorstin gave in his book *The Image; or, What Happened to the American Dream:* "The celebrity," Boorstin wrote, "is a person who is well-known for his well-knownness," which is improved in its frequently misquoted form as "A celebrity is someone famous for being famous." The other standard quotation on this subject is Andy Warhol's "In the future everyone will be world-famous for fifteen minutes," which also frequently turns up in an improved misquotation as "Everyone will have his fifteen minutes of fame."

But to say that a celebrity is someone well known for being well known, though clever enough, doesn't quite cover it. Not that there is a shortage of such people who seem to be known only for their well-knownness. What do a couple named Sid and Mercedes Bass do, except appear in boldface in the *New York Times* Sunday Styles section and other such venues (as we now call them) of equally shimmering insignificance, often standing next to Ahmet and Mica Ertegun, also well known for being well known? Many moons ago, journalists used to refer to royalty as "face cards"; today celebrities are perhaps best thought of as bold faces, for as such do their names often appear in the press (and in a *New York Times* column with that very name, "Bold Face").

The distinction between celebrity and fame is one most dictionaries tend to fudge. I suspect everyone has, or prefers to make, his own. The one I like derives not from Aristotle, who didn't have to trouble with celebrities, but from the career of Ted Williams. A sportswriter once said that he, Williams, wished to be famous but had no interest in being a celebrity. What Ted Williams wanted to be famous for was his hitting. He wanted everyone who cared about baseball to know that he was — as he believed and may well have been — the greatest pure hitter who ever lived. What he didn't want to do was to take on any of the effort off the baseball field involved in making this known. As an active player, Williams gave no interviews, signed no baseballs or photographs, chose not to be obliging in any way to journalists or fans. A rebarbative character, not to mention often a slightly menacing s.o.b., Williams, if you had asked him, would have said that it was enough that he was the last man to hit .400; he did it on the field, and therefore didn't have to sell himself off the field. As for his duty to his fans, he didn't see that he had any.

Whether Ted Williams was right or wrong to feel as he did is of less interest than the distinction his example provides, which suggests that fame is something one earns — through talent or achievement of one kind or another — while celebrity is something one cultivates or, possibly, has thrust upon one. The two are not, of course, entirely exclusive. One can be immensely talented and full of achievement and yet wish to broadcast one's fame further through the careful cultivation of celebrity; and one can have the thinnest of achievements and be talentless and yet be made to seem otherwise through the mechanics and dynamics of celebrity creation, in our day a whole mini- (or maybe not so mini) industry of its own.

Or, another possibility, one can become a celebrity with scarcely any pretense to talent or achievement whatsoever. Much modern celebrity seems the result of careful promotion or great good luck or something besides talent and achievement: Mr. Donald Trump, Ms. Paris Hilton, Mr. Regis Philbin, take a bow. The ultimate celebrity of our time may have been John F. Kennedy Jr., notable only for being his parents' very handsome son — both his birth and good looks factors beyond his control — and, alas, known for nothing else whatsoever now, except for the sad, dying-young-Adonis end to his life.

Fame, then, at least as I prefer to think of it, is based on true achievement; celebrity on the broadcasting of that achievement, or the inventing of something that, if not scrutinized too closely, might pass for achievement. Celebrity suggests ephemerality, while fame has a chance of lasting, a shot at reaching the happy shores of posterity.

Oliver Goldsmith, in his poem "The Deserted Village," refers to "good fame," which implies that there is also a bad or false fame. Bad fame is sometimes thought to be fame in the present, or fame on earth, while good fame is that bestowed by posterity — those happy shores again. (Which doesn't eliminate the desire of most of us, at least nowadays, to have our fame here and hereafter, too.) Not false but wretched fame is covered by the word "infamy" — "Infamy, infamy, infamy," remarked the English wit Frank Muir, "they all have it in for me" — while the lower, or pejorative, order of celebrity is covered by the word "notoriety," also frequently misused to mean noteworthiness.

Leo Braudy's magnificent book on the history of fame, *The Frenzy of Renown,* illustrates how the means of broadcasting fame have changed over the centuries: from having one's head engraved on coins, to purchasing statuary of oneself, to (for the really high rollers — Alexander the Great, the Caesar boys) naming cities or even months after oneself, to commissioning painted portraits, to writing books or having books written about one, and so on into our day of the publicity or press agent, the media blitz, the public relations expert, and the egomaniacal blogger. One of the most successful of public relations experts, Ben Sonnenberg Sr., used to say that he saw it as his job to construct very high pedestals for very small men.

Which leads one to a very proper suspicion of celebrity. As George Orwell said about saints, so it seems only sensible to say about celebrities: they should all be judged guilty until proven innocent. Guilty of what, precisely? I'd say of the fraudulence (however minor) of inflating their brilliance, accomplishments, worth, of passing themselves off as something they aren't, or at least are not quite. If fraudulence is the crime, publicity is the means by which the caper is brought off.

Is the current heightened interest in the celebrated sufficient to form a culture — a culture of a kind worthy of study? The anthropologist Alfred Kroeber defined culture, in part, as embodying "values which may be formulated (overtly as mores) or felt (implicitly as in folkways) by the society carrying the culture, and which it is part of the business of the anthropologist to characterize and define." What are the values of celebrity culture? They are the values, almost exclusively, of publicity. Did they spell one's name right? What was the size and composition of the audience? Did you check the receipts? Was the timing right? Publicity is concerned solely with effects and does not investigate causes or intrinsic value too closely. For example, a few years ago a book of mine called *Snobbery: The American Version* received what I thought was a too greatly mixed review in the *New York Times Book Review*. I remarked on my disappointment to the publicity man at my publisher's, who promptly told me not to worry: it was a full-page review, on page 11, right-hand side. That, he said, "is very good real estate," which was quite as important as, perhaps more important than, the reviewer's actual words and final judgment. Better to be tepidly considered on page 11 than extravagantly praised on page 27, left-hand side. Real estate, man, it's the name of the game.

We must have new names, Marcel Proust presciently noted — in fashion, in medicine, in art, there must always be new names. It's a very smart remark, and the fields Proust chose seem smart, too, at least for his time. (Now there must also be new names, at a minimum, among movie stars and athletes and politicians.) Implicit in Proust's remark is the notion that if the names don't really exist, if the quality isn't there to sustain them, it doesn't matter; new names we shall have in any case. And every sophisticated society somehow, more or less implicitly, contrives to supply them.

I happen to think that we haven't had a major poet writing in English since perhaps the death of W. H. Auden or, to lower the bar a little, Philip Larkin. But new names are put forth nevertheless — high among them in recent years has been that of Seamus Heaney — because, after all, what kind of a time could we be living in if we didn't have a major poet? And besides there are all those prizes that, year after year, must be given out, even if so many of the recipients don't seem quite worthy of them.

Considered as a culture, celebrity does have its institutions. We now have an elaborate celebrity-creating machinery well in place — all those short-attention-span television shows *(Entertainment Tonight, Access Hollywood, Lifestyles of the Rich and Famous);* all those magazines (beginning with *People* and far from ending with the *Na-*

tional Enquirer). We have high-priced celebrity-mongers — Barbara Walters, Diane Sawyer, Jay Leno, David Letterman, Oprah — who not only live off others' celebrity but also, through their publicity-making power, confer it and have in time become very considerable celebrities each in his or her own right.

Without the taste for celebrity, they would have to close down the whole Style section of every newspaper in the country. Then there is the celebrity profile (in *Vanity Fair, Esquire, Gentlemen's Quarterly;* these are nowadays usually orchestrated by a press agent, with all touchy questions declared out-of-bounds), or the television talk-show interview with a star, which is beyond parody. Well, *almost* beyond: Martin Short in his parody of a talk-show host remarked to the actor Kiefer Sutherland, "You're Canadian, aren't you? What's that all about?"

Yet we still seem never to have enough celebrities, so we drag in so-called It Girls (Paris Hilton, Cindy Crawford, other super-models), tired television hacks (Regis Philbin, Ed McMahon), back-achingly boring but somehow sacrosanct news anchors (Walter Cronkite, Tom Brokaw). Toss in what I think of as the lower-class punditi, who await calls from various television news and chat shows to demonstrate their locked-in political views and meager expertise on major and cable stations alike: Pat Buchanan, Eleanor Clift, Mark Shields, Robert Novak, Michael Beschloss, and the rest. Ah, if only Lenny Bruce were alive today, he could do a scorchingly cruel bit about Dr. Joyce Brothers sitting by the phone wondering why Jerry Springer never calls.

Many of our current-day celebrities float upon hype, which is really a publicist's gas used to pump up and set aloft something that doesn't really quite exist. Hype has also given us a new breakdown, or hierarchical categorization, of celebrities. Until twenty-five or so years ago great celebrities were called "stars," a term first used in the movies and entertainment and then taken up by sports, politics, and other fields. "Stars" proving a bit drab, "superstars" were called in to play, this term beginning in sports but fairly quickly branching outward. Apparently too many superstars were about, so the trope was switched from astronomy to religion, and we now have "icons." All this takes Proust's original observation a step further: the need for new names to call the new names.

This new ranking — stars, superstars, icons — helps us believe that we live in interesting times. One of the things celebrities do for us is suggest that in their lives they are fulfilling our fantasies. Modern celebrities, along with their fame, tend to be wealthy or, if not themselves beautiful, able to acquire beautiful lovers. Their celebrity makes them, in the view of many, worthy of worship. "So long as man remains free," Dostoyevsky writes in the Grand Inquisitor section of *The Brothers Karamazov,* "he strives for nothing so incessantly and painfully as to find someone to worship." If contemporary celebrities are the best thing on offer as living gods for us to worship, this is not good news.

But the worshiping of celebrities by the public tends to be thin, and not uncommonly it is nicely mixed with loathing. We also, after all, at least partially, like to see our celebrities as frail, ready at all times to crash and burn. Cary Grant once warned the then-young director Peter Bogdanovich, who was at the time living with Cybill Shepherd, to stop telling people he was in love. "And above all," Grant warned, "stop telling them you're happy." When Bogdanovich asked why, Cary Grant answered, "Because they're not in love and they're not happy . . . Just remember, Peter, people do not like beautiful people."

Grant's assertion is borne out by our grocery press, the *National Enquirer,* the *Star,* the *Globe,* and other variants of the English gutter press. All these tabloids could as easily travel under the generic title of the *National Schadenfreude,* for more than half the stories they contain come under the category of "See How the Mighty Have Fallen": Oh, my, I see where that bright young television sitcom star, on a drug binge again, had to be taken to a hospital in an ambulance! To think that the handsome movie star has been cheating on his wife all these years — snakes loose in the Garden of Eden, evidently! Did you note that the powerful senator's drinking has caused him to embarrass himself yet again in public? I see where that immensely successful Hollywood couple turn out to have had a child who died of anorexia! Who'd've thought?

How pleasing to learn that our own simpler, less moneyed, unglamorous lives are, in the end, much to be preferred to those of these beautiful, rich, and powerful people, whose vast publicity has diverted us for so long and whose fall proves even more diverting now. "As would become a lifelong habit for most of us," Thomas McGuane writes in a recent short story in *The New Yorker* called

"Ice," "we longed to witness spectacular achievement and mortifying failure. Neither of these things, we were discreetly certain, would ever come to us; we would instead be granted the frictionless lives of the meek."

Along with trying to avoid falling victim to schadenfreude, celebrities, if they are clever, do well to regulate the amount of publicity they allow to cluster around them. And not celebrities alone. Edith Wharton, having published too many stories and essays in a great single rush in various magazines during a concentrated period, feared, as she put it, the danger of becoming "a magazine bore." Celebrities, in the same way, are in danger of becoming publicity bores, though few among them seem to sense it. Because of improperly rationed publicity, along with a substantial helping of self-importance, the comedian Bill Cosby will never again be funny. The actress Elizabeth McGovern said of Sean Penn that he "is brilliant, *brilliant* at being the kind of reluctant celebrity." At the level of high culture, Saul Bellow used to work this bit quite well on the literary front, making every interview (and there have been hundreds of them) feel as if given only with the greatest reluctance, if not under actual duress. Others are brilliant at regulating their publicity. Johnny Carson was very intelligent about carefully husbanding his celebrity, choosing not to come out of retirement except at exactly the right time or when the perfect occasion presented itself. Apparently it never did. Given the universally generous obituary tributes he received, dying now looks, for him, to have been an excellent career move.

Careful readers will have noticed that I referred above to "the actress Elizabeth McGovern" and felt no need to write anything before or after the name Sean Penn. True celebrities need nothing said of them in apposition, fore or aft. The greatest celebrities are those who don't even require their full names mentioned: Marilyn, Johnny, Liz, Liza, Oprah, Michael (could be Jordan or Jackson — context usually clears this up fairly quickly), Kobe, Martha (Stewart, not Washington), Britney, Shaq, J-Lo, Frank (Sinatra, not Perdue), O.J., and, with the quickest recognition and shortest name of all — trumpets here, please — W.

One has the impression that being a celebrity was easier at any earlier time than it is now, when celebrity-creating institutions, from paparazzi to gutter-press exposés to television talk shows, weren't as intense, as full-court press, as they are today. In the *Times Literary Supplement,* a reviewer of a biography of Margot Fonteyn noted that Miss Fonteyn "was a star from a more respectful age of celebrity, when keeping one's distance was still possible." My own candidate for the perfect celebrity in the twentieth century would be Noël Coward, a man in whom talent combined with elegance to give off the glow of glamour — and also a man who would have known how to fend off anyone wishing to investigate his private life. Today, instead of elegant celebrities, we have celebrity criminal trials: Michael Jackson, Kobe Bryant, Martha Stewart, Robert Blake, Winona Ryder, and O. J. Simpson. Schadenfreude is in the saddle again.

American society in the twenty-first century, received opinion has it, values only two things: money and celebrity. Whether or not this is true, vast quantities of money, we know, will buy celebrity. The very rich — John D. Rockefeller and powerful people of his era — used to pay press agents to keep their names out of the papers. But today one of the things money buys is a place at the table beside the celebrated, with the celebrities generally delighted to accommodate, there to share some of the glaring light. An example is Mort Zuckerman, who made an early fortune in real estate, has bought magazines and newspapers, and is now himself among the punditi, offering his largely unexceptional political views on *The McLaughlin Group* and other television chat shows. Which is merely another way of saying that, whether or not celebrity in and of itself constitutes a culture, it has certainly penetrated and permeated much of American culture generally.

Such has been the reach of celebrity culture in our time that it has long ago entered into academic life. The celebrity professor has been on the scene for more than three decades. As long ago as 1962, in fact, I recall hearing that Oscar Cargill, in those days a name of some note in the English department of New York University, had tried to lure the then-young Robert Brustein, a professor of theater and the drama critic for the *New Republic,* away from Columbia. Cargill had said to Brustein, "I'm not going to bulls—t you, Bob, we're looking for a star, and you're it." Brustein apparently wasn't looking to be placed in a new constellation, and remained at Columbia, at least for a while longer, before moving on to Yale and thence to Harvard.

The academic star, who is really the academic celebrity, is now a fairly common figure in what the world, that ignorant ninny, reckons the Great American Universities. Richard Rorty is such a star; so is Henry Louis Gates Jr. (who as "Skip" even has some celebrity nickname recognition); and, at a slightly lower level, there are Marjorie Garber, Eve Sedgwick, Stanley Fish, and perhaps now Stephen Greenblatt. Stanley Fish doesn't even seem to mind that much of his celebrity is owed to his being portrayed in novels by David Lodge as an indefatigable, grubby little operator (though Lodge claims to admire Fish's happy vulgarity). Professors Garber and Sedgwick seem to have acquired their celebrity through the outrageousness of the topics they've chosen to write about.

By measure of pure celebrity, Cornel West is, at the moment, the star of all academic stars, a man called by *Newsweek* "an eloquent prophet with attitude." (A bit difficult, I think, to imagine *Newsweek* or any other publication writing something similar of Lionel Trilling, Walter Jackson Bate, Marjorie Hope Nicolson, or John Hope Franklin.) He records rap CDs and appears at benefits with movie stars and famous athletes. When the president of Harvard spoke critically to West about his work not constituting serious scholarship (as if that had anything to do with anything), it made front-page news in the *New York Times*. When West left Harvard in indignation, he was instantly welcomed by Princeton. If West had been a few kilowatts more the celebrity than he is, he might have been able to arrange for the firing of the president of the university, the way certain superstars in the National Basketball Association — Magic Johnson, Isiah Thomas, Larry Bird, Michael Jordan — were able, if it pleased them, to have their coaches fired.

Genuine scholarship, power of ratiocination glowing brightly in the classroom, is distinctly not what makes an academic celebrity or, if you prefer, superstar. What makes an academic celebrity, for the most part, is exposure, which is ultimately publicity. Exposure can mean appearing in the right extra-academic magazines or journals: the *New York Review of Books,* the *London Review of Books,* the *Atlantic Monthly; Harper's Magazine* and the *New Republic* possibly qualify, as do occasional cameo performances on the op-ed pages of the *New York Times* or the *Washington Post*. Having one's face pop up on the right television and radio programs — PBS and NPR certainly, and enough of the right kinds of appearances on C-SPAN — does not hurt. A commercially successful, much-discussed book helps hugely.

So does strong public alignment with the correct political causes. Harvey Mansfield, the political philosopher at Harvard, is a secondary academic celebrity of sorts, but not much in demand, owing to his conservatism; Shelby Steele, a black professor of English who has been critical of various aspects of African-American politics, was always overlooked during the days when universities knocked themselves out to get black professors. Both men have been judged politically incorrect. The underlying and overarching point is, to become an academic celebrity you have to promote yourself outside the academy, but in careful and subtle ways.

One might once have assumed that the culture of celebrity was chiefly about show business and the outer edges of the arts, occasionally touching on the academy (there cannot be more than twenty or so academic superstars). But it has also much altered intellectual life generally. The past ten years or so have seen the advent of the "public intellectual." There are good reasons to feel uncomfortable with that adjective "public," which drains away much of the traditional meaning of intellectual. An intellectual is someone who is excited by and lives off and in ideas. An intellectual has traditionally been a person unaffiliated, which is to say someone unbeholden to anything but the power of his or her ideas. Intellectuals used to be freelance, until fifty or so years ago, when jobs in the universities and in journalism began to open up to some among them.

Far from being devoted to ideas for their own sake, the intellectual equivalent of art for art's sake, the so-called public intellectual of our day is usually someone who comments on what is in the news, in the hope of affecting policy, or events, or opinion in line with his own political position, or orientation. He isn't necessarily an intellectual at all, but merely someone who has read a few books, mastered a style, a jargon, and a maven's authoritative tone, and has a clearly demarcated political line.

But even when the public intellectual isn't purely tied to the news, or isn't thoroughly political, what he or she really is, or ought to be called, is a "publicity intellectual." In Richard A. Posner's interesting book *Public Intellectuals*, intellectuals are in one place ranked by the number of media mentions they or their works have garnered, which, if I am correct about publicity being at the heart of the enterprise of the public intellectual, may be crude but is not foolish. Not knowledge, it turns out, but publicity is power.

The most celebrated intellectuals of our day have been those most skillful at gaining publicity for their writing and their pronouncements. Take, as a case very much in point, Susan Sontag. When Susan Sontag died at the end of last year, her obituary was front-page news in the *New York Times,* and on the inside of the paper it ran to a full page with five photographs, most of them carefully posed — a variety, it does not seem unfair to call it, of intellectual cheesecake. Will the current prime ministers of England and France when they peg out receive equal space or pictorial coverage? Unlikely, I think. Why did Ms. Sontag, who was, let it be said, in many ways the pure type of the old intellectual — unattached to any institution, earning her living (apart from MacArthur Foundation and other grants) entirely from her ideas as she put them in writing — why did she attract the attention she did?

I don't believe Susan Sontag's celebrity finally had much to do with the power or cogency of her ideas. Her most noteworthy idea was not so much an idea at all but a description of a style, a kind of reverse or anti-style, that went by the name of Camp and that was gay in its impulse. Might it have been her politics? Yes, politics had a lot to do with it, even though when she expressed herself on political subjects, she frequently got things mightily askew: during the Vietnam War she said that "the white race is the cancer of human history." As late as the 1980s, much too late for anyone in the know, she called communism "fascism with a friendly face." (What do you suppose she found so friendly about it?) To cheer up the besieged people of Sarajevo, she brought them a production of Samuel Beckett's *Waiting for Godot.* She announced in *The New Yorker* that the killing of three thousand innocent people on 9/11 was an act that America had brought on itself. As for the writing that originally brought her celebrity, she later came to apologize for *Against Interpretation,* her most influential single book. I do not know any people who claim to have derived keen pleasure from her fiction. If all this is roughly so, why, then, do you suppose that Susan Sontag was easily the single most celebrated — the greatest celebrity — intellectual of our time?

With the ordinary female professor's face and body, I don't think Ms. Sontag would quite have achieved the same celebrity. Her attractiveness as a young woman had a great deal to do with the extent of her celebrity; and she and her publisher took that (early) physical attractiveness all the way out. From reading Carl Rollyson and Lisa Paddock's biography *Susan Sontag: The Making of an Icon,* one gets a sense of how carefully and relentlessly she was promoted by her publisher, Roger Straus. I do not mean to say that Sontag was unintelligent or talentless, but Straus, through having her always dramatically photographed, by sending angry letters to the editors of journals where she was ill reviewed, by bringing out her books with the most careful accompanying orchestration, promoted this often difficult and unrewarding writer into something close to a household name with a face that was ready, so to say, to be Warholed. That Sontag spent her last years with Annie Leibovitz, herself the most successful magazine photographer of our day, seems somehow the most natural thing in the world. Even in the realm of the intellect, celebrities are not born but made, usually very carefully made — as was, indubitably, the celebrity of Susan Sontag.

One of the major themes in Leo Braudy's *The Frenzy of Renown* is the fame and celebrity of artists, and above all writers. To sketch in a few bare strokes the richly complex story Braudy tells, writers went from serving power (in Rome) to serving God (in early Christendom), to serving patrons (in the eighteenth century), to serving themselves, with a careful eye cocked toward both the contemporary public and posterity (under Romanticism), to serving mammon, to a state of interesting confusion, which is where we are today, with celebrity affecting literature in more and more significant ways.

Writers are supposed to be aristocrats of the spirit, not promoters, hustlers, salesmen for their own work. Securing a larger audience for their work was not thought to be their problem. "Fit audience, though few," in John Milton's phrase, was all right, so long as the few were the most artistically alert, or aesthetically fittest. Picture Lord Byron, Count Tolstoy, or Charles Baudelaire at a lectern at Barnes & Noble, C-SPAN camera turned on, flogging (wonderful word!) his own most recent books. Not possible!

Some superior writers have been very careful caretakers of their careers. In a letter to one of his philosophy professors at Harvard, T. S. Eliot wrote that there were two ways to achieve literary celebrity in London: one was to appear often in a variety of publications; the other to appear seldom, but always to make certain to dazzle when one did. Eliot, of course, chose the latter, and it worked smashingly. But he was still counting on gaining his reputation through his actual writing. Now good work alone doesn't quite seem to make it; the publicity catapults need to be hauled into place, the walls of indifference stormed. Some writers have decided to steer shy from publicity altogether: Thomas Pynchon for one, J. D. Salinger for another (if he is actually still writing or yet considers himself a writer). But actively seeking publicity was thought, for a writer, somehow vulgar — at least it was until the last few decades.

Edmund Wilson, the famous American literary critic, used to answer requests with a postcard that read:

> Edmund Wilson regrets that it is impossible for him to: Read manuscripts, Write articles or books to order, Make statements for publicity purposes, Do any kind of editorial work, Judge literary contests, Give interviews, Conduct educational courses, Deliver lectures, Give talks or make speeches, Take part in writers' congresses, Answer questionnaires, Contribute to or take part in symposiums or "panels" of any kind, Contribute manuscripts for sale, Donate copies of his books to libraries, Autograph books for strangers, Allow his name to be used on letterheads, Supply personal information about himself, Supply photographs of himself, Supply opinions on literary or other subjects.

A fairly impressive list, I'd say. When I was young, Wilson supplied for me the model of how a literary man ought to carry himself. One of the things I personally found most impressive about his list is that everything Edmund Wilson clearly states he will not do, Joseph Epstein has now done, and more than once, and, like the young woman in the Häagen Dazs commercial, sitting on her couch with an empty carton of ice cream, is likely to do again and again.

I tell myself that I do these various things in the effort to acquire more readers. After all, one of the reasons I write, apart from pleasure in working out the aesthetic problems and moral questions

presented by my subjects and in my stories, is to find the best readers. I also want to sell books, to make a few shekels, to please my
publisher, to continue to be published in the future in a proper
way. Having a high threshold for praise, I also don't in the least
mind meeting strangers who tell me that they take some delight in
my writing. But, more than all this, I have now come to think that
writing away quietly, producing (the hope is) good work, isn't any
longer quite sufficient in a culture dominated by the boisterous
spirit of celebrity. In an increasingly noisy cultural scene, with
many voices and media competing for attention, one feels — perhaps incorrectly but nonetheless insistently — the need to make
one's own small stir, however pathetic. So, on occasion, I have
gone about tooting my own little paper horn, doing book tours,
submitting to the comically pompous self-importance of interviews, and doing so many of the other things that Edmund Wilson
didn't think twice about refusing to do.

"You're slightly famous, aren't you, Grandpa?" my then eight-
year-old granddaughter once said to me. "I am slightly famous,
Annabelle," I replied, "except no one quite knows who I am." This
hasn't changed much over the years. But of course seeking celebrity in our culture is a mug's game, one you cannot finally hope to
win. The only large, lumpy kind of big-time celebrity available, outside movie celebrity, is to be had through appearing fairly regularly
on television. I had the merest inkling of this fame when I was walking along one sunny morning in downtown Baltimore, and a red
Mazda convertible screeched to a halt, the driver lowered his window, pointed a long index finger at me, hesitated, and finally, the
shock of recognition lighting up his face, yelled, "C-SPAN!"

I was recently asked, through e-mail, to write a short piece for a
high price for a volume about the city of Chicago. When I agreed
to do it, the editor of the volume, who is (I take it) young, told me
how very pleased she was to have someone as distinguished as I
among the volume's contributors. But she did have just one request. Before making things final, she wondered if she might see a
sample of my writing. More than forty years in the business, I
thought, echoing the character played by Zero Mostel in *The Pro-
ducers,* and I'm still wearing the celebrity equivalent of a cardboard
belt.

"Every time I think I'm famous," Virgil Thomson said, "I have only to go out into the world." So it is, and so ought it probably to remain for writers, musicians, and visual artists who prefer to consider themselves serious. The comedian Richard Pryor once said that he would deem himself famous when people recognized him, as they recognized Bob Hope and Muhammad Ali, by his captionless caricature. That is certainly one clear criterion for celebrity. But the best criterion I've yet come across holds that you are celebrated, indeed famous, only when a crazy person imagines he is you. It's especially pleasing that the penetrating and prolific author of this remark happens to go by the name of Anonymous.

EUGENE GOODHEART

Whistling in the Dark

FROM THE SEWANEE REVIEW

A VERY HOT AND HUMID DAY. I am reading Ruth Prawer
Jhabvala's *Heat and Dust.* Watertown, Massachusetts, a suburb of
Boston where I live, is not India. The streets are clean and are not
occupied by the homeless. I am writing this in my air-conditioned
study, grateful to be in the most advanced country of the techno-
logically advanced West, because with my asthma and mechanical
incompetence I would not be able to survive in the heat and dust
where millions live. As it is, the humidity of the New England summer is barely tolerable. An asthmatic, I awake in the morning with
a constricted chest, congested sinuses, telling myself to be calm
while coughing up phlegm and trying to breathe normally. Then I
am swept by fatigue. Retired from my teaching position at the university, I am free to do as I please. The day will unfold slowly, and it
will take determination to resist letting it fritter away.

My wife and I have no plans to travel. Friends and acquaintances, retired and unretired, seem to be traveling everywhere on
business, to conferences, for pleasure. Traveling for the sake of it,
seeing the world and often remembering little or remembering
events and circumstances without experiencing them, traveling to
the point of exhaustion — all so they can have the pleasure of returning home. I travel in my own mind, in my reading, in my writing. The secret of happiness, a French friend of mine once said, is
alternance (change). But not for me: my wife, less afflicted and
more enterprising, seems to have caught something of my affliction. Or have I caught her affliction? It takes such an effort to get
ourselves up to go somewhere. Inertia settles in. I read and write
and fidget. I am fearful of lacking for something to say, to write.

Yet I cannot imagine myself without pen in hand, scribbling my thoughts. Though I am uncertain about the value of what I write and need the assurance of friends, I can't imagine not writing, even if those friends confirmed my worst suspicions. It is a compulsion, more so now than when I was younger and I wrote exclusively about books and ideas, about other people's thought and expression. I have become my own irresistible subject. A writer of the personal essay speaks of it as a genre of maturity. I think of it as the genre of the posthumous. It belongs to a feeling that you have already lived, that life is no longer a matter of new departures. Your thoughts and emotions have become retrospective. Who are you? What have you been? What have you done? These are questions you don't usually ask yourself (I didn't) as you make a career, a life. You may be seized by ambition, feel triumphant over a success, plunged into despair by failure. You may even take stock from time to time. But to reflect continuously about your life, and by implication about the lives of others, you need to enter the zone of the posthumous in which you are no longer exalted or depressed by events, but have become calm and self-possessed. Or so I tell myself.

Looking backward, you don't recover the past in tranquility. I have taken to looking at old family photos. Photographs are lies. They fix moments in the past in which what was really felt and experienced is unrevealed. All surface and seduction, they present a beautifully composed past that tells us nothing of the real life of the moment. Reflecting on the past brings it up to the present. You reopen wounds and recall forgotten injuries and pleasures as if they were present injuries and pleasures. Writing comes out of the disturbances in our lives, or maybe it is writing itself that is the disturbance, an unwillingness to take our daily existence for granted. In recalling and rewriting the past, you find there is no closure. Present and future remain open.

I take a perverse pleasure in being out of it, by which I mean the competition for rewards, the yearning for approval. I know that I begin to matter less and less in what was my professional life. It's not a matter of the intrinsic value of anything I've done, but rather the passing of generations, the inflection of younger voices and of their interests. Not to be lamented. We too at one time were the younger voices — and except for the rare older voice with an authority that persisted into the next generation, we (I am no longer among the we) look upon the elderly, the aging, with condescending tolerance. Now I can think and care about only what *I* think and care about. My days are filled with reading (diffusely), with writing (sporadically), with giving an occasional lecture, having lunches and dinners with friends, conversing on the phone, making forays to the cinema and the concert hall, gorging on the news of the day, time wasting. As I say, there is no strong urge to travel or for adventure or for accumulating experiences to report to the interested or uninterested or to admiring or envious acquaintances. What I want is to be able to write (and be in my writing) without the need to ingratiate, please, or worry about success, to make sentences about my life that belong together and correspond to the truth. I am of the generation that still believes in truth.

As a college student, I read Montaigne's essay "On Solitude." What could I have possibly gotten out of it? Retreat into yourself, devote yourself to what gives you pleasure in your advanced years, renounce ambition, please yourself, not others, acquire knowledge not to impress others, but for your own sake (not for its sake). What could an undergraduate, uncertain of himself, driven by hormones and by ambition, make of such advice? Not much. Then, it may have had the sententious resonance of wisdom, but it was remote from my life. But what about now, at age seventy-three and retired? Wonderful advice, but try following it (meant without irony). Dr. Johnson warns of the illusoriness of the pleasures of retirement. Your community of friends shrinks; calls and visits become fewer and fewer. Not entirely a bad thing. When the phone rings now, I experience something of a shock. I both want it to ring and find it unwelcome. Who was it who said that the cure for loneliness is solitude?

Everyone alive ages, but one reaches an age when distinct *aging* occurs. I have reached that age. Does it need to be said? No place for aging, America is the country of the young, where wisdom is knowing the latest fashion, and who knows the latest fashion better than the young? It's an old story: the young rebel, the old conserve, partly a matter of the economy of energy. Rebellion feeds off enthusiasm; enthusiasm wanes as one grows older. Two views: the illusions of youth and the wisdom of age; the idealism of youth and the cynicism of age. Here's another way of seeing the difference: youth, unshadowed by mortality, rejects limitation; age, shadowed by mortality, has no choice but to accept limitation. But in our time youth, too, is shadowed by mortality — of its own self-destructive making.

A friend of mine in her sixties says she still feels herself as twelve, about the age E. B. White thought of himself throughout his life. Shouldn't development occur in the psyche as well as in the body? Shouldn't they evolve in harmony? Then there would be no fear of dying, but rather a sense of exhaustion, such as the one that over-takes us late at night when we want to sleep. Rilke said: "Only those who have unlived lines in their bodies are afraid of death." Has such a creature ever existed? I, too, continue to feel young inside, a kind of perpetual adolescence that doesn't disappear with age. But the body tells another story. People see me in my body. When the young hear me tell a joke or kid around, they must perceive the disparity (gross, or grotesque?) between what they hear and what they see — an old man trying to sound or be young. I want to pro-test that I am not trying. But why protest if I am accommodated with a smile? Who says that I am trying too hard? It must be that I am protesting against my own self-perception. A friend called to tell me that he saw a photograph in a newspaper of a former stu-dent of mine who had become famous. "He looks older than you." Meaning? "You look young compared to him," or, what's more likely, "You may look young compared to him, but you are the stan-dard for aging." Another very youthful-looking friend my age in-troduced me to a stranger as his father. With such friends, who needs enemies?

Aging recalls our youth. Philip Larkin wakes in the night "grop-ing back to bed after a piss" and is "startled by . . . the moon's cleanliness." (I know about the groping but am too groggy to no-tice the moon.) We are startled by the rhyme of "piss" and "clean-liness," which emphasizes rather than erases the contrast. The moon, a "lozenge of love," "is a reminder of the strength and pain / Of being young; that it can't come again, / But is for others un-diminished somewhere." Would Larkin, or any of us, want to re-turn to the strength and pain of when we were young? We say, un-thinking, If only we could go back and do things over again, given what we know now. But what I know now is the "wisdom" of old age, which would only diminish the strength we had when we were young. If E. M. Cioran is right that "the wise man is hostile to the new," then being young with the advantage of wisdom is hardly an advantage. And as for the wisdom of old age, Larkin again: "Most people know more as they get older: / I give all that the cold shoulder." So why does he continue writing? Is he selling out for the moment, for a rhyme? He tells us that there is nothing left to say about aging and dying: "All that's left to happen / Is some deaths (my own included). / Their order, and their manner, / Remain to be learnt." And the poet who has nothing more to say about the subject says once more: "Unresting death, a whole day nearer now / Making all thought impossible but how / And where and when I shall myself die." Terror freezes thought. How different from Keats's line "Now more than ever seems it rich to die." Perhaps not so different, for in dying he would "cease upon the midnight with no pain." Rilke's line embraces Keats and Larkin: "Only those who have unlived lines in their bodies are afraid of death." Keats, despite his death at age twenty-five, may have lived out the lines of his body — and spirit. Larkin and most of us are among the "only those." It makes no difference whether one is young or old. Temperament is all.

We outgrow relationships, but cling to them out of habit or fear that we will wind up alone. Sometimes we meet someone late in life who we feel could be a friend, who has the qualities we've been looking for but never found. Maybe it's an illusion that would be shattered once the friendship has been formed. But it may be too late, for friendship depends upon a common fund of memories, of shared experience. There's nothing more desolating than for the old to learn of friends who are dying off. Nothing is more devastating than watching a beloved spouse die. But what of the singular person who was never able to choose another to share his life? Larkin had never "met that special one / Who has an instant claim / On everything I own / Down to my name." He preferred the selfishness of solitude. "To find such seems to prove / You want no choice in where / To build, or whom to love." He admits "*All solitude is selfish,*" and he asserts with a cynic's confidence: "No one / Now believes the hermit with his gown and dish / Talking to God (who's gone too); the big wish / Is to have people nice to you, which means / Doing it back somehow." Larkin inured himself to the isolation of old age by embracing it as a young man.

"Aging gracefully": a phrase of flattery, uttered by those who do not yet think of themselves as aging. Even old people find other old people less and less appealing. To think of yourself as old is to overcome an enormous resistance — like the resistance put up on the psychoanalyst's couch. We joke about our aging to avoid taking it seriously. Two elderly men, friends, are seated on a park bench in Miami Beach. After a while, one of them indicates that he has to leave, and he raises himself slowly with groans. The seated friend says, "What's the rush?" Or take the age-defying eighty-five-year-old man (the age varies depending upon the auditor) who enters an old-age home and puts a sign on the door of his new room: STUD. Shortly afterward, a little old lady knocks on the door, is let in by the old geezer, who gives her the options: $25 on the linoleum, $50 on the sofa, and $100 on the bed. The old lady extricates a hundred-dollar bill from her purse. The old man understands: "On the bed?" "No," the old lady says, "four times on the lino-leum."

The consolation of aging, of course, is that we have escaped the alternative. In nature, in the vegetable world, we discard the over-ripe, any vegetable or fruit that shows signs of decay. Only the monsters in humanity would apply such a rule to the human world. What protects us aging human beings from being discarded is our sentience and consciousness. We don't need a belief in the immortality of the soul to affirm the survival of the unfittest. Dar-win tells us that "when we reflect on [the struggle for existence], we may console ourselves with the full belief, that the war of nature is not incessant, that no fear is felt, that death is generally prompt, and that the vigorous, the healthy and the happy survive and multi-ply." But modern human existence is dedicated to the fear of death, the prolongation of life, and the survival of the unhealthy and the disabled. The survivors are not consoled by a quick death.

Elias Canetti once said, "The highly concrete and serious, the admitted goal of my life, is to achieve immortality for men." (From an earlier time, he folded women into men.) I have wondered what this extremely intelligent and sophisticated European could mean by such a preposterous statement. Did he think of himself as the Messiah? Was he on a personal search for the elixir of life? Had he joined a biological laboratory? None of these things offers itself as an explanation. The desire for physical immortality is the ulti-mate egoism. It is unseemly to want to cling to life forever. There is grace in self-sacrifice for others, for a cause and in the capacity for simply letting go. Maybe it was a question of what he means by immortality, but no answer is available. We might begin with the fact that most people don't want to die. Some, too many, do, because they find life intolerable. Let us say that those of us who don't want to die and who fear death were given the choice of immortality on earth (I assume that's what Canetti means). What would we make of it? I think that the no vote would be large, and it would include me, if it were not accompanied by eternal youth. In his beautiful poem "Tithonus," Tennyson evokes the pathos of the goddess Aurora's lover, whom she granted immortal life but not eternal youth. (Was it the negligence of a god who knows only youth?)

> The woods decay, the woods decay and fall,
> The vapours weep their burthen to the ground,
> Man comes and tills the field and lies beneath,
> And after many a summer dies the swan.
> Me only cruel immortality
> Consumes: I wither slowly in thine arms . . .

But would eternal youth be sufficient? Reacting against Canetti, I once wrote the following: "Wouldn't the boredom of a several-hundred-year existence become unbearable? Moreover, what of its consequences for new birth and new life? The virtue of a Christian conception of an afterlife is that it satisfies a desire for immortality that doesn't threaten future life on earth." One thing is certain: Canetti has set himself against the philosopher's creed that wisdom lies in the graceful acceptance of death. So what is there to say for Canetti's protest against the authority of death? We all join in protesting and resisting death inflicted by murder. But what of natural death? Is it not also a judgment, an exercise in humiliation? In the nonhuman world, it disposes of the inferior or weaker species, or of the inferior, the weaker, and the aged within a species. Darwin called it natural selection, which differs from human killing "only" (a large only, to be sure) in the fact that it is without intention, without design, but the effect of which may be the same. Ask the person who has been struck by a paralytic stroke, who is imprisoned in his body and knows his life is very short. He has been humiliated by nature.

Death, we say, is the great equalizer, the one indubitable universal, if one is not a believer. If one is, then depending on the creed, you may be saved or damned, reincarnated into a lord or a worm. For the survivor, believer or not, there are the different ceremonies: those who are brought to their final resting place in pomp and ceremony, and those who are given a pauper's burial. Sholem Aleichem's Berel Isaac, a teller of tall tales about his visit to America from the shtetl of Kasrilevka, describes three classes of funerals: for the very rich (not only is the carriage richly adorned, the crowd enormous, but the day is gloriously bright), the middle class (the carriage more austere, the crowd thinner, the sky cloudy), and the lower class (the carriage nondescript, the crowd small, the sky overcast). And then there is the impoverished homeless person who has to walk to his own funeral, held up by two friends in a pouring rain. The humiliation of death is not enough: the world and nature have to rub it in. I leave God out of it.

Almost every day in the newspapers or on television, some old geezer in his late nineties, or at the one hundred mark, becomes the object of amused, condescending attention. The old are no longer tribal elders, awe-inspiring or terrifying. The wisdom of old age has been a ruse of the aged to protect and justify their place in the world. But as the cohort of the old gets very, very old, the justification wears thin. "What is the secret of your longevity?" "I stayed away from alcohol, didn't smoke, and was happily married." Sometimes the answer is the opposite: "drank martinis every evening, smoked cigars daily, and remained single." The great "achievement" of the very old lies in their genes. The aged now are like old pets. In nursing homes, dogs are brought in to comfort their human counterparts.

My wife, Joan, opens the newspaper and turns to the obituary page; I turn to the sports pages (my insurmountable youth). I used to ignore the obituaries, but now I, too, find myself drawn to them. I look first at the ages of the deceased. On certain days they are all or mostly young, victims of catastrophes: AIDS, cancer, accidents, suicide. On most other days, the ages are closer to home. Joan says I will survive her, what with the difference between my family's history and hers. I say it's all nonsense, but what she says sinks in. Prepare to live alone. Harder for men than for women.

Death itself doesn't distress us, but instead the prospect of the experience of dying. Tolstoy should have had Ivan Ilych say, "Dying [not Death] is finished." Beyond death, for Ivan Ilych, is the light at the end of the tunnel. Tolstoy had made Ivan, like himself, a believer. When ill, the Chinese writer Lu Hsun thought that "if [dying] happens once, I can take it." Of course death happens once, but we may die more than once — and, if we are possessed of morbid imaginations, many times. Though I am not a believer, the idea of an absolute extinction of consciousness and dissolution of the body are hard for me to imagine.

Death does distress the human race. I sometimes imagine death as a claustral experience. Fully conscious in the confines of a coffin or an urn, aware of those whom I have left behind — wife, children, friends — free of the ills of the physical life, but not of regret for what I failed to do or apprehension about the fate of the living. Knowing in life how the dead are forgotten, how in order to live you have to forget them most of the time, I imagine myself, in death, bereft of all those who cared for me while I was alive, as those whom I have left behind would be bereft of me. Death as absolute solitude. No, not solitude, a benign condition, but loneliness.

Beckett was imagining death in *Happy Days,* in which a character in succeeding scenes is gradually covered up to her neck by the earth, suggesting that it will soon cover her entirely. If she were covered entirely, she could not speak. At least she has an audience every night. The theater keeps her alive. This is not the immortality promised by religion. But it makes me understand why religion tells another story about immortality. At times I am struck by the injustice of having been born into life. To be born is to be sentenced to death. This is hardly news, and yet you are not struck by this cold fact until you age, until you can begin to count on the fingers of both hands how long you are expected to live. What is novel about this thought, novel for me at least, is being *struck* by it, by the thought turning quickly into sharp feeling.

In *Antimémoires,* Malraux writes: "Even that night, dying seemed banal to me. What interested me was death." Only someone cut from heroic cloth could find dying banal. It is the most fearful experience for ordinary souls. Malraux does not want the consolations of faith. "On the road, I might have received the bullets in the head, like the driver, instead of the legs. I felt strongly that all faith dissolves life into the eternal, and I was cut off from the eternal. My life was one of those human adventures which Shakespeare justifies by calling dreams and which are not dreams." Malraux does not deny the eternal; he rejects it, preferring instead the heroic intensity of mortal life. I read him, but he does not speak to me.

Why do we, in the relative comfort and security of our existence, indulge in thoughts of morbidity? Think of the millions around the world barely surviving or dying. They do not have the luxury of such thoughts because they have no time for them. While in the concentration camps, the inmates thought only of survival. After liberation, many survivors, reflecting on the price paid for survival, killed themselves. Aging and mortal illness everywhere level the playing field. What some learn and some do not is the grace in facing death that heroes come by instinctively. E. M. Cioran knows "one mad old woman who expects her house to fall to pieces from one minute to the next; she spends her days and her nights on the alert; creeping from room to room, ears cocked for every sound, she is furious that the *event* takes so long to occur." Writing about collapse, you want the event to take as long as possible so that you can meditate upon it. Instead of dying, you turn the thought of dying into a state of mind.

I read an obituary the other day of a prominent professor who took her own life in her late seventies. No explanation was given by her son. Was she physically ill, was she suffering from depression? In a book published years before, she had written that she was prepared to take her own life when the time came, when she felt that the journey of her life had concluded. The self-possession of her manner was Socratic. She had also written that her mother had felt that she was dying of boredom. Was it boredom (a legacy from the mother), that feeling of utter emptiness, that drove her accomplished daughter to suicide? And what about her son, her family? She apparently was not so desperate as to forget them. She was calm and imaginative enough to know the effect of her action on others. Was she saying to them that her love, assuming that she loved, was insufficient to counteract the feelings of emptiness? Or maybe that she was empty of love as well. I am imagining, even inventing a character from the bare facts, because the bare facts by themselves are incomprehensible. Not that contemplating suicide is incomprehensible. A person of imagination cannot fail to have

these thoughts at some time during a life. What is hard to fathom is
the action taken without the pressure of unbearable physical or
mental illness. The woman who took her life was a writer. Had her
desire to write evaporated? Did she feel that she had nothing more
to say? Or was writing simply not enough?

I visit a friend, old and bedridden from a stroke. He looks pitiful
and ancient. His mouth is open and he is having trouble breathing. It looks like dying to me. But he says through a smile that he
can still manage: "I'm sorry I couldn't report what my father
said about my being a writer." This very old and very distinguished
Jewish writer was back in his childhood. "Where's the *tachlis?*"
("Where's the reward?") I say to him, "Does it bother you that your
father didn't believe in your work?" He says no, this time with a little laugh. I tell him a joke (he loves jokes) about the Jew who
crosses the street and is hit by a car. A man runs over to him to ask
if he's comfortable. Yes, he replies, I make a good living. My friend
laughs, saying, "How sweet." How sweet! I think he will die laughing.

Weeks later there is a celebration of a work that he composed
fifty years earlier. The event occurs in a large, packed auditorium.
Admirers read from his work, which is life-affirming but unsenti-
mental. He cannot appear in person, for he is lying in a hospital
bed at home. Hours before the occasion, friends come to his home
to toast him. He is in the bedroom on the second floor; the party is
happening on the floor below. Then, at the appointed time, the
party of thirty or more ascends the stairs to surround his bed,
glasses of champagne in hand, to toast him. He is frail, feeble, lids
struggling to stay open, but with a smile of pleasure at the scene.
Someone in the party approaches the bed, speaks, and kisses him
on the cheek. And then we all follow, each of us recognized and
greeted. It is a strange scene, like one in a funeral home. We stand
around the bed in an awkward silence, occasionally interrupted by
a pleasantry, a witticism. Someone remarks on the lavender-col-
ored sweater he is wearing, and he says that he prefers it to a
shroud. His wit is irrepressible. My friend appears ready for anything in this farewell scene. But life is still in him. He is prepared to
die, but he does not welcome death.

I recur almost obsessively to the cremation of my mother. There
was the social embarrassment of carrying the urn (by train, plane,

and, after a hotel stay, by taxi) to the gravesite while my family looked on. No one said anything about it. I read nothing on their faces except respectful attention, but I suspected their thoughts. The decision to cremate was my mother's, probably encouraged by me, who asked her how she wanted to be buried. Just the asking meant that I didn't take for granted what every Jewish person of her and previous generations assumed — that the body would be placed in a coffin. An old friend with whom she spoke daily on the phone for years had decided to be cremated against the wishes of his son. He had an aversion to worms. Mother took to the idea of cremation; maybe she intuited my feeling about the inconvenience of transporting a body from one state to another. So my father, who is buried next to her, is bones and she is ashes. Anxiety, guilt, not because it goes against Jewish tradition, but because it is an act of annihilation, destroying rather than preserving the cadaver. My mother now is an idea, a sentiment, a memory, without bones. The deepest reason for my guilt is the crematoria of the camps, which were intended to annihilate memory as well.

So what about me? Can I possibly *not* be cremated after what Mother and I decided? Is my body more deserving of preservation than hers? I confess to anxiety about the intensity of the heat of the fire, for I have difficulty in thinking of myself as utterly without sentience. Since no one knows how it feels (if it feels) to be dead, how do we know that there is no life in our bodies, despite appearances? I buried the urn, did not place it on the mantel of a fireplace or hide it in a closet, as do those for whom cremation is the natural thing. The mantel is a risky place: a cleaning woman might knock it over and empty its contents on the rug, the ashes winding up in a vacuum cleaner. And then there is the grandiose gesture of hiring a plane and scattering the ashes over the ocean. There is modesty in cremation; the cremated occupy no space in the earth. Does it matter if the body leaves no trace of itself? Would it make a difference to human history if all the dead were cremated? It would, of course, to archeologists, who are the professional custodians of our past. The Nazis cremated the Jews so that they would be erased from the human record.

We think of lives that are happy or tragic, successful or failed — as if it ultimately matters to the particular consciousness of any life. Death not only ends a life, it extinguishes all consciousness of it, all memory of having lived. It is the ultimate form of Alzheimer's. To die is to achieve the condition of not having been born. It is as if you have never lived. So, as Marcus Aurelius tells us, it ultimately makes no difference whether we have lived three days or three generations. A difference does lie in the names Shakespeare, Newton, Beethoven, and for that matter Marcus Aurelius himself, who fortunately lived more than three days. They are legacies to the living, consolation while you are alive. But the legacies mean nothing to the dead. The body, already perishing in life, is disposable. The belief in immortality, however, is a refusal to accept the extinction of consciousness. It is a belief I don't share, but the need for which I understand.

The fact of individual life is so extraordinary, why shouldn't personal immortality be a possibility? Before we were born we had no way of knowing the fact of life, so why, then, should we know of the possibility of an afterlife? And why should our not knowing be an argument against its possibility? The unbelieving rationalist says there is no evidence for the afterlife, and he trusts only evidence. The biologist tells us that life itself has no meaning, no purpose except for reproduction. Meaning is the creation of human beings. But human beings are the production of biology and so the ultimate source of human creation, including meaning, the belief in God, and immortality. Why should evolution give us these beliefs if they are simply false? Anyway, according to natural selection, the unfit do not survive, and what has survived longer than religious belief, the enemy of natural selection? And don't tell me that the productions of humanity are different from those of nature, for humanity, too, as the biologists tell us, is part of nature. I am not a believer, but I have no confidence in my unbelief.

If life is a vale of tears, as it is and has been for millions, why should these millions desire personal immortality, unless it is the paradise that religion dreams of? But, as Proust tells us, all paradises are lost paradises. Genesis got it wrong: suffering and death are not punishment for our sins. Suffering may be punishment; death, however, is relief. We are given suffering so that we would not regret the extinction of consciousness. Colm Tóibín, in his novel *The Master*, endows his protagonist, Henry James (endows him with what in life he already possessed), with the imagination of the rightness of our mortality. "Here in this cemetery, which they began to stroll around once more, the state of not-knowing and not-feeling which belonged to the dead seemed to him closer to resolved happiness than he had ever imagined possible." So when death visited him, his last words were "So here it is at last, the distinguished thing."

Cemeteries are rarely a subject for conversation. When I bring it up with friends, they say they haven't given it a thought, and change the subject or look as if I have suddenly become odd. Death these days is something you don't prepare for. My immigrant parents and their *landsleit* created a burial society when they were relatively young, wanting to maintain their community in death. But now families are scattered to the four winds. The salesman who accompanied me on a visit to a cemetery pointed out half-occupied family plots that would never be filled because members of the family had departed for far-flung places, never to return. Or couples had divorced and neglected to tend the gravesite.

In any event, all thoughts nowadays are on the search for the fountain of youth. A scientist friend tells me that the cell is, in theory, immortal. If the cell, why not human beings? I'll tell you why not. Imagine the current lot of humanity filling the earth forever, leaving little space for anything new. And to think that we would have to endure others and ourselves eternally, as in Sartre's *No Exit*! But mine is a minority opinion. My daughter Jessica, miles away in another part of the country and many years away from James's "resolved happiness," is amused by the visit my wife and I made to a cemetery to buy a plot. She has turned it into a poem: "It makes no difference. / Willow or duck pond. Lilies, asters, roses. / Soon, you'll be tooth, shard and nail. And some time this long limbed, / upright woman will join you, bone on your bone."

Well, let me set her straight: there will be ashes, but no bones. The salesman, of course, made much of the difference between willow and duck pond. Why $5,000 for this site and $10,000 for the other? "It's the view that makes all the difference" (*gravely* said). The view (!) for those who will never or hardly ever visit? On reflection, I saw the salesman's point. My parents lie in a vast city of the dead, grave pressed against grave endlessly to the horizon. Though I rarely visit, the image of the overcrowded city of the dead reminds me of the overcrowded street of tenements where they lived. The dead leave memories of themselves behind, so the view matters. Jessica guessed right about our spirits as my wife and I walked through the cemetery: "Right now, you giggle together. / It's a lark, a walk down the path of 'here lies,' / the laughable dead on each side, / somber as straight men / in a comedy routine, / a vaudeville of cold stone / and beating heart." The salesman, commercially grave-faced, didn't hear the giggle. And my son Eric, living close by, in the same spirit as his sister's, suggests that we arrange a picnic in the cemetery. A wake before the event — and we aren't even Irish.

Socrates is mortal . . . We all know the syllogism, which modern biologists are determined to refute, not simply by extending life but by demonstrating that cells are theoretically immortal, making us potentially immortal. At a wedding, of all places, I found myself sitting next to a cardiologist who got me talking (or did I get him talking?) about my mitral valve prolapse. When I told him that my doctor prescribed an echocardiogram every six months in order to see whether my heart had enlarged (if so, requiring a valve replacement), he said without missing a beat that either my condition must be very serious or my doctor was insane. I reported the episode to my cardiologist, without mentioning the suspicion of insanity. He wondered about the tact (why not sanity?) of his colleague and brushed aside the question about how serious my leaky heart valve was with the reassurance that the only thing certain is that I will die. Suddenly feeling giddy, I challenged him to prove it. Hadn't he read David Hume? Nothing in our empirical past can *prove* what the future holds. My doctor looked puzzled. Had he never read philosophy? I told a friend I was writing about aging and dying, and he said you have to be funny or lighthearted, otherwise who would want to read it? So I whistle in the dark.

ADAM GOPNIK

\

Death of a Fish

FROM THE NEW YORKER

WHEN OUR FIVE-YEAR-OLD DAUGHTER Olivia's goldfish, Bluie,
died the other week, we were confronted by a crisis larger, or at
least more intricate, than is entirely usual upon the death of a pet.
Bluie's life and his passing came to involve so many cosmic elements — including the problem of consciousness and the plot line
of Hitchcock's *Vertigo* — that it left us all bleary-eyed and a little
shaken.

To begin with, Bluie, as his name suggests, was not actually a
goldfish. He was a betta, a goldfish-size fish that the people in pet
stores encourage you to buy in place of the apparently tetchy and
sickly true Asian goldfish. The betta is a handsome fish with long,
sweeping fins. It can be red or black or violet or blue, and it is, at
least according to the pet-store people, the Vietcong of pet fish,
evolved in rugged isolation in the rice-paddy puddles of Indochina
and just about impossible to kill off. The only drawback is that
male bettas fight with each other, and have to be kept apart. It is
not surprising, these days, to see a set of them on a child's dresser
in Manhattan, held in separate containers, in a kind of glass-bowl
parody of the co-op apartment building that surrounds them, each
fish furiously pacing its cubic foot of space and waiting for the
other to turn up the stereo.

And then, in a deeper, damper sense, Bluie was not really a fish
at all. He was, like so many New York fish and mice and turtles, a
placeholder for other animals, which the children would have preferred to have as pets, but which allergies and age and sheer self-
preservation have kept their parents from buying. Olivia and her

ten-year-old brother, Luke, desperately want a dog, and at Christmas Olivia brought the class hamster, Hamu, home from her preschool as an experiment in pet-keeping. Hamu stayed with us for a mostly happy, if sometimes jittery, holiday week, and we reluctantly agreed to add a hamster to the family.

We went to the second floor of Petco, the mallish store on East Eighty-sixth Street, where all the rodents are kept together — rats and mice and guinea pigs and hamsters and gerbils. Looking at them, my wife, Martha, had a foreboding sense of what Darwin must have felt, looking at the Galápagos finches: that these things were not nearly so distinct as they had been trying to make you believe. A hamster and a guinea pig and a gerbil are all rats, and the differences, tails and no tails, cute noses and not, are really bells and whistles, niche-marketing gimmicks. Having spent twenty-five years of her New York life struggling to keep rodents out, Martha couldn't see spending time and money to bring one in.

So we talked the children into goldfish, and then the weary fish salesman talked us into bettas instead. ("The goldfish will die," he said, shortly. "Then what?") We bought them bowls and gravel and decorative architecture to swim around in, and took them home. Luke named his Django, and Olivia gave hers the descriptive name of Bluie. For a while, she seemed to accept his provisional, placeholding nature with equanimity.

For a pet condemned to live in so many brackets of meta-meaning, a fish passing as a hamster hoping to be a dog, Bluie had a pretty good life. In the constant struggle of parents of two children — one obviously large and one (especially to herself) irrefutably, infuriatingly small — to even life up, we got Bluie a castle, a bigger *objet* for his tank than we got for Django. It sat on the gravel and rose almost to the surface — a Disney-like princess's residence, with turrets and castellations and plastic pennants. There was even a route from the base of the castle to the top turret which Bluie could swim up. A second betta, won at a street fair, joined Bluie on Olivia's dresser, but this new guy, named Reddie, had only a bowl to swim in. Reddie, we thought, kept pressing to the edge of his bowl to stare at Bluie's real estate with a certain resentment, the way a guy who lives in a condo on Broadway and teaches at City College might regard a colleague who writes bestsellers and lives in a penthouse on Central Park West.

One Sunday night around bedtime, my wife called me into Olivia's room. Bluie was stuck in one of the windows of his castle, wriggling and huffing, with just his head out, looking ahead and trying to swim away. He wasn't supposed to be able to swim up there into the windows — he was supposed to stay within the channel in the castle. But the castle obviously had an architectural flaw.

"Bluie's stuck in the window!" Olivia cried.

"Calm down, Olivia," Luke said. "He's just a fish."

"Bluie is my best friend," Olivia said. "I could tell him things I couldn't tell anyone else!" Until that moment, Bluie had seemed to be just a finny bit of decor, but at that moment, at least, he mattered to her crucially.

I watched Bluie wriggling in his window, staring out, stuck. I felt for him, another victim of grandiose Manhattan real estate, undone by his own apartment. It was one of those moments, of which parenting is full, where you scream inside, "I do not know what to do about this!" while the parent you are impersonating says calmly, "I'll fix it." I picked up Bluie's bowl and took him into the kitchen, leaving Martha to console Olivia.

I slid the kitchen door shut, and then reached into the water and tried gently to draw Bluie out of the window. I tugged lightly, and then realized that he was really wedged in. I tugged again, just a touch harder. Nothing. I saw that if I pulled at all firmly I was likely to rip his fins right off. I tried pushing him on the nose, urging him back out the way he came. Still nothing. He was stuck.

I looked around the kitchen. The remains of a sea bass that we had eaten for dinner — and that had doubtless had a lot more personality than Bluie ever did — rested on the counter, filleted skeleton and staring, reproachful head, waiting to be tossed out.

"Why can't Bluie think, I got into this mess by swimming forward, I'll go back the other way?" Luke said. "It's like he doesn't have a rewind function in his brain."

He had slipped quietly into the kitchen beside me and was watching, an intern to my baffled surgeon. Like many ten-year-olds, he is obsessed by what philosophers call the problem of consciousness but he calls the thinking and feeling thing. "Does Bluie know he's Bluie?" he would ask when we watched the fish swimming in his bowl in Olivia's room. "I mean, I know he doesn't think, Oh, I'm Bluie! But what *does* he think — does he know he's *him* swimming around? Or is he just like a potato or something, only with fins, who swims but doesn't think anything?" What does it feel like, he wanted to know, to be a fish, a hamster, a monkey, a chimp? What does it feel like to be someone else?

When my sister, a developmental psychologist at Berkeley, came to visit, she sat Luke down and said, smoothly, that scientists once thought that life was a problem, but then they had not so much solved the problem as dissolved it, by understanding ever simpler forms of life. Luke's problem, why we know what it feels like to be alive, would probably dissolve into its parts, too. Luke had nodded politely, but I could see he still held that the problem of thinking and feeling certainly felt like a problem when you thought about it.

"Swim backward, Bluie," I implored. "Get out of there."

Bluie, of course, did nothing but wiggle some more within his window.

"Is he thinking, I'm dying?" Luke asked at last.

Finally, I settled on a cowardly postponement of what even then I knew to be inevitable. I walked back to Olivia's room. "Let's take Bluie to Petco in the morning and see if the experts there can help him," I said to Olivia as we tucked her in. "They've probably got a whole team of guys who are specialists in castle-extraction."

At five in the morning, I woke up to look in on Bluie. He was dead. I tried to think about what to do. I decided to take him out, still stuck in his castle window, and put him and the castle into a white plastic bag. Then I sat down to read at the kitchen table, in the gray light of the June Manhattan dawn, spring in Manhattan feeling so much more accelerated, so much quicker and time-lapsed and vivid than it does in any other city, a wave of pollen and warmth and renewal blowing in the window.

My sister had given me a kind of reading list to help me answer Luke's questions at a deep level, and I had read many of the philosophers who have something to say about his problem. I read David Chalmers, who thinks that consciousness is the ghost in the machine, the secret irreducible presence in the mind that distinguishes us from computers and goldfish and other creatures who provide only a zombie-like imitation of our self-knowledge. I read those philosophers who think that what we call consciousness is just an illusion, and bears the same relation to the workings of our real minds that the White House press spokesman bears to the workings of the Bush White House: it is there to find rationalizations and systematic reasons for feelings and decisions made by dim, hidden powers of whose pettish and irrational purposes it is aware only long after the fact.

Of all the theories that I came across, the most impressive was Daniel Dennett's. He argues that consciousness is a byproduct, not a point — that it is just the sound that all those parallel processors inside our heads make as they run alongside one another, each doing its small robotic task. There is no "consciousness" apart from the working of all our mental states. Consciousness is not the ghost in the machine; it is the hum of the machinery. The louder the hum, the more conscious you feel. If Bluie had had a more interesting life, he would have known that he was having it. Bluie did not know that he was Bluie because there was not enough Bluie going on in his head to make being Bluie interesting even to Bluie.

Luke woke up and padded into the kitchen. He asked what had happened to Bluie, and I told him. We decided that we would bury Bluie before Olivia woke up, and then tell her that we had taken him to Petco. That would buy some time, anyway. I emptied Bluie's bowl, hid it in the closet of my office, and Luke and I got dressed. We carried Bluie, in his castle, in his white bag, down the hall to the trash room. We held our caps over our hearts as he went down the chute. Then I took Luke to school. He was silent on the way, but at the school door he turned to me.

"Dad, whatever you tell her, don't do a big Bluie's-in-the-fish-hospital thing," he counseled me. *"That* she'll never buy."

When I got home, I woke up Martha. "Bluie didn't make it," I whispered. "What are we going to do?"

"We're doing the full *Vertigo*," she announced, almost before her eyes were open. She had obviously been thinking about it since last night. "You're going to Petco and buying a fish that looks just like Bluie, and then we're going to put him in the fishbowl and tell her that it's Bluie. If it worked with Kim Novak, it can work with a betta."

She was referring, of course, to the plot of the fifties Hitchcock classic, which we had seen, as part of an impromptu Hitchcock festival, about a week before. In *Vertigo,* James Stewart falls in love with a mysterious, cool blond beauty, played by Kim Novak, who he comes to believe is a mystical reincarnation of her long-dead great-grandmother, compelled to imitate her actions. When, like her great-grandmother, she launches herself to her death from a bell tower in a restored mission town, Stewart is devastated. Haunted and desperate, he stumbles on a brunette shopgirl who looks eerily like Kim Novak, and forces her to dye her hair blond and dresses her in tailored gray suits, turning her into a precise replica of the Kim Novak character.

Actually, though, she is the Kim Novak character. She had been hired by the bad guy to play the part of the first Kim Novak charac-ter — another woman was thrown off that tower, as part of an in-surance scam — and, to make it even odder, the fact that this is so is given away by the second Kim Novak character (in a flashback) right in the middle of the movie, so that the viewer, unlike poor Jimmy Stewart, is never in doubt about the reason the new Kim Novak looks like the old Kim Novak. The meaning of Hitchcock's choice to give away the key plot point in the middle of the movie, against the advice of everyone around him, is, I have discovered, a subject as much argued about among the cinéastes as the nature of consciousness is among the philosophers.

Martha went to wake Olivia and get her dressed for school.

"Bluie's in the fish hospital, darling," I heard her say. Boys and men don't believe in the fish hospital; mothers know that it is where all problems should be sent, while we wait to solve them.

"She'll just walk in, like Jimmy Stewart, and will be strangely re-minded of Bluie — then he'll become Bluie for her," Martha said a few hours later, as we watched the new fish swim around in Olivia's tank, though I could tell that she was trying to reassure herself that this would work. I had gone to Petco and bought a Bluie look-alike. It was easy — the bettas all looked like Bluie.

But I was beginning to doubt that this was such a good idea. I re-membered that in the movie Jimmy Stewart goes nuts, and Kim Novak ends up throwing herself off that bell tower for real.

"Are we doing the wrong thing?" I asked. "I mean, won't she fig-ure out at ten or so that Bluie died?"

All this while, Martha, as a New York mother in crisis, had her cell phone cradled under her jaw. Everybody had had a dead-pet problem. Goldfish had floated to the tops of bowls; hamsters had been found dead in their cages, their furry feet upward; and more gruesome inter-pet homicides had taken place, too. Each family had a different tack, and a different theory. There were those who had gone the full *Vertigo* route and regretted it; those who had gone the tell-it-to-'em-straight route and regretted that. In fact, about all one could say, and not for the first time as a parent, is that whatever one did, one regretted it afterward.

I made only one call, and that was to my sister, the developmental psychologist. She explained to me instantly that it was normal for children to develop intense attachments to pets, even "zombie" ones that did not reciprocate affection, and that a pair of Japanese psychologists, Hatano and Inagaki, had done studies of how children develop intuitive theories of biology by having pets.

"They claim that all kids, Western and Eastern, go from having primarily just psychology and physics to having a 'vitalist' biology right around age six," she told me. "That is, they start to think there is some vital spirit — you know, kind of like Chinese chi — that keeps animals and humans alive, gets replenished by food, damaged by illness, and so on. And here's the cool thing. Hatano and Inagaki show experimentally that giving kids pet fish accelerates the development of this kind of vitalism. We give them fish as a learning device, though we don't know that when we do it. Olivia is probably in transition from a psychological conception of life to a biological one, which may be why she's so bewildered."

It seemed that the mere presence of a fish in a bowl, despite the barriers of glass and water and the fact of the fish's mindlessness, acted as a kind of empathy pump for five-year-olds, getting into the corners of their minds. Olivia was a vitalist, and Bluie was no longer vital. According to my sister, children's education proceeds in stages. At three, they're mostly psychologists, searching for a theory of mind; at six, they're biologists, searching for a theory of life. At ten, they're philosophers, searching to understand why our minds cannot make our lives go on forever.

"My sister doesn't think we're going to screw up Olivia's mind," I said to Martha a few moments later. "She does think that we're going to screw up her theories of biology." Martha was still watching the tank and trying to see if new Bluie would pass. "Olivia is going to think that dying things go away to Petco and come back as good as new."

Luke was the first one home. He studied the new fish too. "Does new Bluie know that he's not Bluie?" he asked. Reddie was looking at new Bluie, but we couldn't even guess what he was thinking.

In the end, when Olivia came home from school, we did neither the ingenious Hitchcockian thing nor the honest brutal thing but, being New York liberals, the in-between, wishy-washy, split-the-difference thing. Martha told her that Bluie had been successfully extracted from his castle window by the fish specialists, but he had been so stressed by the experience that he was resting, and it might take a long time for him to recover. Meanwhile, they had given us Bluie's brother.

Olivia took one long, baleful look at the new Bluie.

"I hate this fish," she said. "I hate him. I want Bluie."

We tried to console her, but it was no use.

"But, look, he's just like Bluie!" we protested weakly.

"He looks like Bluie," she admitted. "He looks like Bluie. But he's not Bluie. He's a stranger. He doesn't know me. He's not my friend, who I could talk to."

That evening, we took turns staying up with her, sitting in the rocking chair in her room and rocking until she slept. The room, I realized, was full of Bluies: things that she had ascribed feelings and thoughts and intentions to, all the while knowing that they didn't really have them. There were Buzzes and Woodies, American Girl dolls, and stuffed animals from her infancy. Children, small children particularly, don't just have more consciousness than the rest of us. They *believe* in consciousness more than the rest of us; their default conviction is that everything might be able to think, feel, and talk. This conviction is one that entertainment companies both recognize and exploit, with talking toys and lovable sharks, though at some other level, of course, the children are entertained by them because they know it's all made up — no child believes that her own toys in her own bedroom talk like Woody and Buzz in the movie. Ascribing feelings to things is a way of protecting your own right to have feelings. Expanding the circle of consciousness extends the rule of feelings.

Olivia loved Bluie because it is in her nature to ascribe intentions and emotions to things that don't have them, rather as Hitchcock did with actresses. She knows that she is Olivia because one of the things that she is capable of doing is imagining that Bluie is Bluie. Though you read about the condition "mind-blindness" in autistic children, the alternative, I saw, was not to be mind-sighted. The essential condition of youth is to be mind-visionary: to see everything as though it might have a mind. We begin as small children imagining that everything could have consciousness — fish, dolls, toy soldiers, even parents — and spend the rest of our lives paring the list down, until we are left alone in bed, the only mind left.

And yet, though I had been instructed by my reading that we imagine minds as much as know them, I also realized, looking at the little girl who had cried herself to sleep, that the difference didn't quite matter. A pet is an act of empathy, a theory of love the child makes, but it is also a living thing, and when it dies it moves briefly but decisively outside the realm of thought, where everything can be given the shape of our own mind, and into the cold climate of physical existence, where things are off or things are on. Science might be dissolving life and mind into smaller parts, but among the higher animals, at least, with eyes and skeletons and hungers, the line between life and nonlife is pretty much fixed and hard; from the other side of that window, no traveler, or goldfish, has yet come home to his bowl.

The real proof of consciousness is the pain of loss. Reddie, swimming in his studio, did not know that Bluie had gone; Bluie himself may in some sense not have known that he had gone. But Olivia did. The pain we feel is not the same as the hum we know, and it is the pain, not the hum, that is the price of being conscious, and the point of being human. I looked at the sleeping child, hoping that she would be over her grief in the morning.

"Mom," Luke said the next morning, "you shouldn't have done that big Bluie's-in-the-fish-hospital thing. It just stretched it out." The three of us were sitting at the kitchen table, waiting for Olivia to wake up.

"I *didn't* do a big Bluie's-in-the-fish-hospital thing," Martha objected querulously. She was pretty tired. "I did a big Bluie's-in-the-rehab-clinic-right-next-to-the-fish-hospital thing."

"Well, that makes it worse," Luke said.

"Let's try this," Martha said. "Let's tell her that, though Bluie did die, this Bluie is kind of Bluie reborn."

I thought she might have something, and in the next fifteen minutes we did a quick, instinctive tour of the world's religions. We made up a risen-from-the-grave Christian story: the Passion of the Bluie. We considered a Buddhist story: Bluie goes round and round. We even played with a Jewish story: Bluie couldn't be kept alive by the doctors, but what a lovely bowl he left for his family!

Then we heard the door of Olivia's room open, and she came to the table, theatrically calm, and sat down. "I'm going to call the new fish Lucky," she announced. "And can I please have the Honey Nut Cheerios?" She knew that the Honey Nut Cheerios were, strictly speaking, off limits, but that no one was going to call her on it this morning.

It was, I thought, an inventive stroke. Did the name refer to new Bluie's unearned good fortune in getting a home after the death of the original Bluie? Or did it refer to his good fortune in being alive at all to swim around in the world a little longer? Certainly luck seemed like a wiser thing to celebrate in a fish than reincarnation.

But then an odd thing happened. After a couple of days of everyone calling him Lucky, we noticed that Olivia, on her own, began to call the new fish Bluie. It was as if, having made a grand and instructive emotional tour, she had ended up right where she started. We begin with the problem of mind, pass through the experience of pain — and end up loving the same old fish.

I understood suddenly why Hitchcock had given the secret away in the middle of *Vertigo*. The surprise is revealed because Hitchcock could not see what was surprising. He didn't think that there was anything bizarre in the idea of someone constantly being remade in the image of someone else's schemes or desires or weird plot points, because he thought that this is what life and love consist of. Suspense, not surprise, was the element Hitchcock swam in — not What next? but How will we get to the inevitable place again? Hitchcock himself, after all, did not adapt to circumstances. He made circumstances adapt to him. When Grace Kelly married a prince, there was Kim Novak, and when Kim Novak rebelled there was Tippi Hedren. Every five-year-old has one fish, as every great director has a single Blonde. What Hitchcock's films of the fifties have in common with all the world's religions is the faith that death can be overcome, or at least made tolerable, by repetitive obsession. First the mind, then the pain, and then the echo: that is the order of life. James Stewart learned this, and now Olivia had, too.

Luke had a much more sinister view about what had happened to Bluie — less *Vertigo* and more *Psycho.*

"What I think is," he said, "Reddie put Bluie up to swimming into that window, and then laughed inside when he saw what happened. It was, like, the Revenge of Reddie. He hated Bluie all this time for having a bigger house than he did, and finally tricked him to his death. Reddie is the bad guy, with all these plots and schemes. Look at him! He's the villain."

And for a moment or two, watching poor Reddie innocently swimming in his low-rent bowl, I did think I could see an evil gleam in his small fishy eye, a startling resemblance to Anthony Perkins in his drawn, nervous excitability and long-simmering rage. I watched him in slightly panicky wonder. He looked like a fish who knows his own mind.

KIM DANA KUPPERMAN

Relief

FROM HOTEL AMERIKA

Has it ever been absent, this desire
for every moment to stand in relief,
the unending row of them set
like solitaires into what passes,
burnished to unbearable depths?

  — MELANIE REHAK, "The Modernist Impulse"

I

I WOKE TO A downpour the March morning in 1989 when I
had to identify my mother's body at the New York City morgue.
Drenched, the island of Manhattan smells cleansed, an idea of
earth under all that granite and steel and glass. When I opened my
eyes the bedroom seemed fashioned not of four walls, but of details. The shade covering the window, a yellow number 2 pencil in
a cup, an address book opened to the B section — all these objects
looked as if they had been placed on top of surfaces and polished
while I slept. In spite of the day before, the day of my mother's
heart stopping, of waiting and her two suicide notes, of possibly
too much wine and definitely not enough sleep, I could make out
with ease the rip in the shade, the eraser's rubbed-down edge, the
phone number for the city coroner penciled next to my mother's
name.

 I dressed and made my way downtown, toting an umbrella, identification, keys to my mother's apartment, all the necessary para-
phernalia of a person attempting to fit into a world where the
rules seem to have suddenly changed. Entering the lobby of the

morgue, I looked up at a large plaque with raised letters that pronounced FIORELLO LA GUARDIA, MAYOR. Contemplating the possibility that news of La Guardia's death forty-two years earlier had somehow not been communicated within this building, I felt the first trick of relief. I embraced the absurdity that you could die and still hold office, at least here where the city keeps the bodies of the unidentified dead.

The previous day I'd confirmed for the police, the paramedics, and the coroner that the naked body stretched out on the bed belonged to my mother.

"Yes, that's her," I said. Why, I wondered, had no one bothered to shut her eyes, wide open in terrified surprise? Her mouth was fixed into a perfect O, a scream I couldn't hear. She regretted her suicide, I thought, and was on the edge of dying when she realized her mistake. My mother had lived on edges — poverty, depression, having to be an adult before she completed childhood — and she died knowing their sharpness.

I was struck then by my mother's swollen feet, and in an attempt to relieve the swelling, I knelt on the floor and rubbed them. Maybe it was my guilt I was trying to rub away. Perhaps this act was simply the final performance of one I'd rehearsed throughout childhood on Saturday nights, when my mother and I would stay up late and watch old horror movies. The toes were almost too hardened to massage, the heels cool, the insteps stiff. As I massaged those feet, I knew it was the last time I would touch my mother's body.

After I'd talked to the police, I signed all the forms in which I acknowledged being the daughter of the deceased woman in the apartment. But because of a law about unattended deaths, I still needed to go downtown the next day to identify her body, and I resented this redundancy.

I see myself standing on the wet floor of the morgue's lobby. Pouring rain outside. Folded, dripping umbrellas hooked over people's arms. The smell of drenched raincoats, the wads of tear-soaked tissues in pockets. Presiding over this frozen moment is Mayor La Guardia, a dead man whose vital record, like my mother's, is incomplete.

The woman at the morgue placed a Polaroid head shot of my mother on the small table between us. I had imagined a more clinical episode, like something from TV, which involved a walk down a corridor, a stranger peeling a sheet off my mother's body in a room of white tile and surgical steel. Instead I sat in a small cubicle that was bare save for a box of Kleenex and some chairs. Painted in a green that is neither sage nor olive, a color I believe is mixed especially for institutions. A liminal zone between the announcement of death and its confirmation. A place governed by hidden people who typed memos, drank coffee, and washed their hands while I sat and stared at a Polaroid. The dead separated from us by walls and photographs.

No one had warned me that the features of my mother's face had experienced a kind of inexplicable shift, as though they had been moved to the right of the meridian defined by her nose. The O her mouth had formed only ten hours ago had collapsed into lips that should have been parallel but were askew. I thought of all the years she had meticulously spent "putting on her face," only to wear a final version that disturbed the structure of her cheekbone and eroded the curve of her lip. What if I had not been able to really identify her? What happens to a daughter who cannot point with defiance and certainty to her own mother and say "Yes, that's her"?

My mother's true identity was as foreign to me, I know now, as her face in that picture. She bleached her hair blond and trained her skin to alabaster by avoiding the sun — who would look for a woman who was half Jewish in all that paleness? To attract men she lined her mouth carefully with fire engine–red lipstick, but refused to kiss lest it smear. She used wigs and powders and different colors with elaborate care. She even paid to have her nose broken and re-set so that no one would notice it. My mother had spent her life mastering the art of disguise, learning how to stand out to be concealed. Hidden in plain sight, as they say.

Perhaps the plunge into suicide had stripped away all that artifice and raised up the true design of her face, which seemed to emerge through the mask she had spent so much time fashioning. The face I saw in the picture was unforgiving, the cheekbones so chiseled they appeared stripped of the softness I'd relied on all my life.

Sitting in that room in the morgue, gazing at the Polaroid, I wondered how I'd confirm my mother's identity. I barely recognized her, and I craved the familiarity of her disguise. How could I

say that her body, which was nowhere in sight, belonged to this image of a face that did not belong to her?

The woman at the morgue shuffled some papers. I looked at
her, but we never made eye contact.

"Yes," I said, "that's her."

Late October 1990. The three days before my older half-brother
Ronnie died, I contemplated sneaking into his hospital room and
opening the morphine drip all the way. Instead I spoke awkward
prayers to a creator I couldn't envision as I stood in a circle with my
family in a hospital corridor on the AIDS ward, my head bent and
eyes closed while a rabbi led us in prayer. How to petition God? I
wondered, just as somebody paged a doctor and people walked
past us. I asked that my brother be relieved of his suffering. But my
father and my brother's mother, I suspected, requested that he remain bound to them. Our prayers would cancel each other's out,
and then what?

When my brother died, he wore such a peaceful expression that
I barely recognized him. There was his salt-and-pepper hair against
the white pillowcase, the same curls that were drenched in sweat
several days ago that now seemed clean and soft. The sheet, which
before had only emphasized his emaciation, appeared to caress his
body as if giving it back its substance. During the last year of his
life, my brother's face seemed pulled down as his cheeks hollowed
and his jawbone protruded. The creases at the corners of his eyes
tightened, squeezed out the gentler laugh lines, and had hardened
into an expression of permanent anger, or perhaps regret. It seems
peculiar now to think that this man, who had raged his entire life,
stopped raging when death approached.

I imagine that my brother welcomed death like a sentry who, relieved of watching for danger, succumbs to sleep. I like to think of
him lifting off from the landscape of pain his body had become.
Like a heron I once saw that unfolded its wings and levitated from
the road. Gone, with just the slightest rustle of feathers.

II

Procrastination and numb dread lay at the heart of my inability to
scatter my mother's ashes, and so they remained on a shelf in my
bedroom closet for almost two years. Sometimes when I opened

the closet door to reach for a dress or a blouse, the sight of that plain cardboard box on the shelf would freeze me in place. What kind of person keeps her mother's ashes on a shelf in the closet as if she's a hat that's gone out of style? I reminded myself that no sacred niches decorated the walls of my apartment. There were no shrines. No one had taught me about the etiquette of ashes. Since I wasn't planning on urns or a mausoleum, the closet seemed the most discreet arrangement.

Arrangements. This is the word for everything that must be completed once someone dies — the repeated telephone conversation with family and friends, the wording of the obituary, the date and time of the service, the crematorium, the paperwork, the transportation, the disposal of personal affairs, the deposition of remains. In arrangements, though, there is a hint of relief, the kind that is brought about by dissolution. "Wind blowing over water disperses it, dissolving it into foam and mist," says the *I Ching*. First there is the gathering, the accumulation of family and friends in one space (too small), the never-ending food (too much) that suddenly appears. In this swell of comfort you feel awkward and exposed, like someone who's the subject of an overheard secret. Then the gathering dissolves: you wrap and store the leftovers, wring out the sponge used to clean the counter, turn out the light on the fingerprints that linger on the refrigerator door. Later you touch and sort and discard and keep for another time the artifacts — a fur hat on my brother's bureau that my father cannot wear but which fits me; a tiny bear carved of jade on my mother's perfume tray. Eventually all these objects are not only handled more than once, but packed into containers, some resurfacing on shelves or from drawers years later, others given to friends, shipped off to the Salvation Army, or carried to landfills. These things we once thought were useful or beautiful disperse or are buried, as if there were no point to having them in the first place. But in the act of letting go of them, there is a relief that they no longer have to be carried or cared for or worried about.

Two months after Ronnie died, I made arrangements to move to France, as if I were another artifact left behind after my mother's death, as if I needed to ship myself off to some place where no one would recognize that I belonged to her. But before I left, I made arrangements to scatter my mother's ashes.

III

A freezing December day, old snow and ice hardened in the New Jersey suburbs where I've come to leave my mother's remains. I'm with Laurie, my mother's goddaughter, whose deceased mother was my godmother, and whose ashes she's come to scatter. We form a private club — gloved hands, cans of ashes hidden in the bags we carry. Something about how we are padded in layers of clothing, how we each chose similar canvas bags for this excursion, makes me feel conspicuous. We stand in the back yard of the house Laurie grew up in, where my mother and I spent Thanksgiving and Christmas when I was a child. The house is now for sale, and it feels eerie out here under the bare trees, two young women in winter coats carrying their mothers' remains in totes. The reflection of our shapes and the contours of the bags seem pasted on the surface of the dark windows. It would be easier, I think, to be that reflection of myself, temporary and raised on glass, than to stand here and shiver in the icy wind, ready to consign to permanence my mother's remains.

"Right here," Laurie says, pointing to two old trees. "We should scatter them right here, under these two maples."

I agree. In the fall, one of these trees burns yellow, the other red, just like our blond and copper-haired mothers. We remove our respective cans from the bags. Remains, the stuff inside is called. Remains, I think, of women who orchestrated holiday lights, gifts, and party dresses. Women who presided over each year's variation on the turkey and pecan pie, twice a year within a month, every year. Women who said things like "beauty hurts" and who taught us that birth control, blush, and bleach are essential for life as a woman. None of this is written on the plain tins. Nothing about how they had invented themselves with ordinary tools like eyeliner and lipstick. It seems a disservice to them both to be reduced to *remains,* packed into containers like small paint cans, without even a label like *Butter Whisper* or *Adobe Dust.* I wrestle briefly with the contradiction of remains as matter that does not remain still, but that drifts and settles, settles and drifts, and refuses to stay anywhere for very long. I fish around in my pocket for a quarter to pry off the top of my mother's can.

I can't open it. Is the lid sealed with Super Glue? The superstitious side of me thinks my failure is the result of having waited so

long to do this. Maybe I was wrong before about remains not remaining, maybe if I don't open this can, my mother will remain
with me forever. I ask Laurie if she has a screwdriver. She doesn't.
She tries to get the lid off and breaks a nail, which makes us both
laugh until we cry, just like both our mothers would have done.

I keep working at the can until what seems like half an hour
elapses. Under all my layers of clothing I feel cold and sweaty at the
same time. The stubborn quality of this moment is not lost on me
as the final complicity of our two mothers, friends who considered
each other sisters. After the sixth or seventh attempt to open the
can, I feel a surge of adrenaline rush down to my toenails and out
of my fingertips. One more pry with the quarter and the lid opens,
releasing a gasp of vacuum-sealed air. In this energy-charged state
I'm also able to open Laurie's container.

I want to say that I felt shocked when I looked into the can and saw
my mother, reduced to ashes inside a plastic bag tied with a twistie.
I wasn't shocked but relieved by the plainness of her remains, how
their dusty grayness obscured the Technicolor complexity of my
mother when she was alive. An emptiness settled over me, flooded
each pore and hair follicle. Even though Laurie stood by my side,
even though her hand was probably on my arm, I felt more alone
than I have ever felt before or since.

I don't recall opening the bag to disperse my mother's ashes underneath the trees, or what I said at that moment, but once the bag
was emptied, I sensed myself as very light and small, almost invisible. Anchored to all things, yet hovering above the world.

My father has come to Paris, where I live, to scatter my brother's remains. Mary, my father's wife, holds his left arm; on his right shoulder he carries a bag holding my brother's ashes. At the hotel, he
unpacks.

The can with the ashes is still inside a cardboard box on whose
surface is inscribed my father's name and address in worn letters. I
imagine him unable to sleep, wandering into the den — where
Mary insists he keep that particular package — and holding the
box in his hands. I picture him absent-mindedly rubbing his
fingers over the name inked on the cardboard, as if that were not
his name and this box did not contain his oldest son. I wonder if

he ever questions what part he might have played in my brother's death.

"Take that home with you tonight," Mary says. She's unable to look at the box, to even say the word "box." I consider her request, the whisper of despair in her voice. It dawns on me: What first-generation Jewish immigrant, raised in a kosher home, would feel comfortable with the incinerated residue of anyone, let alone a child? Into my black canvas satchel it goes. I take the metro home with what remains of my brother in a bag that now hangs from my shoulder.

Writing this, I am unable to summon the faces from the metro that evening. Perhaps I had cast my eyes downward, arms folded on top of the parcel in my lap. Maybe I was too tired to register any more information that described this episode in my family's life. But I can see all the implications now: the father brings the son into heaven, the sister takes the brother underground. They each carry him in the same way to different destinations, one relieving the other of this obligation.

My brother had asked to have his ashes scattered on Mediterranean shores, but my father considers the request too expensive to honor, too complicated to arrange. In his final act as the patriarch against whom my brother revolted, my father decides on the Normandy coastline instead.

It's raining — a June mist promising rain, really — when we take my brother's ashes to Deauville. This is the France of Camembert and apple brandy, of Henry James and Marcel Proust. These are the shores of D-day and the birthplace of impressionism. Of course we are not here for any of that, but as we walk past the casinos along the grand boardwalk, I feel asthmatic ghosts beside me in the damp air.

We stand at the edge of a low soft tide, the open can of my brother's remains at our feet. My father takes the first handful and casts the ashes to the sea. He is crying. I start to curl my fingers around the dry, gray stuff where life once was fleshy and brown when I notice a woman walking toward us. For a moment I'm a little panicked — what if she's patrolling this shore for people just like us, casting the ashes of the dead into the water? That seems unlikely, but perhaps she *is* on the lookout for littering. If I were standing where she is, I might see two people throwing things away.

I point her out to my father, put the lid back on the can, close a tight fist around the handful of my brother's ashes, and thrust that hand into my coat pocket. When the woman nears, I see that her wispy, dark hair is greasy, and her black pants and jacket are faded.

"Do you have a light?" she asks. *Do you have some fire?* is the literal translation of this French query, and I realize she's holding a cigarette in her right hand.

I want to laugh, the absurdity is so complete, but I also want her to keep walking so my father and I can finish what we started. As it is, I happen to have what she needs, a light, but it's in the same pocket as my closed and hidden fist. I reach around my back with my left hand to retrieve my lighter and light her cigarette. She takes a deep draw on it and exhales. I'm relieved she hasn't noticed my awkward movement.

"I simply love smoking in the rain on the beach," she says. She begins to walk away, then stops, her feet just inches from the can of my brother's ashes, which she eyes.

"Collecting seashells?" she asks.

I nod. She smiles at me, continues walking. I've seen no shells on this beach, no starfish or sand dollars either. Nothing that would stop me in my meandering along the shore and beckon me to pocket some proof that I was here. And the birds are strangely absent too, even gulls. It is as if the scene in which I participated occurred just above the surface of things, in a place where evidence becomes so light that it dissolves.

We had gone to that beach to leave something behind, not to collect. Some part of me must have felt obligated to preserve that moment, so I gathered its details. The woman's voice, which seemed to match the wispiness of her hair and the fadedness of her clothing. The almost impossible maneuver of lighting her cigarette. The dialogue. I did what I always do when faced with a potential memory: I chose the most absurd part and catalogued its fragments.

"What was that all about?" my father asks.

Laughter would be a relief right now, but it would be inappropriate — my father will take it the wrong way and never forgive me. I explain to him without the slightest trace of a smile that the woman needed a light.

As soon as she's receded into the distance, I release my fistful of ashes. I watch the smaller flakes hover before they drift to the edge of the sea, and the heavier pieces fall directly to the wet sand. Suddenly all things water here have assumed a cadence that contradicts my urge to laugh: the raised rhythm of the waves against the shore, the rain falling in fat drops now, threatening to drench us if we don't hurry. Something in the splatter, ebb, and flow suggests a flat seriousness that belongs to me simply because I'm standing here now, watching the remains of my brother float in the water and disperse in the air. I'm not too concerned that a fragment of my brother may have lodged in my coat pocket, tangled perhaps in a loose thread, his remains remaining. Instead I concentrate on emptying the can and getting my father and me to shelter before we get soaked.

IV

For most people, rainy days signify sadness, and the cold instills loneliness. It works that way in books sometimes, or in TV movies. But for me, rain and cold backdrop those moments when grief — that ache we carry underneath like a secret aquifer — suddenly subsides into a sense of relief. I'm not talking here of release from distress or sorrow, the relieved sigh when you finally put down your heavy suitcase, or the body's sag after days of weeping. Instead I mean the relief of contrast, of projected or outlined edges — think relief map, or a bas-relief where figures rise out of a stone slab. Or, for me, the shiny Polaroid that surfaces each time I hear the word "morgue." Or the city corner where I stand, transfixed by the sunshine on a building where my dead brother lies, the front of the hospital pushing out from all the architecture next to it. In French, this idea of relief is expressed in the word *relever*, which means to rise again, to be raised. In ballet the raising of the body initiated at the toes is called a *relevé*. This pressing up and onto the balls of the feet begins on the ground, spirals up the turned-out legs and hips into the torso, and lifts the dancer's head. Rising again, raised.

I like the idea that emotional rawness can suddenly sharpen ordinary objects. Amid the monotony of grief, everyday things — window shades, pencil erasers — stand out and help me find my way. Sometimes these projections manifest as the absurd of the ordinary — a dead mayor who presides over the city morgue that holds my mother's body, or the woman who interrupts the solemnity of scattering ashes, asking for a light, only to flick her own ashes away.

But perhaps it's the more subtle experience of relief as a kind of lifting up that most interests me. Relief lifts us up and lets us go — a daughter floats above the shadows while releasing her mother's ashes; a sister grips the edge of stifled laughter, suspended between the shards of her brother that drift in all directions. I observe as I participate, like those figures in the stone who are both grounded in and raised above the slab. There I am, my feet firmly planted on the beach at Deauville, or in a frozen suburban yard in New Jersey, and there at the same time is my own absence, the shape of what is not there. Relieved of my weight, yet holding on to it.

MICHELE MORANO

Grammar Lessons:
The Subjunctive Mood

FROM CRAB ORCHARD REVIEW

THINK OF IT THIS WAY: learning to use the subjunctive mood is like learning to drive a stick shift. It's like falling in love with a car that isn't new or sporty but has a tilt steering wheel and a price you can afford. It's like being so in love with the possibilities, with the places you might go and the experiences you might have, that you pick up your new used car without quite knowing how to drive it, sputtering and stalling and rolling backward at every light. Then you drive the car each day for months, until the stalling stops and you figure out how to downshift, until you can hear the engine's registers and move through them with grace. And later, after you've gained control over the driving and lost control over so much else, you sell the car and most of your possessions and move yourself to Spain, to a place where language and circumstance will help you understand the subjunctive.

Remember that the subjunctive is a mood, not a tense. Verb tenses tell *when* something happens; moods tell *how true*. It's easy to skim over moods in a new language, to translate the words and think you've understood, which is why your first months in Spain will lack nuance. But eventually, after enough conversations have passed, enough hours of talking with your students at the University of Oviedo and your housemate, Lola, and the friends you make when you wander the streets looking like a foreigner, you'll discover that you need the subjunctive in order to finish a question, or an answer, or a thought you couldn't have had without it.

In language, as in life, moods are complicated, but at least in language there are only two. The indicative mood is for knowledge, facts, absolutes, for describing what's real or definite. You'd use the indicative to say, for example:

> I was in love.
> Or, *The man I loved tried to kill himself.*
> Or, *I moved to Spain because the man I loved, the man who tried to kill himself, was driving me insane.*

The indicative helps you tell what happened or is happening or will happen in the future (when you believe you know for sure what the future will bring).

The subjunctive mood, on the other hand, is uncertain. It helps you tell what could have been or might be or what you want but may not get. You'd use the subjunctive to say:

> I thought he'd improve without me.
> Or, *I left so that he'd begin to take care of himself.*

Or later, after your perspective has been altered, by time and distance and a couple of *cervezas* in a brightly lit bar, you might say:

> I deserted him (indicative).
> *I left him alone with his crazy self for a year* (indicative).
> *Because I hoped* (after which begins the subjunctive) *that being apart might allow us to come together again.*

English is losing the subjunctive mood. It lingers in some constructions ("If he *were* dead . . . ," for example), but it's no longer pervasive. That's the beauty and also the danger of English — that the definite and the might-be often look so much alike. And it's the reason why, during a period in your life when everything feels hypothetical, Spain will be a very seductive place to live.

In Spanish, verbs change to accommodate the subjunctive in every tense, and the rules, which are many and varied, have exceptions. In the beginning you may feel defeated by this, even hopeless and angry sometimes. But eventually, in spite of your frustration with trying to explain, you'll know in the part of your mind that holds your stories, the part where grammar is felt before it's understood, that the uses of the subjunctive matter.

1. With Ojalá

Ojalá means "I hope" or, more literally, "that Allah is willing." It's one of the many words left over from the Moorish occupation of Spain, one that's followed by the subjunctive mood because, of course, you never know for sure what Allah has in mind.

During the first months in Spain, you'll use the word by itself, a kind of dangling wish. "It's supposed to rain," Lola will say, and you'll respond, "*Ojalá.*" You'll know you're confusing her, leaving her to figure out whether you want the rain or not, but sometimes the mistakes are too hard to bear. "That Allah is willing it wouldn't have raining," you might accidentally say. And besides, so early into this year of living freely, you're not quite sure what to hope for.

Each time you say *ojalá,* it will feel like a prayer, the *ja* and *la* like breaths, like faith woven right into the language. It will remind you of La Mezquita, the enormous, graceful mosque in Córdoba. Of being eighteen years old and visiting Spain for the first time, how you stood in the courtyard filled with orange trees, trying to admire the building before you. You had a fever then, a summer virus you hadn't yet recognized because it was so hot outside. Too hot to lift a hand to fan your face. Too hot to wonder why your head throbbed and the world spun slowly around you.

Inside, the darkness felt like cool water covering your eyes, such contrast, such relief. And then the pillars began to emerge, rows and rows of pillars supporting red-and-white brick arches, a massive stone ceiling balanced above them like a thought. You swam behind the guide, not even trying to understand his words but soothed by the vastness, by the shadows. Each time you felt dizzy you looked up toward the arches, the floating stone. Toward something that felt, you realized uncomfortably, like God. Or Allah. Or whatever force inspired people to defy gravity this way.

Ten years later, after you've moved to Oviedo, the man you left behind in New York will come to visit. You'll travel south with him, returning to La Mezquita on a January afternoon when the air is mild and the orange trees wave tiny green fruit. He'll carry the guidebook, checking it periodically to get the history straight, while you try to reconcile the place before you with the place in your memory, comparing the shadows of this low sun with the light of another season.

You'll be here because you want this man to see La Mezquita. You want him to feel the mystery of a darkness that amazes and consoles, that makes you feel the presence in empty spaces of something you can't explain. Approaching the shadow of the door, you'll both untie the sweaters from around your waists, slipping your arms into them and then into each other's. He will squint and you will hold your breath. *Ojalá*, you'll think, glimpsing in the shadows the subjunctive mood at work.

2. *After Words of Suasion and Negation*

In Oviedo, you'll become a swimmer. Can you imagine? Two or three times a week you'll pack a bag and walk for thirty-five minutes to the university pool, where you'll place clothes and contact lenses in a locker, then sink into a crowded lane. The pool is a mass of blurry heads and arms, some of which know what they're doing and most of which, like you, are flailing. You keep bumping into people as you make your way from one end of the pool to the other, but no one gets upset, and you reason that any form of motion equals exercise.

Then one day a miracle happens. You notice the guy in the next lane swimming like a pro, his long arms cutting ahead as he glides rhythmically, stroke-stroke-breath. You see and hear and feel the rhythm, and before long you're following him, stroking when he strokes, breathing when he breathes. He keeps getting away, swimming three laps to your every one, so you wait at the edge of the pool for him to come back, then follow again, practicing. At the end of an hour, you realize that this man you don't know, a man you wouldn't recognize clothed, has taught you to swim. To breathe. To use the water instead of fighting against it. For this alone, you'll later say, it was worth moving to Spain.

Stroke-stroke-breath becomes the rhythm of your days, the rhythm of your life in Oviedo. All through the fall months, missing him the way you'd miss a limb, your muscles strain to create distance. Shallow end to deep end and back, you're swimming away.

From memories of abrupt mood shifts. From the way a question, a comment, a person walking past a restaurant window could transform him into a hunched-over man wearing anger like a shawl. From the echo of your own voice trying to be patient and calm, saying, "Listen to me. I want you to call the doctor." In English you said "listen" and "call," and they were the same words you'd use to relate a fact instead of make a plea. But in Spanish, in the language that fills your mind as you swim continually away, the moment you try to persuade someone, or dissuade, you enter the realm of the subjunctive. The verb ends differently so there can be no mistake: requesting is not at all the same as getting.

3. *With* Si *or* Como Si

Si means "if." *Como si* means "as if." A clause that begins with *si* or *como si* is followed by the subjunctive when the meaning is hypothetical or contrary to fact. For example:

If I'd known he would harm himself, I wouldn't have left him alone.

But here we have to think about whether the if-clause really is contrary to fact. Two days before, you'd asked him what he felt like doing that night, and he'd responded, "I feel like jumping off the Mid-Hudson Bridge." He'd looked serious when he said it, and even so, you'd replied, "Really? Would you like me to drive you there?" *As if* it were a joke.

If you had known he was serious, that he was thinking of taking his life, would you have replied with such sarcasm? In retrospect it seems impossible not to have known — the classic signs were there. For weeks he'd been sad, self-pitying. He'd been sleeping too much, getting up to teach his freshman composition class in the morning, then going home some days and staying in bed until evening. His sense of humor had waned. He'd begun asking the people around him to cheer him up, make him feel better, please.

And yet he'd been funny. Ironic, self-deprecating, hyperbolic. So no one's saying you should have known, just that maybe you felt a hint of threat in his statement about the river. And maybe that angered you because it meant you were failing to be enough for him. Maybe you were tired too, in need of cheering up yourself because suddenly your perfect guy had turned inside out. Or maybe that realization came later, after you'd had the time and space to develop theories.

The truth is, only you know what you know. And what you know takes the indicative, remember?

For example: You knew he was hurting himself. The moment you saw the note on his office door, in the campus building where you were supposed to meet him on a Sunday afternoon, you knew. The note said, "I'm not feeling well. I'm going home. I guess I'll see you tomorrow." He didn't use your name.

You tried calling him several times, but there was no answer, so you drove to the apartment he shared with another graduate student. The front door was unlocked, but his bedroom door wouldn't budge. You knocked steadily but not too loudly, because his housemate's bedroom door was also closed and you assumed he was inside taking a nap. *If* you'd known that his housemate was not actually home, you would have broken down the door. That scenario is hypothetical, so it takes the subjunctive — even though you're quite sure.

The human mind can reason its way around anything. On the drive to your own apartment, you told yourself, He's angry with me. That's why the door was locked, why he wouldn't answer the phone. You thought, If he weren't so close to his family, I'd really be worried. If today weren't Mother's Day. If he didn't talk so affectionately about his parents. About his brother and sisters. About our future. If, if, if.

When the phone rang and there was silence on the other end, you began to shout, "What have you done?"

In Spain, late at night over *chupitos* of bourbon or brandy, you and Lola will trade stories. Early on, you won't understand a lot of what she says, and she'll understand what you say but not what you mean. You won't know how to say what you mean in Spanish; sometimes you won't even know how to say it in English. But as time goes on, the stories you tell will become more complicated. More subtle. More grammatically daring. You'll begin to feel more at ease in the unreal.

For example: *If* you hadn't gone straight home from his apartment. *If* you hadn't answered the phone. *If* you hadn't jumped back into your car to drive nine miles in record time, hoping the whole way to be stopped by the police. *If* you hadn't met him on the porch, where he had staggered in blood-soaked clothes. *If* you hadn't rushed upstairs for a towel and discovered a flooded bedroom floor, the blood separating into water and rust-colored clumps. *If* you hadn't been available for this emergency.

As the months pass in Spain, you'll begin to risk the *then*. His housemate would have come home and found him the way you found him: deep gashes in his arm, but the wounds clotting enough to keep him alive, enough to narrowly avoid a transfusion. His housemate would have called the paramedics, ridden to the hospital in the ambulance, notified his parents from the emergency room, and greeted them after their three-hour drive. His housemate would have done all the things you did, and he would have cleaned the mess by himself instead of with your help, the two of you borrowing a neighbor's wet-dry vac and working diligently until you — or he — or both of you — burst into hysterical laughter. Later this housemate would have moved to a new apartment, just as he has done, and would probably be no worse off than he is right now.

You, on the other hand, would have felt ashamed, guilty, remiss for not being available in a time of crisis. But you wouldn't have found yourself leaning over a stretcher in the emergency room, a promise slipping from your mouth before you could think it through: "I won't leave you. Don't worry, I won't leave you." *As if* it were true.

4. *After Impersonal Expressions*

Such as *it is possible, it is a shame, it is absurd.*

"*It's possible* that I'm making things worse in some ways," you told the counselor you saw on Thursday afternoons. He'd been out of the hospital for a few months by then and had a habit of missing his therapy appointments, to which you could respond only by signing up for your own.

She asked how you were making things worse, and you explained that when you told him you needed to be alone for a night and he showed up anyway at eleven, pleading to stay over, you couldn't turn him away. She said, "*It's a shame* he won't honor your request," and you pressed your fingernails into the flesh of your palm to keep your eyes from filling. She asked why you didn't want him to stay over, and you said that sometimes you just wanted to sleep, without waking up when he went to the bathroom and listening to make sure he came back to bed instead of taking all the Tylenol in the medicine cabinet. Or sticking his head in the gas oven. Or diving from the balcony onto the hillside three stories below. There is nothing, you told her, nothing I haven't thought of.

She said, "Do you think he's manipulating you?" and you answered in the mood of certainty, "Yes. Absolutely." Then you asked, "*Isn't it absurd* that I let him manipulate me?" and what you wanted, of course, was some reassurance that it wasn't absurd. That you were a normal person, reacting in a normal way to a crazy situation.

Instead she said, "Let's talk about why you let him. Let's talk about what's in this for you."

5. After Verbs of Doubt or Emotion

You didn't think he was much of a prospect at first. Because he seemed arrogant. Because in the initial meetings for new instructors, he talked as if he were doing it the right way and the rest of you were pushovers. Because he looked at you with one eye squinted, as if he couldn't quite decide.

You liked that he was funny, a little theatrical, and a great fan of supermarkets. At ten, after evening classes ended, he'd say, "Are you going home?" Sometimes you'd offer to drop him off at his place. Sometimes you'd agree to go out for a beer. And sometimes you'd say, "Yeah, but I have to go to the store first," and his eyes would light up. In the supermarket he'd push the cart and you'd pick items off the shelf. Maybe you'd turn around and there would be a whole rack of frozen ribs in your cart, or after you put them back, three boxes of Lucky Charms. Maybe he'd be holding a package of pfeffernusse and telling a story about his German grandmother. Maybe it would take two hours to run your errand because he was courting you in ShopRite.

You doubted that you'd sleep with him a second time. After the first time, you both lay very still for a while, flat on your backs, not touching. He seemed to be asleep. You watched the digital clock hit two-thirty A.M. and thought about finding your turtleneck and sweater and wool socks, lacing up your boots, and heading out into the snow. And then out of the blue he rolled toward you, pulled the blanket up around your shoulders, and said, "Is there anything I can get you? A cup of tea? A sandwich?"

You were thrilled at the breaks in his depression, breaks that felt like new beginnings, every time. Days, sometimes even weeks, when he seemed more like himself than ever before. Friends would ask how he was doing, and he'd offer a genuine smile. "Much better," he'd say, putting his arm around you. "She's pulling me through the death-wish phase." Everyone would laugh with relief, and at those moments you'd feel luckier than ever before, because of the contrast.

Do you see the pattern?

6. To Express Good Wishes

Que tengas muy buen viaje, Lola will say, kissing each of your cheeks before leaving you off at the bus station. *May you have a good trip.* A hope, a wish, a prayer of sorts, even without the *ojalá.*

The bus ride from Oviedo to Madrid is nearly six hours, so you have a lot of time for imagining. It's two days after Christmas, and you know he spent the holiday at his parents' house, that he's there right now, maybe eating breakfast, maybe packing. Tonight his father will drive him to Kennedy Airport, and tomorrow morning, very early, you'll meet him at Barajas in Madrid. You try to envision what he'll look like, the expression on his face when he sees you, but you're having trouble recalling what it's like to be in his presence.

You try not to hope too much, although now, four months into your life in Spain, you want to move toward instead of away. Toward long drives on winding mountain roads, toward the cathedral of Toledo, the mosque at Córdoba, the Alhambra in Granada. Toward romantic dinners along the Mediterranean. Toward a new place from which to view the increasingly distant past. You want this trip to create a separation, in your mind and in his, between your first relationship and your real relationship, the one that will be so wonderful, so stable, you'll never leave him again.

Once you've reached Madrid and found the *pensión* where you've reserved a room, you'll get the innkeeper to help you make an international call. His father will say, "My God, he can't sit still today," and then there will be his voice, asking how your bus ride was, where you are, how far from the airport. You'll say, "I'll see you in the morning." He'll reply, "In seventeen hours."

The next morning, the taxi driver is chatty. He wants to know why you're going to the airport without luggage, and your voice is happy and excited when you explain. He asks whether this boyfriend writes you letters, and you smile and nod at the reflection in the rearview mirror. "Many letters?" he continues. "Do you enjoy receiving the letters?" In Spain you're always having odd conversations with strangers, so you hesitate only a moment, wondering why he cares, and then you say, "Yes. Very much." He nods emphatically. "*Muy bien.*" At the terminal he drops you off with a broad smile. "*Que lo pases bien con tu novio,*" he says. *Have a good time with your boyfriend.* In his words you hear the requisite subjunctive mood.

7. In Adverbial Clauses Denoting Purpose, Provision, Exception

How different to walk down the street in Madrid, Toledo, Córdoba, to notice an elaborate fountain or a tiny car parked half on the sidewalk, and comment aloud. You've loved being alone in Spain, and now, even more, you love being paired.

On the fifth day you reach Granada, find lodging in someone's home. Down the hallway you can hear the family watching TV, cooking, preparing to celebrate New Year's Eve.

In the afternoon you climb the long, slow hill leading to the Alhambra and spend hours touring the complex. You marvel at the elaborate irrigation system, the indoor baths with running water, the stunning mosaic tiles and views of the Sierra Nevada. Here is the room where Boabdil signed the city's surrender to

Ferdinand and Isabella; here is where Washington Irving lived while writing *Tales of the Alhambra*. Occasionally you separate, as he inspects a mural and you follow a hallway into a lush courtyard, each of your imaginations working to restore this place to its original splendor. When you come together again, every time, there's a thrill.

He looks rested, relaxed, strolling through the gardens with his hands tucked into the front pockets of his pants. When you enter the Patio of the Lions — the famous courtyard where a circle of marble lions projects water into a reflecting pool — he turns to you wide-eyed, his face as open as a boy's.

"Isn't it pretty?" you keep asking, feeling shy because what you mean is "Are you glad to be here?"

"*So* pretty," he responds, taking hold of your arm, touching his lips to your hair.

The day is perfect, you think. The trip is perfect. You allow yourself a moment of triumph: I left him *so that* he would get better without me, and he did. I worked hard and saved money and invited him on this trip *in case* there's still hope for us. And there is.

Unless. In language, as in experience, we have purpose, provision, exception. None of which necessarily matches reality, and all of which take the subjunctive.

On the long walk back down the hill toward your room, he turns quiet. You find yourself talking more than usual, trying to fill the empty space with cheerful commentary, but it doesn't help. The shape of his face begins to change until there it is again, that landscape of furrows and crags. The jaw thrusts slightly, lips pucker, eyebrows arch as if to say, "I don't care. About anything."

Back in the room, you ask him what's wrong, plead with him to tell you. You can talk about anything, you assure him, anything at all. And yet you're stunned when his brooding turns accusatory. He says it isn't fair. You don't understand how difficult it is to be him. Your life is easy, so easy that even moving to a new country, taking up a new language, is effortless. While every day is a struggle for him. Don't you see that? Every day is a struggle.

He lowers the window shade and gets into bed, his back turned toward you.

What to do? You want to go back outside into the mild air and sunshine, walk until you remember what it feels like to be completely alone. But you're afraid to leave him. For the duration of his ninety-minute nap, you sit paralyzed. Everything feels unreal: the darkened room, the squeals of children in another part of the house, the burning sensation in your stomach. You tremble, first with sadness and fear, then with anger. Part of you wants to wake him, tell him to collect his things, then drive him back to the airport in Madrid. You want to send him home again, away from your new country, the place where you live unencumbered — but with a good deal of effort, thank you. The other part of you wants to wail, to beat your fists against the wall and howl, *Give him back to me.*

Remember: purpose, provision, exception. The subjunctive runs parallel to reality.

8. After Certain Indications of Time, If the Action Has Not Occurred

While is a subjunctive state of mind. So are *until, as soon as, before,* and *after.* By now you understand why, right? Because until something *has happened,* you can't be sure.

In Tarifa, the wind blows and blows. You learn this even before arriving, as you drive down Route 15 past Gibraltar. You're heading toward the southernmost point in Spain, toward warm sea breezes and a small town off the beaten path. You drive confidently, shifting quickly through the gears to keep pace with the traffic around you. He reclines in the passenger's seat, one foot propped against the dashboard, reading from *The Real Guide,* open against his thigh. "Spreading out beyond its Moorish walls, Tarifa is known in Spain for its abnormally high suicide rate — a result of the unremitting winds that blow across the town and its environs."

You say, "Tell me you're joking." He says, "How's that for luck?" Three days before, you'd stood in Granada's crowded city square at midnight, each eating a grape for every stroke of the New Year. If you eat all twelve grapes in time, tradition says, you'll have plenty of luck in the coming year. It sounds wonderful — such an easy way to secure good fortune — until you start eating and time gets ahead, so far ahead that no matter how fast you chew and swallow, midnight sounds with three grapes left.

*

In Tarifa, you come down with the flu. It hits hard and fast — one minute you're strolling through a whitewashed coastal town, and the next you're huddled in bed in a stupor. He goes to the pharmacy and, with a handful of Spanish words and many gestures, procures the right medicine. You sleep all day, through the midday meal, through the time of siesta, past sundown, and into the evening. When you wake the room is fuzzy and you're alone, with a vague memory of him rubbing your back, saying something about a movie.

Carefully you rise and make your way to the bathroom — holding on to the bed, the doorway, the sink — then stand on your toes and look out the window into the blackness. By day there's a thin line of blue mountains across the strait, and you imagine catching the ferry at dawn and watching that sliver of Morocco rise up from the shadows to become a whole continent. You imagine standing on the other side and looking back toward the tip of Spain, this tiny town where the winds blow and blow. That's how easy it is to keep traveling once you start, putting distance between the various parts of your life, imagining yourself over and over again into entirely new places.

Chilly and sweating, you make your way back to bed, your stomach fluttering nervously. You think back to Granada, how he'd woken from a nap on that dark afternoon and apologized. "I don't know what got into me today," he'd said. "This hasn't been happening." You believe it's true; it hasn't been happening. But you don't know *how true.*

You think: He's fine now. There's no need to worry. He's been fine for days, happy and calm. I'm overreacting. But overreaction is a slippery slope. With the wind howling continuously outside, the room feels small and isolated. You don't know that he's happy and calm right now, do you? You don't know how he is today at all, because you've slept and slept and barely talked to him.

You think: If the movie started on time — but movies never start on time in Spain, so you add, subtract, try to play it safe, and determine that by ten forty-five your fretting will be justified. At eleven you'll get dressed and go looking, and if you can't find him, what will you do? Wait until midnight for extra measure? And then call the police? And tell them what? That he isn't back yet and you're afraid because you're sick and he's alone and the wind here blows and blows, enough to make people crazy, the book says, make them suicidal? This is the *when,* the *while,* the *until.* The *before* and *after.* The real and the unreal in precarious balance. This is what you moved to Spain to escape from, and here it is again, following you.

The next time you wake, the room seems brighter, more familiar. You sit up and squint against the light. His cheeks are flushed, hair mussed from the wind. His eyes are clear as a morning sky. "Hi, sweetie," he says, putting a hand on your forehead. "You still have a fever. How do you feel?" He smells a little musty, like the inside of a community theater where not many people go on a Sunday night in early January. He says, "The movie was hilarious." You ask whether he understood it, and he shrugs. Then he acts out a scene using random Spanish words as a voice-over, and you laugh and cough until he flops down on his stomach beside you.

Here it comes again, the contrast between what was, just a little while ago, and what is now. After all this time and all these miles, you're both here, in a Spanish town with a view of Africa. You feel amazed, dizzy, as if swimming outside yourself. You're talking with him, but you're also watching yourself talk with him. And then you're sleeping and watching yourself sleep, dreaming and thinking about the dreams. Throughout the night you move back and forth, here and there, between what is and what might be, tossed by language and possibility and the constantly shifting wind.

9. In Certain Independent Clauses

There's something extraordinary — isn't there? — about learning to speak Spanish as an adult, about coming to see grammar as a set of guidelines not just for saying what you mean but for understanding the way you live. There's something extraordinary about thinking in a language that insists on marking the limited power of desire.

For example: At Barajas Airport in Madrid, you walk him to the boarding gate. He turns to face you, hands on your arms, eyes green as the sea. He says, "Only a few more months and we'll be together for good. Right, sweetie?" He watches your face, waiting for a response, but you know this isn't a decision, something you can say yes to. So you smile, eyes burning, and give a slight nod. What you mean is, *I hope so.* What you think is, *Ojalá.* And what you know is this: The subjunctive is the mood of mystery. Of luck. Of faith interwoven with doubt. It's a held breath, a hand reaching out, carefully touching wood. It's humility, deference, the opposite of hubris. And it's going to take a long time to master.

But at least the final rule of usage is simple, self-contained, one you can commit to memory: Certain independent clauses exist only in the subjunctive mood, lacing optimism with resignation, hope with heartache. *Be that as it may,* for example. Or the phrase one says at parting, eyes closed as if in prayer: *May all go well with you.*

Lost Dog

FROM THE NEW YORKER

ON AUGUST 6, 2003, Stephen Morris parked his car at the Atlanta History Center, expecting to spend half an hour or so edifying himself and his nephew on the particulars of the Civil War. It was the beginning of what would turn out to be a very bad day. At the time, though, everything seemed fine. Morris, a sinewy guy in his fifties with a scramble of light brown hair and the deliberative air of a nonpracticing academic, was at work on his doctoral dissertation — a biography of William Young, a seventeenth-century composer in the court of the Archduke of Innsbruck. Morris's teenage nephew was visiting from British Columbia, and Morris had taken a break to show him the highlights of Atlanta. Morris's wife, Beth Bell, a compact, gray-haired, dry-witted epidemiologist whose specialty is hepatitis, was at her job at the Centers for Disease Control and Prevention, where she is a senior investigator; that day, she was knee-deep in a disease outbreak among attendees of jam-band concerts.

Morris found parking at the History Center easily enough — the open-air three-story garage is small but had plenty of available spaces. A sign above the entrance reads, "Help Us Keep Your Vehicle Safe While You Are Here. Please Remove All Valuables from Vehicle," but the History Center is in Buckhead, a prosperous, bosky section of the city where people and vehicles are generally out of harm's way. Morris and Bell's car — a dinged-up but serviceable 1999 Volvo station wagon — was not the sort to attract much attention anyway. The only noteworthy thing about the car was that Morris and Bell's dog, Coby — a black Border collie with a false hip and a missing tooth — was in it, and so was a rather nice viola da gamba that Morris was looking after in his capacity as a rental-program director of the Viola da Gamba Society of America.

August 6 was a hot, soupy Wednesday in Atlanta. On Coby's behalf, Morris left the car in the History Center garage with its doors locked but with the engine running and the air conditioner on — a bit of animal husbandry that is not unheard of in southern climates if you leave your dog in a parked car and don't want to return to find him cooked. Uncooked dog notwithstanding, an unoccupied but idling car in a relatively empty parking garage might present to a certain kind of person an irresistible temptation. But if anyone saw such a person in the vicinity, he didn't make an impression. Meanwhile, Morris and his nephew wandered through the cool, white halls of the museum, did a quick appraisal of the War Between the States, and then got ready to leave. At first, they thought they had misremembered where they'd parked the car, but after looking through the whole garage they came back to where they were sure they had left it. The Volvo, the viola da gamba, and the dog were gone. All that marked the spot was a glittering blue sprinkle of broken glass.

Around eighty cars are stolen in greater Atlanta every day — a steady but not exceptional amount, putting the city's number of disappearing cars a little behind Houston's and a little ahead of Seattle's. Most of the thefts reward the perpetrator with, in addition to a car, nothing more than a couple of cassette tapes, some fast-food flotsam, and a clutch of exhausted air fresheners. Stephen Morris and Beth Bell's car, though, offered its unusual booty of dog and viola da gamba. The best guess is that the thief never even noticed; he was probably too excited about finding a car with a key in the ignition to take stock of its contents. Morris and Bell were upset about losing the viola da gamba — it was a fine reproduction of a fifteenth-century instrument and worth thousands of dollars — and they were not happy about losing their car, but those were trifling concerns compared with how they felt about losing their dog. In the report that Morris filed as soon as police arrived at the History Center, he didn't even mention the viola da gamba, but he brought up Coby's kidnapping a number of times.

Generally speaking, people love their dogs. Morris and Bell may be particularly devoted to Coby because they have nursed him through a variety of misadventures. They first spotted him at a sheepherding event nearly seven years ago when they were out bicycling in the Georgia countryside, but the breeder had promised the puppy to someone else, then decided that she wanted him for herself. Only after a day of negotiating did Coby end up with Morris and Bell. By the time he was two, he had full-blown dysplasia in his hips and needed a $4,000 surgery to replace one of them. At two and a half, he busted a tooth playing catch. Sometime later, he caught a stick wrong, and it jammed down his throat a few millimeters from his windpipe. Coby's vet likes to describe him as a dog with nine lives. In this life, anyway, Coby is a bushy-haired, prick-eared dog with tensed shoulders, an arresting stare, and an avid fetch-centric attitude. His dedication to retrieving bounceable rubber objects is so inexhaustible that it is exhausting. He has worn a deep, dusty path in Bell and Morris's yard between where they like to stand when they throw his Kong toy and where he likes to lie in wait for it. Morris has, thanks to Coby, developed a hot pitching arm and a firm way of saying, "That will do, Coby," when he runs out of steam.

So here was the problem: a dog on foot can travel at about five miles an hour, but a dog in a car can travel at sixty or seventy miles an hour. If Coby had jumped out of the car and walked away from the History Center, a perimeter of his possible whereabouts could have been plotted according to his likely pace. If he was still in the car — well, there was no way of knowing where he might be. Within an hour or two, he could have been in Alabama or South Carolina or Tennessee. Epidemiological science was of some help. That evening, a number of Bell's CDC colleagues joined Morris, who had set out to search the thirty-three acres of the History Center and the surrounding area. "We were in the hypothesis-generation stage of the investigation," Bell said recently. "We first developed the hypothesis that Coby might still be at the History Center." Bell advanced the theory that the guy who had taken the car did not want a dog, and that it was likely that as soon as he noticed Coby, he let him out. Her secondary theory was that as soon as the thief broke the window to get in, Coby had escaped. Both theories led to the Tullie Smith Farm — an antebellum homestead on the grounds of the History Center, where maidens in muslin churn butter and dip candles, and which, in the interest of total authenticity, also features a small herd of sheep. Border collies love sheep, so the crew of epidemiologists headed straight for the farm, and went there the next day, too. "We looked around and didn't see Coby, but we stopped everyone who passed us," one of the searchers told me. "We got some interesting responses. We approached one older woman and asked her if she had seen the dog, and she said no. Then she said that she had just lost her family, and she asked us if we'd seen them." The search party hung some hastily made posters on light poles; they checked around trash cans and Dumpsters; they flagged down cars driving past on West Paces Ferry Road; they crisscrossed the History Center's Mary Howard Gilbert Memorial Quarry Garden and its Victorian Playhouse and its Swan Woods Trail. They searched until eleven on Wednesday, and most of the day Thursday, but there was no dog, and no sign of the dog.

In all sorts of circumstances, dogs go missing. They slip out the door with trick-or-treaters; they burrow under fences; they take off after unattainable squirrels and pigeons. Some dogs are repeat offenders. Recently, I heard the story of Huey and Dewey — Shetland-sheepdog siblings living in Massachusetts — who took exception to a visit to the veterinarian and ran off. Huey was recovered a quarter mile from the clinic by a dog-search volunteer after forty-three days, but Dewey was gone for good. A year and a half after that, Huey took exception to a visit to a kennel and was found eighty-nine days later a few feet from where she'd escaped. Sometimes a dog, presumed irretrievable, unexpectedly reappears: a certain Doberman pinscher from San Francisco, capable of standing on its head, vanished for three years; his owner finally located him when she overheard a waiter in a restaurant discussing his roommate's new dog, a Doberman with a knack for standing on its head. According to the American Pet Product Manufacturers Association, there are sixty-five million pet dogs in this country, and an estimated ten million of them go astray every year. About half of those are returned. Others end up in new homes under assumed names, or are killed by cars; most, though, disappear without a trace.

Dog identification contraptions are a gigantic subset of the gigantic $34.3-billion-a-year pet care industry. Aside from tags shaped like hearts and stars and hydrants in aluminum, gold, steel, and rhinestone, there is a brisk business in microchip tags — grain-size data-bearing devices that are implanted under the skin between an animal's shoulder blades. Microchips were introduced in the early eighties; AVID Identification Systems, of Norco, California, one of the largest microchip companies in the world, now has more than eleven million pets in its international database, and HomeAgain, another major microchip supplier, has chips in close to three million. And GPS Tracks, a Jericho, New York–based company, will soon introduce the world's first global positioning system for dogs — a fist-size transmitter called a GlobalPetFinder, which will attach to the animal's collar and transmit its exact location every thirty seconds to a cell phone, computer, or a PDA. Before the device was even officially announced, the company had a waiting list of more than three thousand customers. "One night, it was pouring rain, my dogs had run away, the kids were hysterically crying, and I thought, This has to stop," Jennifer Durst, the founder and CEO of GPS Tracks, said recently. "If they have Lo-Jack for cars, why can't there be a Lo-Dog for dogs?"

Coby, regrettably, had neither a microchip implant nor an early-release prototype of GlobalPetFinder. He wasn't even wearing his rabies tag, which is one more chance for an animal to be identified. Coby wears a nylon collar printed with his name and phone number and bearing his rabies tag, but Bell and Morris take it off every night so that Coby can sleep in the nude; that particular day, Morris hadn't put the collar on because he expected that the History Center trip would be brief and that Coby would be safely cosseted in the car. So the dog was now at large and anonymous, and everything that could identify him was at home, in a basket by the back door of Bell and Morris's sprawling split-level in Decatur, a suburb of Atlanta.

After Wednesday night's fruitless search, Bell decided that it was time to accelerate into an outbreak investigation — that is, to apply the same techniques she uses when analyzing, say, a wave of contagion among methamphetamine users in Wyoming. She and Morris blast-faxed Atlanta-area animal shelters, local rescue groups, and nearby veterinarian offices. They listed Coby on many of the almost countless Internet lost-pet sites: PetFinder, Pets 911, Pets Missing in Action, Find-Fido, Petznjam, K9Finder, Dog Tracer,

Lassie Come Home. They made hundreds of posters, and on Thursday hung them in high-volume, highly animal-sensitive areas like the parking lots of pet stores. They also hung them along Peachtree Road, which cuts diagonally through northeast Atlanta and is lined with the city's busiest restaurants and bars. Bell reasoned that it was one of the few places in Atlanta where people travel on foot — in other words, at a speed allowing for a close reading of a lost-dog poster.

They got responses immediately. A woman in northern Gwinnett County, about an hour's drive away, called to say that she had found a dog loosely fitting Coby's description; Bell and Morris drove up to take a look, but he turned out to be a Border collie someone else had lost. A woman called from Alabama, but the dog she had found was a small white poodle. The phone kept ringing — some of the calls reported dog sightings, some offered advice, many were from people who had also lost dogs and just wanted to commiserate. Bell and Morris were also flooded with e-mails:

> Hi, This is Amy . . . I'm so sorry to hear about this tragedy.

> Maybe the thieves put him out in Buckhead, but who knows? Wonder why the dog was left in a car on a HOT summer day??????

> I'm sorry your dog is missing, what a sad story.

On Thursday and Friday, they visited animal shelters around Atlanta to make sure that Coby wasn't waiting among the errant terriers and golden retrievers in the urban pounds, or the pit bulls and hounds languishing in shelters out of town. Bell realized that it was also time to start checking with the city employee who was assigned the unpleasant task of cataloguing each day's roadkill. "When you're searching for something, you never know what you're going to find," she said recently. "But you do have to ask the question."

One other question was whether to look for help elsewhere. The cohort of people with lost pets is large and constantly renewed, and forms a significant and often free-spending market to be served. In fact, one of the best-known lost-pet detectives in the country, Sherlock Bones, got into the business on a price-per-pound basis. Fed up with a job in the insurance industry, Bones, whose civilian name is John Keane, decided to start his own business but wasn't sure what to pursue until he noticed an ad for a lost

Chihuahua. Keane said that the ad was an epiphany. "There was a thousand-dollar reward for that Chihuahua," he told me recently. "I thought to myself, That's five hundred dollars a pound." Keane, who started Sherlock Bones twenty-nine years ago and now operates out of Washougal, Washington, works on about five hundred cases a year. He used to do ground searches but now limits his involvement to consulting and to producing materials — primarily posters and mailers — for bereft owners. "Doing actual searches was very stressful," he said. At the time we spoke, he was out for a morning walk with his own dog, a French briard, and he was puffing lightly as he talked. "You're dealing with people in crisis. It's a serious business, since after eight hours it is unlikely someone will find their pet themselves, unless they're very lucky. They need help from someone who has the right information. You don't go to a rabbi to learn how to play baseball." He specializes in dogs and cats. "I don't deal with infrequent animals," he said. "Although I did make up a poster for a lost llama once, named Fernando Llama."

Bell and Morris decided to call Bones on Monday if they hadn't had any success; they also got in touch with a volunteer dog searcher named Debbie Hall, a member of a loose community of people across the country who trace lost pets for free. Hall helped them redesign their flyer, suggesting that they describe their car as well as the dog, and sent them extensive recommendations — eight long documents — on pet searches. Hall and her husband live in southeastern Massachusetts with a Yorkie-Chihuahua mix, a Yorkie-poodle mix, and three parakeets, two of which they got as a gift and a third that is probably someone's lost pet, because it just showed up in their yard one day. An entire room in the Halls' house is taken up by pet-detective appurtenances — a rack of camouflage clothes, a few Havahart traps, and half a dozen notebooks detailing her searches. Hall often stays out all night on cases. "It's a long-ass day," she explained, "but I love what I do. This is the one thing in my life that I'm good enough at to call my work." It has not been without its mishaps. She had a gun pulled on her while searching for a German shepherd in Virginia and once got trapped in her own six-foot Havahart trap. Worst of all, she has spent countless days mourning dogs that she found only after they had died. "It still hurts," she said, flipping to a page in her notebook about her first case — Tia, a runaway Border collie who eventually was found drowned. "But I am always optimistic that you will find your dog."

Late Saturday night, three days after Coby had disappeared, Bell and Morris got a break. A young guy walking down Peachtree had noticed one of their posters, and called to say that a few days earlier he had been playing rugby in a park downtown and had seen a dog that looked like Coby. "He said a man had been walking around the park with the dog, saying someone had just dropped it off," Bell said.

First thing Sunday morning, Bell and Morris headed over to the park, a weary-looking plot of land in a hard-luck section of the city known as Old Fourth Ward. At the nearby Tabernacle Baptist Church and Mount Sinai Baptist Church, services were just ending, so Bell and Morris stopped and asked if anyone there had seen the dog, but no one had. They walked down Boulevard, the wide road on the western edge of Old Fourth Ward, past men playing dice in mini-mart parking lots and loitering in front of signs saying PRIVATE PROPERTY DO NOT SIT ON WALL. They passed out flyers and asked after Coby. "My brother has that dog," one of the men told Bell. "If you give me two dollars, I'll go get him." Someone else said he'd played catch with the dog. Bell and Morris handed out more flyers. A young man took one, walked away, and then turned on his heel and came back to talk to them. He said that his name was Chris Walker and that he didn't know anything about the dog, but he did know something about their car: he had seen it near the park over the last few days, and he recognized the driver because they'd been in police detention together a few months earlier.

"This guy Chris was a true scientist," Bell said admiringly. "He said there were only three other people released from detention with him. One was Egyptian, one was elderly, and the third was the car thief, and that all we needed to do was get the detention records, eliminate those other two, and we would end up with this guy's name." Walker insisted that they call the police right away, so that they could check his story. He waited with them for almost an hour until a cruiser responded, and was disgusted that the police didn't have a computer in the car that could review detention records on the spot. Walker was so determined to have his tip substantiated that he accompanied Bell and Morris to a nearby precinct house to see if a police officer there would pull up the records. The officer wouldn't oblige them but he did believe that Walker was telling the truth, and he suggested that Morris and Bell contact Midtown Blue, an organization of police officers who do security work when they're off duty, which he thought might help them. Morris and Bell gave Walker reward money, but he seemed more interested in making sure that they followed up on his tip. "It's a family curse," Walker's uncle Lee Harris told me when I visited him last summer. "We'll just bend over backward to help anyone in pain." Later that Sunday, after leaving Bell and Morris, Walker tangled with a police officer again, and on Monday, when he called Bell to find out if she'd found her car, he was calling from jail.

As astonishing as Walker's story seemed, Bell and Morris came to believe that he had indeed seen their car, and that, from what the rugby player who had called them from Peachtree had told them, the thief had let the dog out in the park. On a shallow slope near the playing fields, they talked to the homeless people who sleep there under a small stand of oak trees, and they all remembered Coby. Some of those same people were still in the park this summer when I went to Atlanta. It was another blistering day; someone was listlessly banging tennis balls against a wall, and muffled cheers and hollers from a soccer game at the far end of the park rose up in the heavy air. Under a cement pavilion in a sliver of shade, a man was sitting on a bench, plunking on a guitar held together with duct tape. He said that his name was Ben Macon, that he had lived in the park for ten years, and that he had spent several days during the previous summer with Coby, whom he described precisely, down to Coby's striking stare and predatory crouch while playing catch. "That dog was unbelievable," Macon said. "He was someone you could play with. He'd be your friend. You could tell he was a people dog." Macon strummed a little and then leaned on the guitar. "If I had a place of my own, I'd like a dog like that. But people with dogs, those are people who have good jobs." He paused for a moment and then added, "A dog like that gives you a warm feeling. I miss him."

By midafternoon that Sunday, Bell and Morris had spent hours searching in the park and going up and down Boulevard, so they took a break from handing out flyers and hanging posters and went home to shower and eat. Their phone rang. A woman on the line said that on Saturday she and her partner had picked up a black male Border collie with no collar as he chased a tennis ball across Boulevard. They had had no luck finding his owner through rescue groups, and they were currently in their car with the dog on their way to the veterinarian because they had decided to keep him. But en route to the vet they had seen one of Bell and Morris's posters — they had probably hung it no more than an hour before. The woman, Danielle Ross, suggested that Bell and Morris meet them at the vet's. When she got off the phone, Ross, who also works at the CDC but had never met Bell, decided to say the name of the dog on the poster to the dog in her car. First she pronounced it "Cobbie," and the dog, who looked reasonably healthy but was totally exhausted, didn't lift his head. Then she tried another pronunciation — "Co-bee" — and he sat up. By the time she and her partner, Debbie Doyle, and the dog arrived at the Pets Are People, Too clinic, she knew the dog was going home.

When Bell and Morris pulled into the parking lot, they could see the dog through the front window of the clinic, and they knew it was Coby. As exhausted as he was, he raced to meet them at the door. Late that night, a police officer called Bell and Morris at home. There had been an automobile accident; the driver had fled; the car, which had been impounded, belonged to them. When Bell and Morris went to the police station the next day to claim it, they were first told that they were mistaken — that no car matching their car's identification numbers had been impounded. But then the officer checked the records again and determined that they did in fact have the car. It had been totaled.

Now, with both Coby and the car accounted for, Bell and Morris felt they might be on a streak. All they needed was to find the viola da gamba. They decided to look in the phone book for pawn shops; there are nearly three hundred in the Atlanta area, so they concentrated on ones near the park where Coby had spent his time. One of them, Jerry's Pawn Shop, listed musical instruments among its specialties. It was a long shot — there are some ten thousand items pawned each month in downtown Atlanta alone, and it was just a guess that the car thief would have decided to cash in the instrument, that he would have chosen to do it at a pawn shop, and that he would have taken it to one near the park. Morris called Jerry's and asked after the viola da gamba. Yes, they had just got one from a fellow who had pawned it for twenty-five dollars. It was Morris's loaner. The man who pawned it? "Well, he didn't strike me as a viola da gamba player," Bill Hansel, who handled the transaction, recalled. According to Hansel, the man was youngish, in a hurry, and happy to sell the viola da gamba outright rather than pawn it. A Georgia law requires fingerprints and identification from anyone doing business with pawn shops. The police later traced the address that the non–viola da gamba player had provided; it turned out to be an empty house.

At this point, the police certainly knew the thief's name — it was on the pawn voucher and in the detention records from his previous lockup with Chris Walker, and there were fingerprints on the Volvo, the viola da gamba, the pawn voucher, and probably on Coby, but the man was still at large. Before the car was towed to a wrecking yard, Morris went through it one more time to see if there were any last belongings of his or Bell's still inside. There was nothing of theirs, but the thief had left behind some of his clothes, a bunch of computer parts, notes from his girlfriend, poetry he had written, and a stack of address labels bearing someone else's name.

SAM PICKERING

George

FROM SOUTHWEST REVIEW

THIS SUMMER I had my dog George put to sleep. He was four-teen years old. Shortly before my father died in 1990, he urged me to get the children a dog. Four months later I bought George for $250. George was five weeks old. He was a dachshund and lived with his littermates on a screened porch in Lebanon, Connecticut. When the door to the porch was opened, he scampered outside, barking and infested with fleas. The breeder said she would mail me George's papers. The papers never arrived. George's hind legs eventually stretched into stilts, and his eyes rolled into soft bis-cuits, turning him into a country dachshund, one with an amiable beagle somewhere in his ancestry. George was affectionate and lov-able, and he fast became the children's medicinal blanket. Edward named him, and when mood lowered heavy over Edward, he car-ried George to his room and, after setting him on his bed, shut the door and kneaded away the dark, rubbing George. For Eliza, George was a sofa companion. When books or sports became bur-densome, she sat on our red couch and watched television, George a brown throw spread across her lap.

Despite the children's affection, George was only part of their lives, rich with new friendships and studies, summer camps and bright fall afternoons on playing fields. George was a bigger part of my life. He was my pal, the dog of my late middle years, forty-eight to sixty-two, that time when the long shadow slips over the horizon and rises in the mind, confining thought. I spent more time with George than any people outside my family. I was physically closer to him than any person, forever rubbing and picking him up, squeezing him until he grunted. Often I talked to him, telling him things I never mentioned to my family. People from my background, southern Americans whose umbilical cords stretch back to dank Britain, are not demonstratively affectionate. Only rarely do we touch others. When we talk, we stand at attention and shout, almost as if brambles separated us from the people with whom we are chatting. When we kiss, even family members, more often than not we avoid faces and, slipping to flanks, brush our lips along the sides of heads, usually above and behind the ear.

Although all middle-aged men live "enisled" after their breeding years end, I suspect I spent more time with George than most males spend with dogs. Writing isolates, turning the gregarious into observers. No matter how much a writer wants to belong, he will always remain slightly apart, his notebook and pencil, though hidden or left on his desk, inevitably separating him from others. In part George became my companion because he didn't talk, though he read my moods, and I his. He never told me a sad tale that awakened me at two o'clock in the morning. His politics and religion, his views of the world, never raised welts of irritation. While I wrote, he snoozed on a bed of old blankets beside my chair. He accompanied me on hundreds of walks, maybe a thousand or more in fact. He didn't complain about high meadow grass or stony ridges. He just made his way. Together we roamed icy downpours, heat that popped like grease in a skillet, and at midnight snow gathered in pleated curtains. No matter the weather, our ambles were silent. I escaped the me that people knew, and as we roamed into woods, trees swung open like gates and I could ponder writing, shaping the buffoons who wandered my essays, characters who caused me to smile and made me thankful to be alive.

I housebroke George carrying him outside at night, first at one, then again at four in the morning. I don't remember how long housebreaking took. The puppy I trained has vanished from memory, as indeed have the young parents who cared for me when I was little. Would that my memories of them were vivid. Would that I could recall them in their middle years. Alas, all I remember are diminished people in old age. Of course after my death, when the children recall me, they won't see me laughing or reading, looking at their mother with affection, even throwing a ball with them. Instead I will totter into imagination as a nuisance, leaning heavily upon them, causing them to stagger through days. They will remember me only as a responsibility and a burden, the shedding of which will bring more relief than grief, as is meet.

No, the dog I remember best and most fondly was old, at first pestered by yeasty ears, then deaf, only able to hear a high whistle. On walks this past year George began to lose his way. If I drifted from sight, he became frantic and set off to find me, usually in the wrong direction, head bent over, skin hanging loosely from his neck like a sail on a boat stranded in the doldrums. When he did not lose me, he often lagged behind. He was game, though. Although his back hips jutted up bony with arthritis and his legs sometimes collapsed, throwing him to the ground, he plugged along, only stone walls bringing him to a standstill. Once upon a time he clambered over walls, almost smiling in the muscular enjoyment of life. This year I lifted him over walls, afterward cradling him for a moment or two so he could rest.

At home he trailed me from room to room, pasting himself to my legs, as if my presence reassured him. Often I became impatient and made him go to bed, forgetting that George's debility foreshadowed my weakness to come, that time when I, too, would need reassurance. Mornings I got up at six o'clock and carried him outside so he could pump himself dry. Throughout days when we did not go for walks, I took writing breaks and carted him outside. He wobbled about, sniffing, and again I grew impatient, ways of coupling sentences suddenly coming to mind and making me want to return to pen and pencil.

"George isn't George," Edward said when he came home in February after spending a semester at St. Andrews University in Scotland. "He's just old," I said. "He's still George." "How much longer will he live?" Edward asked. "A long time," I said. "I hope so," Edward said. "Me too," I said, pausing then adding, "He'll be here when you graduate from Middlebury next summer." Kind words make liars. This past spring the Institute for Advanced Studies in the Humanities at the University of Edinburgh awarded me a fellowship. In January Vicki and I plan to fly to Scotland and spend eight months in Edinburgh, making a flying trip home for Edward's graduation in June. In the past when we went abroad, graduate students lived in our house and took care of George and

Penny, our other dog. George now needed a nurse more than a keeper, and the gap between my assuring Edward and my own wishes was vast. If George did not die, I worried that I'd have to cancel the trip to Scotland. "Just for a dog," I fumed.

George had aged into expense as well as frailty. In September 2002 a local veterinarian gelded him and patched a perineal hernia, charging $616.10. Twice the vet pulled rotten teeth. This June before we left for Nova Scotia, the vet ran a series of tests on him because, Vicki said, "George didn't seem like himself." The vet reported that George had a "remarkable heart, that of a puppy." "All those walks with you," Vicki said. "Yes," I said, looking at the bill, "but do you realize how much keeping George healthy has cost us during the last six hundred and fifty-one days?" Before Vicki could reply, I forged ahead, explaining that I had added the bills for his licenses, operations, teeth, and tests. I had, of course, excluded the cost of his food and the occasional toy, usually a stuffed animal. "Fifteen hundred and seventy-six dollars and six cents, or two dollars and forty-one cents a day," I said. "Spending that much money on a dog isn't rational, and in a world in which vast numbers of people starve and never see a doctor, it's immoral." Words determine thoughts, not thoughts words. In calculating the cost of taking care of George, I was prepping myself to have George euthanized — not, of course, I assured myself, for my convenience, but for his sake. So he wouldn't suffer and would not die a death punctuated by silent howls, I thought, picking up a pencil and writing down the phrase "silent howls."

In truth George was already suffering, and I didn't realize it. The death for which I longed in hard rational moments was fast approaching. In spring, George began drinking water incessantly. Often he stood over his bowl for minutes before he drank, his jaw quivering. When he drank, he sloshed water on the floor in great puddles. In April, Vicki started putting his water bowl in the sink before she went to bed, so he couldn't reach it and overnight turn the kitchen floor into a marsh. At dinner he pushed his food bowl around the kitchen, spilling food on the floor, so much food that she set the bowl in the middle of a heavy horseshoe, not one thrown by a horse, but a big shoe used in the game of horseshoes. In May, George's breath became mucky, smelling worse than it did before the vet pulled his teeth.

The first week in June, I noticed George wasn't lapping water but scooping it into the side of his mouth. That night I pried his jaws apart, and Vicki shined a flashlight down his throat. His tongue had shrunk, drying and curling on itself like old lettuce, red spotting it measly like rust. The vet noticed George's tongue, but because we were leaving for Nova Scotia, he did not have time to take a biopsy and send the specimen to a lab. "George probably has an infection," he said, writing down a prescription for twenty days of antibiotics. "Cancer of the tongue is rare."

When we arrived in Nova Scotia, George jumped out of the car and scampered around the barn, sniffing. For a time he seemed almost youthful. He accompanied Vicki and me when we walked to Port Maitland or Black Point, the walks sometimes four miles. The antibiotics cleaned his breath, and in sunny moments when George dozed in a pile of rugs on the porch, I thought him better. I forgot Edinburgh. George was my pal again, a companion to whom I confided worries about the children and to whom I pointed out moths and dragonflies. He was my friend — my only friend, I sometimes thought.

Sadly, although the drugs sweetened George's breath, drinking and eating became noticeably more difficult for him. When he finished drinking, a custard of brown drool caked the top of the water bowl, the remainder of the drool hanging from his muzzle. Vicki and I wiped his jaw, and George learned to cope with the batter. If we missed a tablespoon, he went into the back parlor and brushed his muzzle across the rug. George also slept a lot, saving himself for walks, I said. At five-thirty in the morning I got up and carried him outside. The steps leading from the porch to the side meadow were steep, so I took him down into the grass and then lifted him back up on the porch. If he went down on his own, his front legs invariably buckled. "An old man with an old dog," Vicki said one afternoon as I put George down on the grass. "Yep," I said, "my puppy, my dear old puppy."

Every day George and I walked along the headland, the path hanging above the bluff like an eyebrow. Blueberries and strawberries grew beside the path. In past summers George chased hares and dug though the roots of broken spruce pursuing red squirrels. His efforts to catch animals were only playful, at least in comparison to his foraging for blueberries. Vicki called him our berry hound, and he ate pints, sweeping them out of the grassy scrub. On a walk early in July, Vicki found not only the first blueberries of the summer but also the last wild strawberries of spring. "What a treat for George," she said, sitting down to pick them. I walked ahead, stalking a sulphur. When the butterfly sliced into grass and shut, snapping its wings together, I turned around. Vicki was crying. "He can't eat them," she said, "not a single berry. He tried and tried." "Oh, shit," I said, looking over the water. A loon laughed, and my chest tightened.

Suddenly I became angry at myself. Grieving for an animal was unseemly. George was a dog, not a human. I breathed deeply and choked my emotion. When a person cared more for a pet than for people, something was out of joint. Had channeling affection toward animals contributed to making the United States the world's most brutal nation? At breakfast Americans dropped bombs. At dinner they talked baby talk to dogs. Twenty-five years ago in Syria, a student interrupted discussion of Keats's "To Autumn." Why, she abruptly and inexplicably demanded, did Americans spend more on pets than most of the world spent on medicine? "How could any people do that?" she asked. "When Syrians stop having twelve children," I said, "Americans will get rid of their pets." My response was terrible, a reaction not to the girl's question but to her outburst and the unseemly disruption of class. Why, indeed, are pets more important to Americans than people?

The next morning Vicki and I took George to the Parade Street Animal Hospital in Yarmouth. When I put George on the examining table, he whimpered, sounding pitifully querulous — a bit like me, I thought. "Now that," Sally Clark, the veterinarian, said, "sounds like an old dog." The appointment cost $29.90. Two days later, at eight o'clock in the morning, I dropped George off at Parade Street, and Sally cut a hunk out of his tongue and sent it to a laboratory on Prince Edward Island. The biopsy and appointment cost $189.75. I fetched George at two in the afternoon. When I entered the building, I heard him barking, a low, hoarse, coughing bark. "That's my fellow," I told the receptionist. When George saw me, he stopped barking. "We will get the results in a week," Sally said. "I will probably call you next Thursday."

The following Tuesday was George's fourteenth birthday. Vicki and I put him and Penny into the back of the Toyota and drove to

Kwik-Way at Mavilette. While Vicki fetched medium-size ice cream cones for the dogs, I raised the door to the back of the car and spread an old towel across the trunk. Vicki bought soft cones in hopes "the birthday boy" could eat the ice cream easily. He couldn't. Penny finished her cone almost before George started. Because George could not lick the ice cream, I held the cone beside his muzzle and he nipped at it, sometimes missing the cone completely, other times biting off a thumbnail of cream.

I sat bent over in the back of the station wagon, George pressed against my left thigh. He took so long to finish the cone that my back ached. "He's not going to be able to eat it all," Vicki said. "Yes, he will. It is his birthday," I said, crushing the cone into nibbles and turning my hand into a dog bowl. After George finished and Vicki cleaned the trunk with a damp towel, we washed our hands inside the store and bought birthday cones. While I celebrated with a scoop of Death by Chocolate atop Ginger, Vicki had Bear Tracks and Cookies and Cream. Then we walked west along the beach at Cape St. Mary to the high bluffs. When the children and George were young, we picnicked beneath the bluffs, afterward raking rockweed off the surface of tidal pools, hunting treasure: Irish moss and limpets, crabs and moon snails. George dutifully plodded up then back along the beach with us, looking, Vicki said, "like a motorized log," his eyes focused on the ground immediately in front of him, never staring down the beach in expectation of seeing another dog. More like a slab of old kindling, I thought, the bark peeling in strips, the heartwood gray, but still solid.

Although we anatomized George after every meal and talked about him almost constantly, life spun along as usual. A friend in Nashville sent me a goofy story. "Perfect for changing the mood of a paragraph," he wrote. The day after they graduated from the University of Tennessee this past June, two new alumni walked into a pet store in Knoxville. "I want four budgies," the taller of the two young men said, still wearing his graduation gown. "Certainly," the clerk responded. "We have an aviary. What would you like, two males and two females, all males, or all females?" "Perhaps," he continued, pausing and giggling, "three of one, one of the other, a sort of feathery ménage à trois?" "I don't know nothing about any ménage," the customer responded. "I just want four budgies." "Certainly," the clerk said, "but what colors would you like? We have yellow, blue, green, and Neapolitan." "Are you deaf?" the customer answered. "I don't care about the colors. Just put four budgies in a box for me. Is that too hard for you to do?" "No, sir," the clerk said.

Once the two men received the birds, they drove to Clingman's Dome, the highest peak in the Smoky Mountains. There they parked their car and walked to the lookout. After studying the lip of the lookout, the first man walked ten paces back toward the car, where he paused and, reaching into the box, seized two budgies, holding one in his left hand, the other in his right. Then, after leaning back like a broad jumper preparing his approach to the bar, he sprinted to the edge of the mountain, hurdled the guardrail, and leaped off the cliff, flapping his arms, the birds firmly in his hands. He hung in the air for a moment, then he fell heavily, smashing onto boulders, body parts snapping off and ricocheting in sundry directions, a leg here, an arm there, his head bouncing into a thicket of laurel like a bowling ball sliding into the gutter beside a lane, his eyes open and spinning like holes in the ball. For a long time his companion stood at the edge of the mountain, rubbing his chin and studying the remains of his friend. Finally he shook his head and said, "Shitfire, this budgie-jumping ain't all that it is cracked up to be."

Thursday passed and the veterinarian did not telephone. "I'm glad," I told Vicki. "I don't want to hear until next week." Back in June I had signed up to run a ten-kilometer race on the next Saturday, part of Yarmouth's summer festival, the Seafest. I hadn't raced for a year. The course was hilly, and I whipped myself into anxiety. Practically every time Vicki and I drove to Yarmouth, I talked about the race. "Ten to one, I won't finish. The rescue squad will have to peel me off the asphalt. But don't worry. The undertaker will be able to tell you the number of my room in the hospital. But don't be late. I won't reside there long." I trained for the run, every day shuffling along shoreline and gravel road, pain a spike in my spine, slicing so sharply through my hips that I rarely thought about George.

During the first kilometer of the race I chatted with a couple from Halifax. I told them some of the jokes my friend sent from Nashville. Their favorite was short. "Clip-clop, clip-clop, clip-clop — bang — clippity-clop, clippity-clop, clippity-clop," I said, then asked, "What's that?" When they did not respond, I answered my own question: "An Amish drive-by shooting." The answer knocked the three of us off stride and into laughter. Pain vanished, and I enjoyed the run, finishing ahead of at least six people.

After the race I showered in a lavatory reserved for yachtsmen, and then Vicki and I climbed the hill from the docks to Alma Square, where I ate two bowls of steamed mussels and listened to 340 South, six country fiddlers and banjo players. The group took its name from Highway 340, the southern part of which ran past most of their homes. When they sang "You Are My Sunshine," I sang with them. Later Vicki and I walked up Main Street to the Yarmouth library, and I checked out novels robust with hard policemen, Ian Rankin's John Rebus and James Lee Burke's Dave Robicheaux, among a squad of others. Afterward we sat on the lawn in front of the library and watched the Seafest parade. In front of us two small boys rolled giggling through endless somersaults. "A good day," I said. "Really good," Vicki repeated. That night George was peppy and ate a big dinner, knocking food across the kitchen but still enjoying his tucker.

The next morning as I sat in the rocking chair beside the stove, George warm in my lap, Vicki told me the veterinarian had telephoned Thursday while I was out jogging. George's tongue was cancerous. "I didn't tell you because you were so worried about the race," Vicki said. "Nuts," I said, tightening my grip on the rug of skin behind George's neck, "oh, nuts." Friday had been Vicki's shopping day, and before going to Sobey's, she drove to Parade Street and paid for putting George to sleep, $30 plus $4.50 tax. If she had wanted the vet to dispose of George's body, the bill would have been $50 plus tax. "Please say 'put to sleep,' " Vicki said later on Sunday, "not euthanize, put down, or kill." She paused before saying "kill." Afterward she said, "But, of course, we are killing him. He can still eat, and he still enjoys walks." "I wish I owned a pistol," I said. "A man should kill his own dog, not a stranger." "Shut up," Vicki said.

Throughout that week we studied George more intensely than ever before, and, as could be suspected, we saw what we imagined we'd see: drool overflowing his muzzle like creeks their banks in spring; his jaw quivering, "chattering," Vicki said. Eating seemed more difficult, each meal taking endless minutes as he stopped frequently to muster strength to push his food into piles that he could grasp with the sides of his jaw. In retrospect, though, George's condition probably did not change much from what it had been early in the summer. What happened was that Vicki and I became tense and anxious. We skidded into an emotion slough. We talked reasonably, knowing well that reason governed little in life, except perhaps a deceptive sentence or two on a page. We muttered weary, self-serving phrases about doing the best for George and not letting him suffer, all the while thinking, If this goes on much longer, I'm going to crack.

We spoke sharply to each other. One night as we ate rhubarb pie, Vicki slammed her fork down on the table and, swinging toward me, shouted, "You turn my blood to vomit." Nothing specific provoked the outburst. During dinner I had described the latest doings in Carthage. Hink Ruunt had bought a zebra and named it Spot, and Raylene McBee's little girl Hostess was pregnant. The news startled Raylene. When Hostess told her, Raylene asked, "Are you sure the baby is yours?" On the other hand, just before dessert, I stuck my tongue out at Penny, so upsetting her that she slunk into her bed and buried her head under an afghan. Penny was a scavenger, and during meals she scoured the linoleum for crumbs, her tags scraping the floor, jangling and sometimes irritating me, particularly when I want to tell Vicki about happenings in Carthage.

Of course, amid the tension and talk about George, days rolled by as they always did. I split kindling and read, solving mysteries before even the best book detectives. Vicki cooked and lectured me, the latest series of lectures being a Dale Carnegie course on public speech. I have a southern accent, and strangers forever ask me where I am from. "Are you from Texas?" a clerk asked me in Kent Hardware the last time I went to town. "Are you from Texas?" a man asked me an hour later in the checkout line at Atlantic Super Store. On my saying "Tennessee," he asked if I played country music. Albeit well meaning and friendly, decades of questions about my birthplace had raised a bunion, and often, Vicki informed me, I scowled before responding. "Not pleasant behavior," she said. To modify my expression, she instructed me to say the word "fresh" silently, "letting the corners of your mouth rise like the tips of the new moon into a smile." Once the smile was luminous, she said, continuing the astronomical imagery, "bright as Arcturus in August," I was supposed to say, "I was born in Tennessee, but now I live in Connecticut. Both places are wonderful."

At least once a day during that week, Vicki conducted smiling drills. She also made me practice ordering coffee at Tim Hortons. In June I told clerks, "I'd like a midsize coffee in a ceramic cup with one pull at the lactator," usually adding that I banned paper products from my mouth because, after several years of allowing paper to touch their lips, people's tongues often ran to ink, making them garrulous beyond endurance. My orders, I am afraid, startled clerks and corked the flow of people by the counter, not a matter that bothered me. Indeed, I thought each order adventurous and verbally intoxicating, if not charming. In contrast, so I learned, my orders embarrassed Vicki, and, she told me, irked customers in a hurry. "They should slow down. I am doing them a medicinal favor," I said. "Most look like they need hernia transplants." "What?" Vicki said. "Nothing," I said, but under my breath muttering, "Both men and women." In any case, after lunch I practiced "efficient speech," repeating, as if I were reciting the litany, the sentence "I would like a medium cup of coffee in a mug with one cream, please."

Every day I read in the study, sitting in a battered gray chair, my feet resting on a faded orange pouf, George lodged between me and the arm of the chair, sleeping against my leg, a pillow atop him, keeping him warm. I rubbed his head, kneaded his shoulders, and ran my hand lightly along his spine. His muzzle was white, and he looked old. Inexplicably, the closer he clung to me, and the more I realized how much his death would cut me up, the more I wanted to put him to sleep. People should control their emotions. Only the selfish or the broken allow mood to surface and affect others. In George's presence my emotions welled and almost lapped into sight, something abhorrent, and maybe frightening.

On Monday, eight days after Vicki told me the news about George's tongue, I telephoned the veterinarian and arranged for George to be put to sleep that Thursday. "I wish he would just fall asleep one night and not wake up. That would be natural," Vicki said. "Are you sure we are doing this for him, not for us?" she asked again. "I am sure," I said, lying. At ten-thirty that morning, I started digging George's grave. I cleared a space under the willow at the edge of the side meadow. I chopped dock, soft rushes, brambles, and knots of grass thick as twine. I sawed dead limbs out of the willow and cut twigs, shaping an inverted basket–like shelter under the tree. Vicki's father had planted the tree in the 1960s, and necklaces of sapsucker holes circled the trunk. The right decoration, I thought.

A curtain of branches dangled behind me, separating me from the meadow. Across the meadow a family of red-breasted nuthatches called to each other, their cries sounding like little tin horns. I stood and looked across the meadow. Yellow-throats hopped through the apple tree, and black-and-white warblers shuffled up a fallen spruce, appearing and disappearing, like pages shuffled by a thumb, then held for a moment at an illustration, then flipped again. From Ma's Property, the field west of the house, came the low throb of a tractor turning newly mown grass. That afternoon Mr. Deveau baled the hay, rolling it into huge cupcakes. Later he loaded the bales on a flatbed truck and hauled them to a field behind his cattle barn.

I enjoyed digging the grave. Perspiration ran down my chin, and the front of my shirt became a damp bib. I dug through moss, a thin layer of topsoil, and rocky till into clay, the top layer of clay orange, the lower and deeper, gray and lifeless. The grave was three and a half feet deep and shaped like a small tub, the sides and bottom almost as smooth as porcelain. I piled the dirt neatly beside the left side of the grave. Dozens of toadlets squirmed through the grass, and I was careful not to crush them. While I dug, George slept on a mat on the porch. After I returned the shovel to the backhouse, I spoke to George. "I dug you a fine grave, old boy," I said. "God!" Vicki exclaimed, "how could you say that to him, even if he is deaf? Don't," she continued, knowing my thoughts, "show him the grave." For once I told the truth. "But Vicki," I said, "it's a good grave. I'm proud of it, and I want him to see it." "That's perverse," she said, adding before going into the kitchen, "You enjoy this, don't you?"

The truth was that I enjoyed the digging, not the prospect of George's death. That night I ate heartily, as I did the night before George died, and as I did again on the day of his death. For dinner I ate beet greens, noodles in cream, a pork chop thick as a hand, sliced tomatoes and onions, a trough of watercress, and for dessert strawberry pie slathered with whipped cream. With the meal I drank a bottle of Keith's India Pale Ale, topping off dessert with a big glass of Cabernet Sauvignon from McWilliams Hanwood Estate in New South Wales. The night before George died I ate rappie pie chunky with chicken, corn, lima beans, and again beet greens and watercress. For dessert I had a chocolate cupcake baked at Comeau's Market in Metaghan and a bowl of raspberry Jell-O, syrupy with fruit cocktail.

The evening after I dug the grave, the air was sweet with the fragrance of new hay, and Vicki and I and the dogs strolled our fields. In the foundation hole of the house that once stood at the front of Ma's Property, I found a gravestone. The stone was narrow at the top and broad and flat on the bottom, and would, I knew, settle nicely into the dirt. The face of the stone was also flat, and across the corners small orange lichens stretched like rambling roses. Later Vicki painted *George* on the face of the stone, using latex paint left over from a previous summer's work on windowsills. We debated whether to paint *George* or *Georgie*. We usually called him Georgie, especially when he snuggled against us. Eventually I decided the *ie* was too informal. "Not proper," I explained, wondering all the while if burying a dog was itself improper. Would George fare better, I thought, if I just tossed his body into the blueberry field? Then he would still live, becoming part of the scavengers who fed upon him. That is what I want to happen to my body. I dream of climbing the air as part of a buzzard and skittering through grass as a weasel. I want beetles to gnaw me, and later a mouse to hide his nest beneath my rib cage. What a person wants for himself, however, won't do for a family pet.

Eight days after I buried George, Vicki painted *George* on the stone, the first *G* a capital three inches high, all the rest small letters one and seven-eighths inches tall, except the second *g*, which was a thumbnail bigger because its lower half hung below the other letters. When we roamed the hayfields, George was lively. While I searched for a gravestone, he nosed sheaves of hay that slipped the baler, finding a decapitated meadow mouse and a garter snake flailed into folds. At the edge of the field three crows racketed in a spruce. I looked at them expecting to see an owl. Suddenly the crows flew out of the spruce, in the bill of the lead bird a broken fledgling.

Wednesday morning, washtubs of rain fell, and the grave became a pool. I bailed the water out, but the ground was saturated, and the next morning water lapped at the top of the grave, humic acid staining it yellow-brown. "We can't bury George in a tub," Vicki said. "Don't worry, I will dry the grave," I said, resisting the temptation to say that no matter how high the water, George wouldn't drown. That night Vicki served George a farewell dinner, mincing slivers of steak into his Pedigree Country Stew and Purina One, thick with "Lamb and Rice Formula." For dessert she dropped a scoop of vanilla ice cream into the bowl. George pushed the ice cream up the side of his bowl with his muzzle. When the ice cream started to slip, he twisted his head and, catching the scoop with the side of his mouth, tossed his head back, bolting the ice cream in one swallow. "Should I give him more?" Vicki said. "I don't suppose it matters." "No, it doesn't matter now," I said. "Give him more." Second thoughts punctuated the evening. Later, after Vicki told George to go to bed, pointing at his bed, a gesture he understood, she exclaimed, "Why should he go to bed? It's the last night of his life."

George's appointment was at eleven o'clock. After breakfast we walked down the lane and along the bluff, "The last mile," Vicki said. We strolled, and George kept pace. Once he scampered ahead and thrust his nose into a patch of blueberries. "Oh, dear," Vicki said, then looked out over the Gulf of Maine. The water was smooth and silver. When we got back to the house, Vicki shredded a piece of jerky and fed it to George. At 10:35 we left for Yarmouth. Vicki wrapped George in a blue acrylic blanket and held him in her lap. "We'll bring him home in the blanket," she said.

Because of an emergency, we sat for a few minutes in the lobby of the clinic. George whimpered, and I squeezed him. A bookkeeper walked out of an office. She was heavy and wore a baggy blue dress. She was also spontaneously, if not thoughtfully, good-natured. She walked over to us and, reaching down, petted George. "You are going on a long journey," she said to him. "You'll be flying." Then she looked up and spoke to Vicki and me. "Maybe you will talk to him tonight." "Maybe," I hurried to say before Vicki could speak. The outer door opened and another woman walked into the office. "What a happy dog," she said, noticing George.

"What is he here for?" "He's being put to sleep," I said. "Oh," the woman exclaimed, "earlier this year I had to put an old cat to sleep," the topic so agreeing with her that she sat near me in order to explore the subject in more detail. "Vicki," I said, "why don't you wait for us in the car?"

Just after Vicki left, Sally appeared. "Sorry to be late," she said, "but I am ready for you now." I wanted to answer politely, but words snagged in my throat, and so I nodded and followed her into an examination room. Sally spread a red cloth over an end of a sterile table. I set George on the cloth. I held him tightly, cradling him against my stomach, clamping his muzzle between my forearm and a rib of fat rippling along my side. Sally cinched a band around George's right front leg, making the radial vein bulge. Then she reached behind her and lifted a syringe off a tray. She stuck the syringe in George's leg. Almost immediately he slumped against me. He died before I could think goodbye. Sally listened to his heart with a stethoscope. "He's dead," she said, and I tightened the muscles in my calves until they hurt. "His bladder will probably let go. Do you want me to put his bottom in a plastic bag?" "Yes," I said, and Sally left the room.

When she returned with a white bag the size of a small grocery sack, I told her I had changed my mind. "I'd rather wrap him in his blanket," I said. Then I thanked her "for all you have done." I did not want to walk out through the lobby, so I asked if I could leave by the side door. "That's fine," she said, and pushed a box from in front of the door. "Is he dead?" Vicki asked when I approached the car. "Yes," I said, handing her George and leaning against the car for a moment and rubbing my right hand hard over my chin. Vicki slid her hand under the blanket. "He's so soft and warm," she said. She pulled the blanket away from George's head. His eyes were half open. "Oh," she said. I put on my sunglasses, started the car, and we drove back to Beaver River. We didn't talk, and the trip seemed long.

The nineteenth-century English painter Edwin Landseer got relations between dogs and people backward. In "The Old Shepherd's Chief Mourner," Landseer painted a sheepdog grieving for his dead master. The dog's muzzle rested atop a blanket covering the shepherd's coffin, the dog's expression as doleful as the light of the declining day that edged, faded, into the room through a window. The truth is that people grieve for dogs, not dogs for people. Landseer should have painted an ancient shepherd standing at the edge of a field, bent over his crook, a single tear sliding down his left cheek, at his feet a nondescript mound, the dirt brown and fresh, a handful of crow flowers scattered yellow over the clods.

In general, people weep more over the deaths of pets than they do over family members. The death of an animal does not disrupt routine or impose responsibility. Consequently a person has the leisure to indulge his emotions. When a family member dies, a person suddenly has so many chores that not only does leisure vanish but the dead person himself disappears. Funerals must be arranged, taxes paid, and estates settled. Clothes must be given away, and houses and apartments sold. In the mail legal forms arrive and thank-you notes go out. Every week I talk to my parents. In the months immediately following their deaths, they so filled my hours that I had little time to miss them, much less chat with them.

Vicki rolled a red wooden wheelbarrow out of the barn. Emile, a caretaker, made it for her in the 1960s, when she was nine or ten. Vicki pushed the wheelbarrow into the sun, stopping by the well cover in the side meadow. She laid George in the wheelbarrow, the blue blanket under him and pulled up over his shoulders. "I've put him in the sun because I don't want him to be cold," she said. While I dug two bushels of peat moss in the boggy spruce woods behind Ma's Property, Vicki gathered a bottle of loose hay from the pasture east of the house. After returning from the woods, I again bailed water out of the grave. This time, though, I spread hay across the bottom of the grave. Once the hay was saturated, I raked it out, carried it across the meadow, and tossed it into a hedge of meadowsweet, the spires of flowers just breaking into white, looking like finials atop posts on dolls' beds.

Next I relined the bottom of the grave with hay. On top of the hay I spread two thick shelves of moss. I laid George on his right side on the moss. We buried him in his collar, tags pressed against his breastbone. A decade ago Eliza suggested that when George died we should keep his collar and every December hang it on the Christmas tree. Before we left Connecticut in June, I mentioned Eliza's suggestion to Edward. "No," he said, "I can't bear to think of Georgie lying naked in the ground."

We arranged the body carefully, tucking George's tail between his legs, pointing his muzzle toward the porch and curling his front legs into his chest so that they looked like sweet rolls. Beside his nose we laid two and a half Milk-Bones, the treat Vicki gave him every day at ten or eleven, the last few months breaking them into small bits so he could eat them. Over him she stretched an old undershirt. She wore the shirt that morning so her scent would be fresh and "George wouldn't feel lost." Over the shirt I scattered rose petals. "For remembrance," I said, "for Francis, Edward, Eliza, and us, and for the housesitters who cared for him when we were in Australia and who sometimes dropped by to see him: Suzy, then Meghan, and Aaron." I then covered George with two more layers of moss. We tossed handfuls of wildflowers on the moss, picking them in part, I think, because wandering about the yard made us aware of the beauty that surrounded us and thus ameliorated sadness: old-fashioned bleeding heart, forget-me-nots, buttercups, dame's rocket, and from the golden elder beside the backhouse, lemony umbels of flowers. Afterward we said goodbye and filled the grave. Vicki tossed on the first shovel of dirt, after which she went into the house. I piled on the rest, tamping the clay down firmly. Once the dirt became a mound, I gathered another bushel of moss and fitted it atop the grave, turning the gray soil green. Because we had churned the ground into mud, I spread a setting of hay around the grave. When I finished, I stood and stretched. A common tan wave caterpillar was inching up my shirt. I slipped a twig under him and, after lifting him, placed him back on the willow. A song sparrow landed on a dead limb at the top of the tree and began to sing. I looked at my wristwatch. The time was 1:50. "So long, sport," I said. "I guess that's the end."

Of course that wasn't the end. I went into the house and took a bubble bath, suds fragrant with kiwi-mango rising in a mound over me — like a grave, I thought at the time. After the bath I changed my socks and put on clean shorts and a T-shirt decorated with fourteen red happy-bugs. At 2:23 I was back under the willow. George was warm and looked almost alive when I buried him. If his head had not flopped loosely over my wrist when I lifted him out of the wheelbarrow, his taproot cut and neck wilting, I would have put off burying him. Now I imagined a paw suddenly clawing through the moss and grabbing at the air frantically before collapsing and curling limply back into the soil. I imagined hearing a choking bark and saw myself on my knees, tearing at the dirt. The fantasy outlived reason. Two dozen times during the next two and a half days I studied the grave, searching for signs of disturbance.

Late that afternoon I walked along the lane. An Atlantis fritillary puddled on a red socket of dirt. Swamp candles flickered beside the blueberry field. A sphagnum sprite perched on black sedge, the minute damselfly fragile as lace. In the shady damp, partridgeberry bloomed, and a schoolyard of young red squirrels scolded me. On the headland, goatsbeard exploded into geodesic domes of seed. A red-eyed vireo called incessantly from an ash, saying, "Hello, hello — hello, you there." I lifted a log, and a shrew whisked out of sight. Under a board a red-bellied snake lay beside a garter snake three times its size. On the slope of the bluff I found three beer cans, a Molson and two Budweisers. I stuffed the Budweisers into the front pockets of my shorts and the Molson into the right rear pocket. At home I threw them into the recycling barrel, shooting them like basketballs.

While I walked, Vicki picked wildflowers: Queen Anne's lace, fall dandelion, purple clover, white and pink yarrow, daisies, knapweed, and tall meadow rue. She put the flowers in a Mason jar and, after filling the jar with water, set it at the foot of George's grave. That night we ate takeout at the Old Mill Seafood and Dairy Bar on Hard Scratch Road. Wooden lobsters perched atop the front corners of the dairy bar. The lobsters were tall and red and stood upright, their tails spread broad beneath them like carpet sweepers. The lobsters' heads rose to a point, the sides resembling roofs falling down from a ridgepole. Smiling, the lobsters waved their left claws above their heads. In their right claws they clutched salmon-colored ice cream cones, the flavor probably strawberry at one time.

Although two picnic tables sat in the gravel surrounding the bar, Vicki and I ate in the car. Mosquitoes swarmed about the bar in a fog, and all customers ate in their cars — or, to be more accurate, in their pickup trucks. While I ate the "big" serving of fried clams, Vicki had fried fish. We both had french fries and drank Pepsis, this a break from Vicki's usual Coca-Cola. After dinner we drove into Yarmouth and watched *I, Robot,* a summertime creature-and-explosion movie. Before the movie, Vicki bought herself a box of

Smarties, and for me a Bounty Bar, at Shoppers Drug Mart. Milk chocolate drenched the bar. Almost never do I eat milk chocolate, preferring bittersweet. Still, because the innards of the bar were coconut, I ate it. Afterward I felt nauseated.

At breakfast the next morning, Vicki said she wished we'd had George cremated. Then, she explained, glancing out the kitchen window, we could have scattered his ashes so we wouldn't associate him with a specific place. "From now on, every time I look at the willow," she said, "I'll think about him and become sad." "For God's sake," I exclaimed, "do you want me to dig him up, build a funeral pyre, and burn him?" "Don't be so cruel," Vicki said. "I just wish we'd cremated him." "Damn," I said, and strode out of the kitchen into the backhouse, letting the screen door slam. I walked along the bluff. Several times I looked behind me, not so much hoping to see George but attempting to slip time and event for a moment, hoping to remember the past before fog billowed off the gulf and swept through the spruces and across the fields, erasing memory.

On returning to the house, I plucked a blanket from George's bed and smelled it. The aroma of dog was strong. My pal, I thought. Vicki wasn't in the room. "Vicki," I yelled, "these blankets have to be washed." "Good God," Vicki said, coming into the kitchen, "didn't hurrying him into the grave satisfy you? Now you want to push him out of thought." Later that week Vicki said she wished we'd bought a movie camera and had filmed George. I replied that I was glad we had never owned a movie camera. I said I didn't want people or pets, Mommy or Daddy, the children when they were younger, flickering out of time and disrupting the present. I said I wanted the children to remember the old, not the young, me. "I want to be the stuff of responsibility happily shed, not of regret and loss." "What do all those words mean, if anything?" Vicki said. "I don't know," I said, "but did I tell you about Proverbs Goforth's trip to Nashville?" Before Vicki answered, I started a story.

Proverbs, it seems, got caught short on Church Street. In desperation, he stopped a stranger and asked directions to the nearest bathroom. "There's a urinal just inside the Tennessee Theater," the man said, pointing across the street. "Urinal, hell," Proverbs said. "I don't give a damn about any urinal. I need an arsenal." At the end of the story, I burst into laughter, beating my fists on my knees and so tiring myself that I lay my head on the kitchen table. Vicki did not laugh. "Jesus, you're insensitive," she said, scowling before she walked into the back parlor. Of course I'm insensitive. Living is impossible if a person is sensitive.

In eighteen days we return to Connecticut. Until then I am going to study Penny. I do not know whether she misses George. For ten years he was her companion. When George was alive, she scurried ahead on walks, even when he lingered behind. Now she stays close to Vicki and me. In the house she follows Vicki from room to room. When I call her, she sometimes hides behind Vicki's legs. Oh, well, three days ago I dug two spruce trees and planted them in the windbreak beside the road. Eliza has arrived after spending two months in St. Petersburg. She said she was glad we put George to sleep while she was in Russia. "Being here would have been terrible," she said. In four days Edward's camp ends. The next night he catches the ferry from Portland and arrives in Yarmouth the next morning. He wrote me that he, too, was glad he wasn't here when George died. Francis remains gainfully unemployed in Storrs. On the telephone he said he was "thankful" he wasn't here during the summer.

The moss on George's grave remains wondrously green. Every afternoon when Vicki drives to the Shore Grocery to pick up the Halifax newspaper, I look at the grave. I miss my dog. Things we did pop into mind; today, for example, the time many years ago when he became overheated on a long walk. To cool him down I dropped him into a cattle trough. Vicki is angry at me. She thinks I am hard-hearted and wants me to cry about George. If I cried in front of her, she'd think better of me. No matter, I won't cry. For years I have kept calm for others. I pay insurance and college tuition, all the household expenses. I have forced myself to be upbeat in hopes of keeping others cheery. I have learned to spin optimism out of dark night. What the hell else can — no, should — a father and a husband, a responsible, arthritic old guy, do? I took care of my pal for fourteen years, then I dug him a humdinger of a grave and found him a crackerjack tombstone.

ROBERT POLITO

Shame

FROM BLACK CLOCK

THIS ALL STARTED with a photograph I saw perhaps once and never again. We were packing up our old house in Dorchester — the first-floor flat of a classic Boston three-decker that Nana, my mother's mother, owned on Semont Road — for our move to Quincy. I had been taken by my father on a Saturday afternoon not long before to look over the new house, our first single-family home, on Hillside Avenue, appropriately near the summit of a minor hill. (The next street up was Summit Avenue.) The place was a wreck, the living room ceiling cracked and at the center dipping perilously, holes as though punched in the walls, bathtub dripping mold. But there were fine compensatory curiosities: a clapboard toolshed out back, a huge skull-shaped rock next to a stone fireplace for burning leaves, oak and fir trees, domed bushes for hiding. Inside off the front entrance hall was the smallest bathroom I've ever seen — even at age seven I could barely sit down without my knees hitting the pipes under the tiny sink. And I would finally have my own room — no longer sharing with Nana, as in Dorchester, the original master bedroom over the street, sleeping side by side in twin beds like a couple from a 1940s Hollywood movie. Whenever I was angry at my parents I would find the printed cardboard sign we used to signal that we needed heating oil and shove it in our bedroom bay window for the silver trucks that prowled the neighborhood, confusion and shouts at the door after a delivery man refilled our tank in summer or topped us off for the third time that winter week.

This would have been late in 1960 — my first Quincy memory is of watching the Kennedy inauguration on a TV that my father set up for us in the basement as workers plastered and painted upstairs. But while moving from Dorchester I helped my father empty his dresser into cartons for the movers — his white work shirts and sleeveless T-shirts, his black socks, his boxer shorts — saving the top drawer, his junk drawer, for last.

I always liked to look through his dresser if there was no one home, or just me and my younger sister and brother. All sorts of objects might spill out of the cigar boxes and trays in his junk drawer. Old coins, some inserted into blue folders, lots of stamps (he worked for the post office), his World War II medals and pins, a few $25 U.S. Savings Bonds with my name on them — for college, he said — and lots of shiny silver shoehorns (on weekends he moonlighted downtown at a women's shoe store). Mornings after he took my mother out for dinner and dancing — maybe once every other month on a Friday night, occasionally to Boston nightclubs with names like the High Hat, more often to VFW posts and church functions — there would be a fresh pack of smokes in his top drawer, always filtered, mostly Kents, with just two or three cigarettes missing. As far as I could see, he never retrieved the old pack the next time they went out. So the Kents tended to pile up, and my parents must have smoked as they drank, taking years to drain the bottle of Seagram's 7 that they stored in a dining room hutch for guests.

In his junk drawer my father kept a locked metal box, though "locked" and "metal" significantly embellish its dime-store, chipped and battered flimsiness. Still, it resisted all my attempts to pick it with a screwdriver and tweezers. But on this day that we were moving, he opened the box right up with a little key that apparently was inside the drawer all along, undetected by me, and out came everything you'd expect someone like my father would consider valuable or at risk: his service discharge papers, his and my mother's Social Security cards, their marriage license, our birth certificates, a red bank book from a decade earlier, and the ring he fashioned during the war for my mother out of a seashell and a New Guinea coin. I can recall all of this because the box came to me, contents more or less intact, after my father died. I keep the mother-of-pearl ring in a dish on a windowsill with both of my parents' wedding rings.

On this day there were photos in the box too: my parents seated by themselves at a table in a dining room I didn't recognize; some soldiers in uniform, young and smiling, my father among them; and what looked like two really ancient photos made — it seemed to me — from the same black metal as the box that held them, individual photos of a man with a mustache and a woman. Though the woman's picture was on top, my father quickly slipped it under the one of the man, as if he were shuffling cards, and said, "That's your grandfather." Since I found out later that my grandfather died when I was four, less than three years before, presumably I had met him. This is the only likeness I have of him. That thin mustache. A dark man in a dark suit and dark hat. Looking incredibly uncomfortable, as if he never wore suits or he just didn't want to be there.

Of course my Irish grandmother, Nana, was still alive, and there were photographs of her family everywhere in the Dorchester house — her parents, her sisters and brothers, her dead husband, and her two other children, my Aunt Mary and Uncle John, both also dead, from cancer before they turned forty. But this Italian grandfather doesn't turn up even among the hundreds of snapshots in my parents' wedding album. I must have asked my father about the woman in the first photo, the dark girl who looked to be (I would say now) in her teens. I understood right away, without being told or knowing why, beyond their same beak-like nose and large black eyes, that she was connected to my father, the way you usually know when someone is about to betray you or hurt you, even though there aren't any obvious signs and warnings; you feel it along your skin.

Orphans fascinated me, and part of my dad's particular fascination for me was that he had lost his mother when he was around my age, was on his own from the age of five, his father always away working. He said he had only one memory of his mother: he was playing in the kitchen, swinging on the door of their icebox, when the whole thing toppled over on him. His mother called out the window for help, and when nobody came she lifted off the icebox herself, even though she was a small woman and frail, perhaps already dying. He told me just one story about his father, too, laughing and shaking his head as he talked. He said that my dockworker grandfather, Luigi Polito, was among the thousands of stupid Bostonians who in 1920 rushed down to 27 School Street to invest their wages in Charles Ponzi's Securities Exchange Company.

I can't remember what I thought my father meant by a "Ponzi scheme," or even if he told me about Ponzi, then or later. I'm guessing that he was trying to distract me from the photograph of the woman — distract me as people will do when they're agitated, as my father visibly was then — by discussing *technique*. We discussed technique a lot. Does that mean we were often agitated? For most of my childhood my father was in many ways my closest friend. A friendship of common interests, like science, rockets, UFOs, and gadgets. Then we got very competitive. He told me that long ago, photographs were first made of glass and then they were made of tin. His information mostly was wrong, of course — or I got it wrong. Daguerreotypes aren't printed on glass; the glass only protects the fragile plates. Tintypes aren't tin at all but thin iron sheets. But tintypes were popular with street photographers into the 1930s, at neighborhood fairs and carnivals. Did my father's tintypes come from one of the Italian summer street fairs — the Saint Anthony Festival? Saint Rocco? — in Boston's North End?

In the tintype, the woman I've always assumed is my grandmother stands on the arc of a little bridge, holding a flower. There was no water under the bridge, so this must have been a set in an impromptu photography studio. A curtain backdrop, I think, provided trees, plus the moon and the outline of a distant river. The woman wore an elaborate dress imprinted with leaves and flowers, and a kind of cape over the dress. There were also flowers and leaves in her hair, which appeared black and curly like my father's and flowed along her shoulders into the swirls of her cape and dress. Her mouth open, smiling almost, she gazes at the camera, or the cameraman, or someone standing behind him, or whoever happens to be looking back at her image.

Later, over the years when I mentioned these photos, my father always denied their existence. He said that he had no photographs of his mother, and that his sister, my Aunt Ann, kept the few pictures there were of my grandfather. My grandfather was an Italian peasant, he said, who didn't like cameras and photographs. He unloaded fish from ships in Boston harbor for the big seafood restaurants. He even tried to force my father to leave school and join him on the docks. He was a laborer. He never wore a suit.

My mentioning the photographs became a funny family story, something like the time I went on a deep-sea fishing trip with my father and supposedly caught thirty-six fish. To my eventual humiliation, it actually was the charter boat captain who caught all the fish; he just handed me the fishing rod whenever he felt a tug on the line. Or the time that my fever spiked to 105 degrees and, as my father recalled, I went off my rocker, babbling deliriously about God knows what. These photos were yet another instance of me going off my rocker.

I never saw that photograph of my grandmother again. No tintypes at all were in the metal box the next time that my sister and I opened it, some thirty-five years later, after my mother died and more than a decade after the death of my father. But as I say, nearly everything else was there, all the papers, the shell ring, the other snapshots — though, oddly, the photograph of my grandfather wasn't a tintype but a photographic postcard. Still, my father told me about tintypes that day we moved, so the photo of the dark, curly-haired woman must have been a tintype. From other tintypes and cabinet cards I've seen since, I realize the woman looked like, or was trying to look like, an opera singer, or an actress.

Once my mother died, I learned more from my sister about my grandmother. This was the way my father apparently told it to my mother, who then told it to my sister. Around 1914 my grandfather arrived in the United States from Naples with his wife and their two children, George and Ann. Soon after, his wife became very ill and returned to Italy, taking the children home with her. A few years later she died, and George and Ann grew up with relatives on a vineyard near Bari. My father, meanwhile, was born in Boston in 1915, to a woman who appears as "Angela DiRuggiero" on his birth certificate and as "Mary Ruggiero" on his marriage license. There's no evidence that she and my grandfather were married then, or any time later. Angela, or Mary, didn't die when my father was five; instead, she left my grandfather, my father, and Boston for New York City. My grandfather summoned George and Ann from Italy, and Ann raised my father, who never saw his mother again.

Because this was a mother abandoning a child, I've always assumed there must have been another man involved. But who knows? Apparently my grandfather was a drunk, and so abusive and violent that he wasn't allowed to attend my parents' wedding. After I got to high school, my father and I fought about the war in Vietnam, Nixon, rock music, and my wanting to be an English professor and not an engineer. Nights when I came in the back door and passed him on the porch with his bound books of *New York Times* crossword puzzles, I thought he looked like the unhappiest person I'd ever met.

Now I don't think he was unhappy so much as ashamed. Something of the world my father must have lived inside, on the porch with his puzzles, hit me the one time I attempted to find out what had happened to my grandmother from my Auntie Ann. "Your father was a good man, Bobby," she snapped back, as though this was the only possible answer to my question, and shut the subject down.

I've looked for that tintype ever since, and on nearly any weekend in upstate New York I will find one at some antiques store, usually for a few dollars, but occasionally for a lot more, if it's tinted or the store is posh. A dealer who gets them for me says that locals will sell old photographs to him even when they know the portraits are of their own family, and he offers practically nothing for them. "I never met these people," they tell him. So sometimes I can buy multiple pictures of the same person, and groups who are clearly related, the tintypes still tucked into their original books, though damaged by water and insects.

I make my living writing about art, and have friends who collect what they call vernacular photography. But this has nothing to do with art. More like I'm assembling an alternate family, the way a childless couple might gather cats and dogs around them. I have stacks of the tintypes now, all over the place. When I see a photograph of a young woman with dark hair who would have been alive in 1915, posed against some fantastic contrived scene, I pay whatever it costs. Then I start looking for her all over again.

DAVID RIEFF

Illness as More Than Metaphor

FROM THE NEW YORK TIMES MAGAZINE

MY MOTHER, Susan Sontag, lived almost her entire seventy-one
years believing that she was a person who would beat the odds.
Even during the last nine months of her life, after she was discovered to have myelodysplastic syndrome, or MDS, a particularly vir-
ulent blood cancer, she continued to persevere in the belief that
she would be the exception. MDS is technically a precursor to
acute myeloid leukemia. On average, its survival rates across the
generational cohorts are no better than 20 percent, and far worse
for a woman in her early seventies who had had cancer twice before. It wasn't that she didn't know that the biological deck was
stacked against her; as someone who prided herself on her ability
to grasp medical facts, she knew it only too well. In the immediate
aftermath of her diagnosis, she went online to learn all she could
about MDS and despaired as the fact of its lethality sank in. But
that despair was almost the flip side of a lifelong confidence in her
ability to defy the odds. "This time, for the first time," she told me,
"I don't feel special."

Remarkably, in only a few weeks she had righted herself psycho-
logically and was gearing up, just as she had done during her successful fights to survive two previous cancers, to find the doctors
and the treatments that seemed to offer her some hope of defying
those terrifyingly long odds and once more becoming the exception. How she did this, I don't know. Perhaps it was the spirit that
had led her, when she recovered from her first cancer, to write a little proudly in her book *AIDS and Its Metaphors* of "confounding my
doctors' pessimism." Perhaps she was able, somehow, to confound

her own as well. What I do know is that the panic attacks that had overwhelmed her after her diagnosis began to lessen, and in the MDS literature that she found on the Web she began to find reasons for hope rather than despair. She even began to work again, writing a fiery piece on the Abu Ghraib torture photographs for this magazine at the same time she was readying herself to become a patient at the Fred Hutchinson Cancer Research Center in Seattle, where the bone-marrow transplant that was her only realistic hope of cure had been pioneered.

Her "positive denial," as I always thought of it, whether with regard to her health, her work as a writer, or her private life, had not been extinguished by the hard facts of MDS after all. On her seventieth birthday, fifteen months before she found out she was ill again, she talked to me at length and with the characteristic passion she brought to her work about how she was only now starting a new and, she thought, the best phase of her writing life. Leaving for Seattle, she began speaking again of projects she would undertake — above all the novel she had been outlining — after her return to New York and even to speculate about whether she would feel strong enough to write during her treatment.

Was it bravado? Doubtless it was, but not bravado alone. During the two years of chemotherapy she underwent in the mid-1970s to treat her first cancer — stage 4 breast cancer that had spread into thirty-one of her lymph nodes — she managed to publish a book on photography and, a year later, her book *Illness as Metaphor.* That time, she *had* beaten the odds. William Cahan, then her principal doctor at Memorial Sloan-Kettering Cancer Center in New York, told me at the time that he saw virtually no hope. (Those were the days when doctors often told patients' relatives things they did not disclose to the patients themselves.) But as her friend Dr. Jerome Groopman, chief of experimental medicine at the Beth Israel Deaconess Medical Center in Boston, told me a few months after her death: "The statistics only get you so far. There are always people at the tail of the curve. They survive, miraculously, like your mother with breast cancer. Her prognosis was horrific. She said: 'No, I'm too young and stubborn. I want to go for it' " — meaning treatment. "Statistically, she should have died. But she didn't. She was at the tail of that curve."

"We tell ourselves stories in order to live." The line is Joan

Didion's, and looking back on my mother's life, I've been wondering lately if we don't tell them to ourselves in order to die as well. In retrospect, I realize that death was never something my mother talked about much. But it was the ghost at the banquet of many of her conversations, expressed particularly in her single-minded focus on her own longevity and, as she got older, by her frequent voicing of the hope of living to be one hundred. She was no more reconciled to extinction at seventy-one than she had been at forty-two. After her death, a theme in many of the extremely generous and heartfelt letters of condolence I received from her friends puzzled me: it was surprise — surprise that my mother *hadn't* beaten MDS, as she had beaten both breast cancer and the uterine sarcoma that struck her in her mid-sixties.

But then, she too was surprised when the doctors in Seattle came in to tell her the bone-marrow transplant had failed and her leukemia was back. She screamed out, "But this means I'm going to die!"

I will never forget that scream, or think of it without wanting to cry out myself. And yet, even that terrible morning, in a pristine room at the University of Washington Medical Center, with its incongruously beautiful view of Lake Union and Mount Rainier in the background, I remember being surprised by her surprise. I suppose I shouldn't have been. There are those who can reconcile themselves to death and those who can't. Increasingly, I've come to think that it is one of the most important ways the world divides up. Anecdotally, after all those hours I spent in doctors' outer offices and in hospital lobbies, cafeterias, and family rooms, my sense is that the loved ones of desperately ill people divide the same way.

For doctors, understanding and figuring out how to respond to an individual patient's perspective — continue to fight for life when chances of survival are slim, or acquiesce and try to make the best of whatever time remains? — can be almost as grave a responsibility as the more scientific challenge of treating disease. In trying to come to terms with my mother's death, I wanted to understand the work of the oncologists who treated her and what treating her meant to them, both humanly and scientifically. What chance was there really of translating a patient's hope for survival into the reality of a cure? One common thread in what they told me was that interpreting a patient's wishes is as much art as science. Dr. Stephen Nimer, my mother's principal doctor, heads the division of hematologic oncology at Memorial Sloan-Kettering and is also one of America's foremost researchers in the fundamental biology of leukemia. As he explained it to me: "The fact is that people are never as educated as the doctor. You have to figure out something about the patient" — by which he meant something that takes both patient and physician beyond the profound, frustrating, and often infantilizing asymmetry between the patient's ability to comprehend the choices to be made and the doctor's.

Still, the doctor's task here is not impossible. As Nimer put it: "There are risk takers and risk-averse. There are those who say, you know: 'I'm seventy years old. If I get another four or five months, that would be fine.' Others say, 'You do everything you can to save my life.' Then it's easy. You can go straight into a discussion of what a patient wants."

For Nimer, as for Jerome Groopman, the ethical challenge, vital for a doctor to recognize and impossible (and ethically undesirable) to deal with formulaically, comes not with the 30 percent of patients Nimer estimates know for certain whether they want aggressive treatment or not, but with the "undecided" 70 percent in the middle. As Nimer told me somewhat ruefully, the doctor's power to influence these patients, one way or the other, is virtually complete. "There are ways to say things," he said. " 'This is your only hope.' Or you could say, 'Some doctors will say it's your only hope, but it has a twenty times better chance of harming you than helping you.' So I'm pretty confident I can persuade people." Groopman, in his clinical practice with patients like my mother, patients for whom, statistically, the prognosis is terrible, at times begins by saying, "There is a very small chance, but it comes with tremendous cost."

In these situations, doctors like Groopman and Nimer see their job as, in effect, parsing the patient's response and trying to determine a treatment plan that is responsive to the patient's wishes but is also not what physicians refer to as "medically futile" — that is, offering no real chance for cure or remission. That is hard enough. What makes the doctor's decision in such situations even more painful is that "medically futile" means different things to different physicians. After my mother's transplant failed and she was medevaced from the University of Washington hospital back to

Memorial Sloan-Kettering, Nimer tried one last treatment — an experimental drug called Zarnestra that had induced remission in some 10 percent of the small number of patients to whom it had been administered. I would learn from the nurses' aides who attended my mother in the last weeks of her life that some of the doctors and nurses on the transplant floor were uncomfortable with the decision, precisely because they saw my mother's situation as hopeless, that is, medically futile. As division head, in consultation with Dr. Marcel van den Brink, the hospital's chief of bone-marrow transplantation, Nimer could overrule these objections. But neither man would have denied the difficulty of drawing a clear line between what is and is not medically futile.

My mother was determined to try to live no matter how terrible her suffering. Her choices had been stark from the outset. Unlike some other cancers that can be halted for years through treatment, there are few long-lasting remissions in MDS. Her only real chance of survival lay in the possibility of an outright cure offered by an adult-blood-stem-cell transplant. Otherwise, to quote from one of the medical Web sites my mother visited repeatedly during the first weeks after her diagnosis, treatment offered her only an "alleviation of symptoms, reduction in transfusion requirements and improvement of quality of life." During their second meeting, Nimer offered her the option of treatment with a drug called 5-azacitidine, which gave many MDS patients some months during which they felt relatively well. But the drug did little to prolong life. My mother replied, with tremendous passion, "I am not interested in quality of life!"

What Nimer knew with the horrified intimacy of long clinical practice, but what my mother could not yet know, was just how agonizing the effects of an unsuccessful stem-cell transplant can be: everything from painful skin rashes to inordinately severe diarrhea to hallucinations and delirium. To me, torture is not too strong or hyperbolic a word. After my mother's declaration, Nimer only nodded and began talking about where the best place might be for her to have the stem-cell transplant, going over with her the variations in different medical research centers' approaches to transplantation. After the transplant failed, and my mother returned from Seattle, Nimer obviously knew how long the odds were against an experimental drug like Zarnestra inducing even a brief extension of her life. But he said he felt that he had to try, both because the drug had had some success and because my mother had told him (and me) from the outset that she wanted her doctors to do everything possible, no matter how much of a long shot it was, to save or prolong her life.

"Always assuming it's not medically futile," he told me a few weeks before her death, "if I can carry out my patients' wishes, I want to do that."

My mother could express herself only with the greatest of difficulty in the last weeks of her life. "Protective hibernation" was how one Sloan-Kettering psychiatrist described it. Like most people who have lost someone dear to them, I would say that one of my dominant emotions since my mother's death has been guilt — guilt over what I did and failed to do. But I do not regret trying to get her to swallow those Zarnestra pills even when her death was near, for I haven't the slightest doubt that had she been able to make her wishes known, my mother would have said she wanted to fight for her life to the very end.

But this does nothing to change the fact that it seems almost impossible to develop a satisfactory definition of what is and is not medically futile. What is the cutoff? A 10 percent chance of success? Five percent? One percent? When does the "very small chance" my mother's doctors bought at the "tremendous cost" in suffering that Groopman described for me become so infinitesimal as to make it no longer worth trying?

I have found no consensus among the oncologists I have spoken with in the aftermath of my mother's death, and I don't believe there is one. There are those who take a strong, consistent stance against not just such treatments but also against the general orientation of American medicine, particularly oncology, toward doing everything possible to save individual patients, no matter how poor their chances. These doctors seem inspired by a public-health model based on better health outcomes for communities rather than individuals, viewing it as the most moral and the only cost-effective way of practicing medicine. This view, often associated with the work of the medical ethicist Daniel Callahan, is increasingly influential.

One reason for this is that the current American medical sys-

tem is breaking down. Several physicians with little sympathy for
Callahan's approach pointed out to me that, like it or not, American society either can't afford or no longer chooses to afford to un-
derwrite the kind of heroic care people like my mother, whose
prognoses are obviously poor, still receive in the United States. Dr.
Diane E. Meier, a palliative-medicine specialist at Mount Sinai Hospital in New York, remarked that if we as a society spent the sort of
money on medical care that we spend, say, on the military, the
challenge facing physicians would be very different. But neither
Meier nor any other doctor I spoke to seemed to believe that there
is much chance of that. If anything, medical financing has moved
and is likely to continue to move entirely in the opposite direction.
As Meier put it to me, "The cost crisis facing Medicare will lead to
substantial and real reductions in access to care."

One illustration of Meier's point is that Memorial Sloan-Kettering already treats, through funds received from private philan-
thropists, many patients whose treatment is not covered by Medicare or who have had their applications for treatment at major
cancer centers refused by their insurance companies. But it is one
of only a few cancer centers in a position to do so. (Even more sobering is the statistic that only a small percentage of Americans
with cancer are treated in a cancer center.) Philanthropy aside —
and even the most generous philanthropy can never make up the
shortfall the continuing cuts in federal financing are likely to produce — it may well be, as Meier suggests, that we are rapidly moving toward a health care system in which "only the rich will be able
to choose the treatment they want."

In a sense, the financial background of my mother's treatment prefigured the world Meier was describing. Once she and
Nimer agreed that she would have a bone-marrow transplant at the
Hutchinson Center, and she was accepted as a patient there, she
applied to Medicare — her primary insurance — for coverage of
the treatment. Medicare refused, saying that coverage could begin
only once her MDS had "converted" to full-blown leukemia; in
other words, when she was far sicker. My mother then applied to
her private insurance company. The response was that her coverage did not extend to organ transplants, which was what it considered a bone-marrow transplant to be. Later, my mother's insurance company relented but still refused to allow her to go "out of

network" to the Hutchinson Center, even though Nimer was convinced that the doctors there stood the best chance of saving her life. Instead, the insurer proposed four "in network" options — hospitals where it would pay for the transplant to be done. But three out of the four said they would not take a patient like my mother (because of her age and medical history). The fourth did agree to take her but admitted, frankly, that it had little experience with patients of her age.

My mother was determined to get the best treatment possible, and Nimer had told her that treatment was to be found in Seattle. So she persevered. She was admitted to the Hutchinson Center as a so-called self-pay patient and had to put down a deposit of $256,000. Even before that, she had to pay $45,000 for the search for a compatible bone-marrow donor.

The knowledge that she was getting the best treatment available, both at Sloan-Kettering and at Hutchinson, was a tremendous consolation to my mother. It strengthened her will to fight, her will to live. But of course she was getting that treatment only because she had the money to pay for it. To be sure, as she was doing so, her doctors both in Seattle and New York very generously helped with her appeal of her insurance company's decision — calling and writing letters providing documentation and expert opinions explaining why the only viable treatment option was the one they had recommended. But both she and they knew that whatever hope she had of cure depended on moving rapidly toward the bone-marrow transplant. This would have been impossible had she not had the money to in effect defy her insurer's verdict, even as she was appealing it legally.

Let me state the obvious: the number of Americans who can do what she did is a tiny percentage of the population, and while I shall always be thankful beyond words for the treatment she received, and believe that she and her doctors made the right choice, I cannot honestly say that there was anything fair about it.

How or whether the realities of the health care system in America today can be reconciled with the fundamental aspiration of science, which is discovery, and the fundamental aspiration of medicine, which is to cure disease, is impossible for me to say. But if the time I have spent in the company of oncologists and researchers convinces me of anything, it is that these aspirations are almost as fundamental in serious doctors as the will to live is in cancer patients. The possibility of discovery, of research, is like a magnet. Marcel van den Brink, the Sloan-Kettering bone-marrow chief, who is Dutch, told me that one of the main reasons he is in the United States is that here, unlike in the Netherlands or, he thought, in the other major western European countries, there is money for his research. For his part, Jerome Groopman emphasized the overwhelming number of foreign researchers in his lab. He described it as "the opposite of outsourcing — it's insourcing."

Researchers find inspiration in the example of AIDS research, an almost paradigmatic example of heroic, cost-indifferent medicine. By public-health standards, AIDS has received a big share of the nation's medical resources, in large measure thanks to the tireless campaigning of gay Americans who have had the economic clout and cultural sophistication to make their voices heard by decision-makers in the medical establishment and in government. As Dr. Fred Appelbaum, clinical-research director of the Hutchinson Center, pointed out to me, understanding AIDS and then devising treatments for it at first defied the best efforts of research scientists. And though a cure has not yet been found, effective treatments have been — albeit extremely expensive ones.

If there is a difference between AIDS research and cancer research, it is that while advances in AIDS came relatively quickly, advances in cancer treatment and, indeed, in the fundamental understanding of how cancer works have come far more slowly than many people expected. Periodically since 1971, when President Nixon declared his war on cancer, the sense that the corner is about to be turned takes hold. We appear to be in such a moment today. The National Cancer Institute has recently put forward ambitious benchmarks for progress in cancer research and treatment. As its director, Dr. Andrew von Eschenbach, a respected surgeon and a cancer survivor himself (he is also acting head of the Food and Drug Administration), put it recently: "The caterpillar is about to turn into a butterfly. I have never known more enthusiasm among cancer researchers. It's a pivotal moment." The suffering of cancer, he argued, will be well on its way to being alleviated by 2015.

The media have mostly echoed this optimism. It is not unusual to read about the latest "breakthrough" in cancer treatment, both in terms of understanding the basic biological processes involved and with regard to innovative new drug therapies. On the level of research, there is no doubt that significant progress has been made. Dr. Harold Varmus, the Nobel laureate who now heads Memorial Sloan-Kettering, is emphatic on the subject. "Fifty or sixty years ago," he told me, "we didn't know what genes were. Thirty or so years ago we didn't know what cancer genes were. Twenty years ago we didn't know what human cancer genes were. Ten years ago we didn't have any drugs to inhibit any of these guys. It seems to me we've made an awful lot of progress in one person's lifetime."

Other research scientists seemed far more pessimistic when I spoke with them. Dr. Lee Hartwell, also a Nobel laureate, is president and director of the Hutchinson Center. He has urged that the focus in cancer treatment shift from drug development to the new disciplines of genomics and, above all, proteomics, the study of human proteins. Though he acknowledged the profound advances in knowledge made over the past two decades, Hartwell emphasized a different question: "How well are we applying our knowledge to the problem? The therapy side of things has been a pretty weak story. There have been advances: we cure most childhood leukemias with chemotherapy, for one thing. But the progress has been surprisingly weak given the huge expenditures that we've made. We're spending over twenty-five billion dollars a year improving cancer outcomes, if you include the spending of the pharmaceutical companies. So you've got to ask yourself whether this is the right approach."

The focus needs to be on "diagnostics rather than therapeutics," Hartwell said. "If you catch a cancer at stage one or two, almost everybody lives. If you catch it at stage three or four, almost everybody dies. We know from cervical cancer that by screening you can reduce cancer up to seventy percent. We're just not spending enough of our resources working to find markers for early detection."

Some researchers are even more skeptical. Mark Greene, the John Eckman Professor of Medical Science at the University of Pennsylvania and the scientist whose lab did much of the fundamental work on Herceptin, the first important new type of drug specifically designed to target the proteins in the genes that cause cells to become malignant, agrees with Hartwell. The best way to deal with cancer, he told me, is to "treat early, because basic under-standing of advanced cancer is almost nonexistent, and people with advanced cancer do little better now than they did twenty years ago."

Varmus, who appears to be somewhere in the middle between the optimists and the pessimists, told me that so far the clinical re-sults are mixed. As he put it: "Many cancers are highly treatable. I am optimistic, but I'm not saying, 'Here's when.' "

The irreducible fact is that failure is the clinical oncologist's con-stant companion. Each of those who treated my mother seemed to have evolved a strategy for coping with this. Stephen Nimer said: "I'd have to be an idiot to think everything I do works. I mean, where have I been the last twenty years? I'm not afraid to fail." Fred Appelbaum put it still more plainly. "You get victories that help bal-ance the losses," he said. "But the losses are very painful."

Appelbaum's almost studied understatement brought home a ques-tion that had recurred through the savage months of my mother's illness and also after her death. I kept wondering how the doctors who were treating her with such determination, against all the odds, could possibly stand swimming in this sea of death that they confronted every day, since they did not have the luxury of pre-tending, at least to themselves, that they didn't know which of their patients were likely to make it and which were not.

The question made sense to some. For Nimer, though, it did not. "I prefer 'swimming in a sea of life,' " he said, adding: "I know I'm not going to save everyone, but I don't think of myself as swim-ming in a sea of death. People who have congestive heart failure, their outcomes are like the worst cancers. People think of it as a cleaner death and cancer as a dirtier death, but that's not the case. I approach things with the question 'What would it be like if I were on the other side?' The first thing is being dependable. I give peo-ple a way to always reach me. They're not going to call me frivo-lously. There's a peace of mind that comes with knowing you can reach a doctor. I think if you have one of these diseases, you know you can die. Before people get to the time of dying, people want to have some hope, some meaning, that there's a chance things can get better."

And when they don't, Nimer continued, "whatever happens is going to happen. But how about the ride? How rough will it be? If I were dying, the thing I'd worry about most is how much I'm going to suffer. I've had a lot of people die over the years. One thing is to reassure people, 'Look, I'm going to do whatever is humanly possible so that you don't suffer.' We're all going to die, but I'm going to spend just as much time paying attention to your last days as I do at the beginning."

And with my mother, that is exactly what he did in the moment of her death — one of the many, too many, Nimer has seen. With all due respect to him, if that's not swimming in a sea of death . . .

If my mother had imagined herself special, her last illness cruelly exposed the frailty of that conceit. It was merciless in the toll of pain and fear that it exacted. My mother, who feared extinction above all else, was in anguish over its imminence. Shortly before she died, she turned to one of the nurses' aides — a superb woman who cared for her as she would have her own mother — and said, "I'm going to die," and then began to weep. And yet, if her illness was merciless, her death was merciful. About forty-eight hours before the end, she began to fail, complaining of generalized low-grade pain (possibly indicating that the leukemia was in her bloodstream). Shortly after, she came down with an infection. Given the compromised state of her immune system, the doctors said, there was little chance that her body could stave it off. She remained intermittently lucid for about another day, though her throat was so abraded that she could barely speak audibly and she was confused. I *feel* she knew I was there, but I am not at all sure. She said she was dying. She asked if she was crazy.

By Monday afternoon, she had left us, though she was still alive. Pre-terminal, the doctors call it. It was not that she wasn't there or was unconscious. But she had gone to a place deep within herself, to some last redoubt of her being, at least as I imagine it. What she took in I will never know, but she could no longer make much contact, if, indeed, she even wanted to. I and the others who were at her side left around eleven P.M. and went home to get a few hours' sleep. At three-thirty A.M. on Tuesday, a nurse called. My mother was failing. When we arrived in her room, we found her hooked up to an oxygen machine. Her blood pressure had already dropped into a perilous zone and was dropping steadily, her pulse was weakening, and the oxygen level in her blood was dropping.

For an hour and a half, my mother seemed to hold her own. Then she began the last step. At six A.M. I called Nimer, who came over immediately. He stayed with her throughout her death.

And her death was easy, as deaths go, in the sense that she was in little pain and little visible anguish. She simply went. First, she took a deep breath; there was a pause of forty seconds, such an agonizing, open-ended time if you are watching a human being end; then another deep breath. This went on for no more than a few minutes. Then the pause became permanence, the person ceased to be, and Nimer said, "She's gone."

A few days after my mother died, Nimer sent me an e-mail message. "I think about Susan all the time," he wrote. And then he added, "We have to do better."

OLIVER SACKS

Recalled to Life

FROM THE NEW YORKER

PATRICIA H. was a brilliant and energetic woman who represented artists and ran an art gallery on Long Island and was a talented amateur painter herself. She had raised her three children,
and, nearing sixty, she continued to lead an active and even, as her
daughters put it, "glamorous" life, with scouting expeditions to the
Village and frequent soirees at home — she was a great cook, and
there would often be twenty people for dinner. Her husband, too,
was a man of many parts — a radio broadcaster, a fine pianist who
sometimes performed at nightclubs, and politically active. Both
were intensely sociable.

In 1989, however, Pat's husband died suddenly of a heart attack.
Pat herself had had open-heart surgery for a damaged valve the
year before, and had been put on anticoagulants. She had taken
this in stride — but now, with her husband's death, as one of her
daughters put it, "She seemed stunned, became very depressed,
lost weight, fell in the subway, had accidents with the car, and
would show up, as if lost, on our doorstep in Manhattan." Pat had
always been somewhat volatile in mood ("She would be depressed
for a few days and take to her bed, then leap up in an opposite
frame of mind, and rush into the city, a thousand engagements of
one sort and another"), but now a fixed melancholy descended on
her.

When, in January of 1991, she didn't answer her phone for two
days, her daughters became alarmed and called a neighbor, who,
with the Long Island police, broke into Pat's house to find her lying in bed unconscious. She had been in a coma for at least twenty

hours, the daughters were told, and had suffered a massive cerebral hemorrhage. There was a huge clot of blood in the left half of her brain, the dominant hemisphere, and it was thought that she would not survive.

After a week in the hospital with no improvement, Pat underwent surgery as a last-ditch measure. The results of this, her daughters were told, could not be predicted.

Indeed, it seemed at first, after the clot was removed, that the situation was dire. Pat would "stare . . . without seeming to see," according to one of her daughters. "Sometimes her eyes would follow me, or seem to. We didn't know what was going on, whether she was there." Neurologists sometimes speak of "chronic vegetative states," zombie-like conditions in which certain primitive reflexes are preserved, but no coherent consciousness or self. Such states can be cruelly tantalizing, for there is often the feeling that the person is about to come to — but the states may last for months or years. In Pat's case, though, it lasted for two weeks and then, as her daughter Lari recalled, "I had a Diet Coke in my hand — she wanted it. I saw her eye it. I asked, 'Do you want a sip?' She nodded. Everything changed at this moment."

Pat was conscious now, recognized her daughters, was aware of her condition and her surroundings. She had her appetites, her desires, her personality, but she was paralyzed on the right side, and, more gravely, she could no longer express her thoughts and feelings in words; she could only eye and mime, point or gesture. Her understanding of speech, too, was much impaired. She was, as neurologists say, aphasic.

"Aphasia" means, literally, a loss of speech, but it is not speech as such that is lost but language itself — its expression, or its comprehension, in whole or in part. (Thus congenitally deaf people who use sign language rather than speech may get a sign aphasia following a brain injury or stroke, an aphasia in every way analogous to the aphasia of speaking people.)

Aphasia is not uncommon — it has been estimated that one person in three hundred may have a lasting aphasia from brain damage, whether this be the consequence of a stroke, a head injury, a tumor, etc. Many people, however, have a complete or partial recovery from aphasia, and there are transient forms that may occur during a migraine or a seizure.

There are many different forms of aphasia, depending on which part of the brain is involved, and a broad distinction is usually made between expressive aphasias and receptive aphasias — if both are present, this is a "global" aphasia.

In its mildest forms, expressive aphasia is characterized by a difficulty finding words, or a tendency to use wrong words, without compromise of the overall structure of sentences.

In more severe forms, a person may be unable to generate full, grammatically correct sentences, and may be able to utter only isolated words ("telegraphic speech"); if the aphasia is very severe, the person may be all but mute, though capable of occasional emotional ejaculations (such as "Damn!" or "Fine!"). John Hughlings Jackson, a pioneer explorer of aphasia in the 1860s and 1870s, considered that such patients lacked "propositional" speech, and he thought that they had lost internal speech as well, so that they could not speak or "propositionize" even to themselves. He felt therefore that the power of abstract thought was lost in aphasia, and on occasion he compared aphasics to dogs.

C. Scott Moss, a psychologist who had a stroke when he was forty-three which rendered him aphasic and paralyzed on the right side, later described his experiences, which were very much in accord with Hughlings Jackson's notions about the loss of inner speech and concepts:

> When I awoke the next morning in the hospital, I was totally (globally) aphasic. I could understand vaguely what others said to me if it was spoken slowly and represented a very concrete form of action . . . I had lost completely the ability to talk, to read and to write. I even lost for the first two months the ability to use words internally, that is, in my thinking . . . I had also lost the ability to dream. So, for a matter of eight to nine weeks, I lived in a total vacuum of self-produced concepts . . . I could deal only with the immediate present . . . The part of myself that was missing was [the] intellectual aspect — the sine qua non of my personality — those essential elements most important to being a unique individual . . . For a long period of time I looked upon myself as only half a man.

But it was very different with Jacques Lordat, an eminent early-nineteenth-century French physiologist, who provided an extraordinary description of his own aphasia after a stroke, sixty-odd years before Hughlings Jackson's studies:

Within twenty-four hours all but a few words eluded my grasp. Those that did remain proved to be nearly useless, for I could no longer recall the way in which they had to be coordinated for the communication of ideas . . . I was no longer able to grasp the ideas of others, for the very amnesia that prevented me from speaking made me incapable of understanding the sounds I heard quickly enough to grasp their meaning . . . Inwardly, I felt the same as ever. This mental isolation which I mention, my sadness, my impediment and the appearance of stupidity which it gave rise to, led many to believe that my intellectual faculties were weakened . . .

I used to discuss within myself my life work and the studies I loved. Thinking caused me no difficulty whatever . . . My memory for facts, principles, dogmas, abstract ideas, was the same as when I enjoyed good health . . . I had to realize that the inner workings of the mind could dispense with words.

Thus in some patients, even if they are totally unable to speak or understand speech, there may be perfect preservation of intellectual powers — the power to think logically and systematically, to plan, to recollect, to anticipate, to conjecture. This was shown, too, with great clarity in the case of a patient who was referred to by his physicians only as Brother John, a monk who would become completely aphasic for several minutes in the course of his epileptic seizures. But even when wholly deprived of language or internal speech Brother John was able to tackle complex problems, to negotiate intricate social situations, to show all the characteristic powers of a human being other than language. Had Hughlings Jackson met Brother John, one feels, he could not have compared aphasics to dogs.

Nevertheless, a feeling remains in the popular mind, and all too often in the medical mind, too, that aphasia is a sort of ultimate disaster which, in effect, ends a person's inner life as well as her outer life. Something along these lines was said to Pat's daughters, Dana and Lari. A little improvement, the neurologists felt, might occur, but Pat would need to be institutionalized for the rest of her life; there would be no parties, no conversation, no art galleries anymore — all that had constituted the very essence of Pat's life would be gone, and she would lead the narrow life of a patient, an inmate.

Scarcely able to initiate conversation or contact with others, patients with aphasia face special dangers in chronic hospitals or nursing homes. They may have therapy of every sort, but a vital social dimension of their lives is missing, and aphasics frequently feel intensely isolated and cut off. Yet there are many activities — card games, shopping trips, movies or theater, dance or sports — that do not require language, and these can be used to draw or inveigle aphasics into a social world of familiar activities and human contact. The dull term "social rehabilitation" is sometimes used here, but really the patient (as Dickens would put it) is being "recalled to life."

Pat's daughters were determined to do everything they could to bring their mother "back into the world," to the fullest possible life her limitations allowed. "We hired a nurse who retaught my mother how to feed herself, how to *be*," Lari said. "Mother would get angry, sometimes strike her, but she, the nurse, would never give up. Dana and I never left her side. We would take her out, wheel her to my apartment . . . We would take her out to restaurants, or bring food in, have her hair done, her nails manicured . . . We never stopped."

Pat was moved from the acute hospital where she had had surgery to a rehabilitation facility, and, after six months, she was finally moved to Beth Abraham Hospital, in the Bronx, where I first met her.

When Beth Abraham Hospital was opened, in 1919, it was called Beth Abraham Home for Incurables, a discouraging name that was changed only in the 1960s. Originally accommodating some of the first victims of the encephalitis-lethargica epidemic (some of whom were still living there more than forty years later, when I arrived), Beth Abraham expanded over the years to become a five-hundred-bed hospital with active rehabilitation programs, aimed at helping patients with all sorts of chronic conditions: Parkinsonism, dementias, speech problems, multiple sclerosis, strokes (and, increasingly, traumatic damage from bullet wounds and car accidents).

Visitors to hospitals for the chronically ill are often horrified at first, at the sight of hundreds of "incurable" patients, many of them paralyzed, blind, or speechless. One's first thought is often: Is life worth living in circumstances like these? What sort of a life can these people have? One wonders, nervously, how one would react to the prospect of being disabled and entering such a home oneself.

Then one may start to see the other side. Even if no cure, or only limited improvement, is possible for most of these patients, many of them may nonetheless be helped to reconstruct their lives, to find other ways of doing things, capitalizing on their strengths, finding compensations and accommodations of every sort. This, of course, depends upon the degree and type of neurological damage, and upon the inner and outer resources of the individual patient.

But if the first sight of a chronic hospital can be hard for visitors, it can be terrifying for a new inmate, who often reacts with horror, mixed with sadness, bitterness, or rage. When I first saw Pat, shortly after her admission to Beth Abraham in October of 1991, I found her angry and frustrated. She did not yet know the staff or the layout of the place, and she felt that a rigid, institutional order was being imposed on her. She could communicate through gestures — these were passionate, if not always understandable — but she still had very little speech (at least of grammatical sentences; she would occasionally, the staff said, exclaim "Hell!" or "Go away!" when she was angry). While she seemed to understand a good deal of what people said to her, it became clear, on examination, that she was responding not to words but to the tone of voice, facial expression, and gestures.

When I tested her in the clinic, Pat could not respond to "Touch your nose," either in speech or in writing. She could count ("one, two, three, four, five . . .") in sequence, but could not say individual numbers or count backward. The right side of her body remained completely paralyzed. Her neurological situation, I noted in my report, was "a bad one. I fear there may not be too much recovery of language functions, but intensive speech therapy, as well as physical therapy and occupational therapy, must certainly be tried."

Pat yearned to speak, but was continually frustrated when, after huge efforts to get a word out, it would be the wrong word, or unintelligible. She would try to correct it, but often would become more unintelligible with every attempt to make herself understood. It started to dawn on her, I think, that her power of speech might never come back, and, increasingly, she retreated into si-

lence. This inability to communicate was, for her, as for many patients with aphasia, far worse than the paralysis of half her body. I
would sometimes see Pat, in this first year after her stroke, sitting
alone in the corridor, or in the patients' dayroom, bereft of speech,
surrounded by a sort of penumbra of silence, with a stricken and
desolate look on her face.

But, a year later, I found Pat much improved. She was able to understand language better, and she could communicate better —
not by speech but by eloquent gesture and pointing. She indicated, for example, fluttering a couple of tickets, that she would go
to the movies if, and only if, a friend of hers could go too. Pat had
become less angry, more sociable, and very aware of all that was going on around her.

This represented an enormous social improvement — an improvement in the ability to communicate — but I was not sure how
much it rested on actual neurological improvement. Friends and
relatives of aphasic patients, indeed, often think that there is more
neurological recovery than there actually is, because many such
patients develop a remarkable compensatory heightening of other,
nonlinguistic powers and skills, especially the ability to "read" others' intentions and meanings from their facial expressions, vocal
inflections, and tone of voice, as well as all the gestures, postures,
and minute movements that normally accompany speech. Such
compensation may give surprising powers to aphasics — in particular, an enhanced ability to see through histrionic artifice, equivo-
cation, or lying. I described this in 1985, when I observed a group
of aphasic patients watching a presidential speech on television,
and, in 2000, Nancy Etcoff and her colleagues at Massachusetts
General Hospital published a study in *Nature* that showed that people with aphasia were in fact "significantly better at detecting lies
about emotion than people with no language impairment." Such
skills, they observed, apparently took time to develop, for they
were not evident in a patient who had been aphasic for only a few
months. This seemed to be the case with Pat, who had initially
been far from expert in picking up others' emotions and intentions but over the years had become preternaturally skillful at it. If
aphasics come to excel in understanding nonverbal language, they
can also become more expert in conveying their own thoughts in
the same way — and Pat was now starting to move toward a con-

scious and voluntary (and often inventive) representation of her thoughts and intentions by mime.

But while gesture and mime, lacking the grammar and syntax of real language, are not compromised in aphasia, they are not enough; they have only a limited ability to convey complex meanings and propositions (unlike a true sign language, such as congenitally deaf people use). These limitations often infuriated Pat, but a crucial change came when her speech pathologist, Jeannette Wilkens, discovered that, though Pat could not read aloud, and could not read a sentence, she could recognize individual words (and that, indeed, her vocabulary was quite extensive). Wilkens had found this with other aphasic patients as they started to recover, and had devised a sort of dictionary, a book of words arranged in categories of objects, people, and events, as well as moods and emotions. Pat always carried the book on her lap or near her, and would leaf through it rapidly with her left hand and point to the words she needed.

While such a book often worked when patients were closeted in one-on-one sessions with Wilkens, many of our aphasic patients had difficulty reaching out to others — were perhaps too shy, or too depressed, or too disabled from other medical conditions to initiate contact with other people. None of this was the case with Pat, who had been outgoing and social all her life: she boldly approached people, opened her book at the right page, thrust it at them, and pointed to the subject she wanted to talk about.

Pat's life expanded in all sorts of ways with her "bible," as her daughters call it. Soon she was able to guide a conversation in any direction she wanted, a conversation that was on her part accomplished solely by gesture and mime — and this had to be done primarily with her left arm, for her right side was still completely paralyzed. But, despite this limitation, gesture and mime, plus the verbal categories in her book, allowed her a remarkably full and exact expression of her needs and thoughts.

Inside the hospital, she became a node of gossip, despite being unable to communicate in the usual way. Even now, Pat calls her daughters "a hundred times a day," though the conversations are all passive on her part, awaiting questions to which she can answer "yes" (she communicates "yes" by kisses), "no," or "fine," or by noises of approbation, amusement, disapproval, etc.

By 1996, five years after her stroke, her receptive aphasia had almost disappeared — she was able to understand speech, though still unable to express herself in speech (she had certain fixed phrases, like "You're welcome!" or "Fine!," but could not name familiar objects or utter a sentence). She started to paint once again, using her left hand, and she was a terror at dominoes — her nonverbal representational systems were unimpaired. (It has long been understood that aphasia does not affect musical ability, visual imagery, or mechanical aptitude, and researchers at the University of Sheffield have shown recently that numerical reasoning and mathematical syntax can be entirely intact even in patients who are unable to understand or produce grammatical language.)

It is often said that after a stroke or a brain injury whatever recovery is possible will occur within twelve to eighteen months. While this may often be so, I have seen this generalization proved false in many individual patients. And in the past few decades neuroscience has shown what physicians have often observed: that, provided the initial damage is not too great, the brain has more powers of repair and regeneration than was formerly believed. There is, too, more "plasticity" — a greater capacity for undamaged brain areas to take over some of the functions of damaged ones. And, above all, there are powers of accommodation: finding new ways, or other ways, of doing things when the original way is no longer available — and here various forms of therapy, with a resourceful patient, can be of paramount importance. With Pat, even five years after her stroke I noted that she was still showing a steady (though now diminishing) improvement of her receptive powers, her ability to understand language.

(I knew another woman, Madeleine G., who had a crippling expressive aphasia, with very little recovery two years after her stroke — her physicians said then that she had "plateaued" — but who, five years after her stroke, could shop, speak to strangers, and hold her own in almost any conversation.)

Pat is the youngest of seven siblings; her extended family had always played a central part in her life, and this extended further still when Lari's daughter Alexa, Pat's first grandchild, was born in 1993. Alexa, said Lari, "was born into Beth Abraham." She would visit her grandmother frequently, and Pat always had a special toy or treat for her ("I don't know how she got these things," Lari mar-

veled). Pat would often ask Alexa to take crackers to a friend down
the hall who could not walk. Alexa and her two younger siblings,
Dean and Eve, are all fascinated by Pat, and like to call her often
on the phone when they cannot visit her. Lari feels that they have a
very active, very "normal" relationship with their grandmother, a
relationship that they all treasure.

One of the pages in Pat's book contained a list of emotional
states (she had picked these out from a word list prepared by the
speech pathologist). When I asked her, in 1998, what her predomi-
nant mood was, she pointed to "happy." There were other adjec-
tives on the mood page, such as "furious," "scared," "tired," "sick,"
"lonely," "sad," and "bored" — all of which she had indicated, on
occasion, in previous years.

In 1999, when I asked her the date, she pointed to "Wednesday,
July 28," a little miffed, perhaps, that I had insulted her with such a
simple question. She indicated, using her "bible," that she had
been, in the past few months, to half a dozen musicals and a couple of art galleries, and that, now that it was summer, she would
visit her daughter Lari on Long Island on the weekends and,
among other things, swim. "Swim?" I asked, incredulous. Yes, Pat
indicated; even with her right side paralyzed, she could still do the
sidestroke. She had been a great long-distance swimmer, she indicated, in her youth. She told me how excited she was that Lari
would be adopting a new baby in a few months. I was especially
struck, on this visit, eight years after her stroke, by the fullness and
richness of Pat's daily experiences, and her voracious love of life in
the face of what one might judge to be devastating brain damage.

In 2000, Pat showed me photos of her grandchildren. She had
visited them all the previous day, for the Fourth of July, and they
had watched the Tall Ships and the fireworks on television. She was
eager to show me the newspaper, with a picture of the Williams sisters playing tennis. Tennis, she indicated, had been one of her favorite sports too, along with skiing, riding, and swimming. She was
at pains to show me that her fingernails were manicured and
painted, and she was dressed in a sun hat and sunglasses, on her
way to sun herself on the hospital patio.

By 2002, Pat had become able to use a few spoken words. This
was achieved by the use of familiar songs like "Happy Birthday" or
"A Bicycle Built for Two," which she would sing along with Connie
Tomaino, Beth Abraham's music therapist. Pat was able to get the

feeling of the music, and some of the words. For a few minutes afterward, this would "release" her voice, and give her the ability to say some of the words, in a singsong fashion. She started carrying a tape recorder with a cassette of familiar songs, so she could get her language powers working. She demonstrated this with "Oh! What a Beautiful Morning," followed by a melodious "Good morning, Dr. Sacks," with a heavy, rhythmic emphasis on "morning."

Music therapy is invaluable for some patients with expressive aphasia, who, finding they can sing the words to a song, are reassured that language is not wholly lost, that they still have access to words somewhere inside them. The question is then whether the language capacities embedded in song can be removed from their musical context and used for communication. This is sometimes possible to a limited extent, by re-embedding words in a sort of improvised singsong.

But I sensed that Pat's heart was not in this — she felt that her real virtuosity lay in her mimetic powers, her appreciation and use of gesture. She had achieved a skill and intuitiveness here amounting almost to genius.

Mimesis, the deliberate and conscious representation of scenes, thoughts, feelings, intentions, etc., by mime and action, seems to be a specifically human achievement, like language (and perhaps music). Apes, which are able to "ape," or imitate, have little power to create conscious and deliberate mimetic representations.

In *Origins of the Modern Mind,* the psychologist Merlin Donald suggests that a "mimetic culture" may have been a crucial intermediate stage in human evolution between the "episodic" culture of apes and the "theoretic" culture of modern man. Mimesis has a much larger and more robust cerebral representation than language, and this may explain why it is so often preserved in patients who have lost language. It is this preservation that can make remarkably rich communication possible for people with aphasia, especially if it can be elaborated and heightened and combined, as in Pat's case, with a lexicon.

Pat has always had a passion to communicate ("This was a woman who talked twenty-four hours a day," Dana said), and it was the frustration of this loquacity that led to absolute fury when she first arrived at the hospital, and to her intense motivation and success in communicating now.

Pat's daughters are sometimes still amazed at her resilience.

"Why isn't she depressed," Dana said, "given her earlier history of depression? How could she live like this, I thought at first . . . I thought she would take a knife to herself." Every so often, her mother makes a gesture that seems to say, "My God, what happened? What is this? Why am I in this room?," as if the raw horror of her stroke had hit her once again. But Pat is aware that she has, in a sense, been very lucky, even though half of her body remains paralyzed. She was lucky that her brain damage, though extensive, did not undermine her force of mind or personality; lucky that her daughters fought so hard from the beginning to keep her engaged and active, and were able to afford extra aides and therapists; lucky, too, that she encountered a speech pathologist who observed her sensitively and minutely, and could provide her with a crucial tool, her "bible," which worked so well.

Pat continues to remain active and engaged with the world. She is, as Dana said, the "darling" of the family, and of the floor at the hospital, too. She has not lost the power to captivate people ("She has even captivated you, Dr. Sacks," Dana said), and she can even do a little painting with her left hand. She is grateful to be alive, and to be able to do as much as she can, and this, Dana thinks, is why her mood and morale have been so good.

Lari expressed herself in similar terms. "It's as if the negativity has been wiped away," she told me. "She is much more consistent, appreciative of her life and gifts . . . of other people, too. She is conscious of being privileged, but this makes her kinder, more thoughtful to other patients who may be physically less disabled than she is but much less 'adapted' or 'lucky' or 'happy.' She is the opposite of a victim," Lari concluded. "She actually feels that she has been blessed."

Last November, on a cool Saturday afternoon, I joined Pat and Dana in one of Pat's favorite activities — shopping on Allerton Avenue, near the hospital. We arrived in Pat's room — it was overflowing with plants, paintings, photos and posters, theater programs — and Pat was awaiting us, already wearing a favorite coat.

As we went up Allerton Avenue, bustling on a weekend afternoon, I saw that half the shopkeepers knew Pat, and shouted "Hi, Pat!" as she bowled past in her wheelchair. She waved at the young woman in the health-food store where she buys her carrot juice, and received a "Hi, Pat!" back. She waved to a Korean woman at the dry cleaner's, blew a kiss, and had a kiss blown back. The woman's sister, Pat was able to indicate to me, used to work in the fruit store.

We entered a shoe shop, where Pat's desires were very clear — she wanted a boot, with fur inside, for the upcoming winter. "Zip or Velcro?" Dana inquired. Pat indicated no preference, but wheeled herself in front of the boot display and then, with great decisiveness, pointed to the boots she wanted. Dana said, "But they have laces!" Pat smiled and shrugged, meaning, "So what! Someone else will tie them." She is not without vanity — the boots must be elegant as well as warm. ("Velcro, indeed!" her expression said.) "What size? A nine?" Dana asked. No, Pat gestured, bisecting her finger, an eight and a half.

We stopped by the supermarket, where she always picks up a few things for herself and for others at the hospital. Pat knew every aisle, and quickly picked two ripe mangoes for herself, a large bunch of bananas (most, she indicated, she would give away), some small doughnuts, and, at the checkout, three bags of candy. (She indicated that these were for the children of an orderly on her floor.)

As we moved on, laden with our purchases, Dana asked me where I had been earlier in the day. I said I had been to a fern meeting, adding, "I'm a plant person." Pat, overhearing, made a wide gesture, and pointed to herself, meaning, "You and I. We are both plant persons."

"Nothing has changed since her stroke," Dana said. "She has all her old loves and passions . . . The only thing is," she added, smiling, "she has become a pain in the neck!" Pat laughed, agreeing with this.

We stopped at a coffee shop. Pat clearly had no difficulty with the menu, indicating that she wanted not home fries but french fries, with whole wheat toast. After the meal, Pat carefully applied lipstick. ("How vain!" Dana exclaimed with admiration.) Dana wondered whether she could take her mother on a cruise. I mentioned the giant cruise ships I had seen go in and out of Curaçao, and Pat, intrigued, inquired with her book whether they set out from New York. I tried to draw a ship in my notebook; Pat laughed, and, left-handed, did a much better one.

PETER SELGIN

Confessions of a
Left-Handed Man

FROM THE LITERARY REVIEW

THE DOG THAT MAULED ME was a black Labrador retriever belonging to a woman I'll call Miss Leachman, who owned a condominium in Westchester. In exchange for using her apartment, from which we would commute to the city, my songwriting partner, Mark (who shared his surname with a twenty-mule-team soap product), and I agreed to water Miss Leachman's plants and take care of Gus, her dog, a stray she had taken in from the street. We were both in our early twenties, and broke.

We'd been there less than a week when, one night when I got up to go to the bathroom, Gus sat in the hallway, blocking my way, baring his teeth and growling. Miss Leachman had instructed us to wave Gus's choke collar at him if he should "get out of hand." The choke collar hung from a hook in the kitchen; to get to it, I had to get past the dog. I made my move. Gus lunged. His jaws went straight for my wrist, the left one.

Luckily Mark was there to hear my cries. He threw a dining room chair at Gus, who finally let go and whimpered away. My torn, bleeding wrist wrapped in a towel, I rode with Mark in his rusting canary-yellow Volkswagen Squareback to the local emergency room. It was a few weeks before Christmas. I remember passing under strung colored lights and thinking to myself what pretty colors, that they should string colored lights like that everywhere, always.

I'm left-handed, mostly. I write with my left hand. I draw with my left hand. I tend to pick up things with my left hand. Like most left-handers I can't tell my left from my right, and tend to flip through magazines backward. The tasks that most define me I've always done with my left hand.

There are lots of myths about left-handedness, myths that tell me, for instance, that I'm eccentric and artistic, that I'm more accident-prone, more subject to autoimmune diseases, more likely to suffer from depression and/or to commit suicide, and likely to die sooner than my right-handed counterparts. And though most if not all of these myths have been scientifically put to bed, still I have a hard time arguing with some of them, since I am an artist; I am accident-prone (case in point: getting mauled by a black Labrador); I have suffered from at least one autoimmune disease (a bout of ulcerative colitis, in my thirties); and I have been, if not suicidal, then suicidally depressed.

Coincidences, I'm sure.

My fraternal twin is right-handed. Although George and I aren't identical, until we were sixteen people couldn't tell us apart. They'd lump us together as "the Selgin boys," as if there were no point trying. Unlike the twins in the Doublemint chewing gum commercials, we didn't walk around dressed alike with tennis rackets slung over our shoulders and big grins on our faces. Our relationship was more like open combat. To this day I have a recurrent nightmare about our fights. In the nightmare, I'm on the ground surrounded by people pointing and laughing as I sit there covered in grass, dirt, blood, and tears. Presumably my brother and I have just finished putting on one of our very popular, Spartacus-like displays, though in the dream George is nowhere to be seen. The inescapable Freudian implication being that I've just beaten the crap out of myself.

George and I grasped at anything we could to set ourselves apart from each other. Since he was astigmatic and had to wear glasses, George became the bookworm, while I seized upon my left-handedness as my most distinguishing trait, in spite of my grandmother doing her damnedest to fix what she saw as a freak of nature, or at best a nasty habit, like picking your nose.

Nonnie had her own apartment tucked away in the back of our Connecticut home, a single small room with a hot plate and a refrigerator. It was its own little world, with its own smells, its own sounds, its own stains, its own dust. To get me to write with my right hand, Nonnie would bribe me with bowls of her homemade rice pudding, the best in the world, topped with a fetching swirl of raspberry syrup and half a maraschino cherry (eventually I'd learn that the "homemade" rice pudding had its source in a can marked "Comstock"). She'd sit me down at her doilied card table with a pencil and paper and feed me Italian phrases to transcribe, saying over and over to me, "*A destra, Piero, a destra!,*" giving my left hand a slap when I'd reach for the pencil or my rice-pudding spoon with it. Nonnie called me *il Mancino* — the left-handed one.

I can't blame my grandmother. She was only following a time-honored tradition, one as old as the prejudice against left-handedness itself, a prejudice stretching as far back as the ancient Greeks, who posted sentries at their temples to make sure those who entered did so right foot first, so as not to offend the gods. Centuries later the Catholics took things a step further, burning their left-handers as witches at the stake. In Victorian times left-handed children would have their left hands strapped behind their backs by means of a ghoulish leather straitjacket-like device. It wasn't unusual for schoolmarms and headmasters to cane pupils for using their "other" hand. To cure their children of left-handedness, the Zulus of southern Africa would plunge a child's left hand into a hole dug in the ground and filled with boiling water, scalding it so severely the child was forced to switch hands.

Luckily for me, my grandmother wasn't a Zulu. Still, when my mother found out what she was up to, she threw a tantrum. I stood by Nonnie's door listening to Mom's Italian curses bounce off her four dusty walls.

My mother needn't have bothered, since I had no intention of betraying my left hand, except to the extent that it would win me an occasional bowl of phony homemade rice pudding. To have done so would have been to surrender the one part of myself that kept me from being George, who, despite having been born first, was, I'd concluded, nothing but a cheap knockoff of me, the original. Like the polymer security thread embedded in our paper money, my left-handedness was proof of my authenticity. No one, not even a Zulu, could or would ever take it away from me.

The emergency room doctor who stitched up my wounds said I might want to visit a neurologist to find out whether there was any nerve damage.

A week after the stitches came out, I did so. I couldn't wiggle my thumb; otherwise everything seemed normal. The hand specialist I saw — I'll call him Dr. Chiu — had his office in Manhattan, in the lower Thirties near First Avenue. I arrived there on a windy, post-Christmas Wednesday afternoon. One wall of the waiting room featured a big poster of a human hand, splayed open to show its hidden circuitry: a bewildering network of red and blue arteries and veins, yellow and purple nerves, green tendons, clay-colored muscles, and layers of golden fat. It looked like a New York highway map, around where the Grand Central Parkway meets the Long Island Expressway. It was, I noted with some dismay, a right hand.

Around me, sitting in the waiting room, were all kinds of people with things wrong with their hands. The guy next to me was about fifty. He wore a green corduroy jacket and had his right hand wrapped in a clear plastic bag, like a sandwich. Across from me, the right hand of a teenager wearing a New York Jets jersey was splinted and bound and lay draped over his thigh like a dead albino reptile. Standing in the corner by the receptionist's desk was a tall, thin woman with a blond bob that looked like a novelty-store wig. Her arm was in a sling — her right arm. I was the only person in the waiting room with something wrong with his left hand. I flashed on a world in which people were divided not by color, religion, or sex, but by left and right, with signs on doors, shop windows, and drinking fountains saying RIGHTS ONLY.

Someone tapped my shoulder.

"Mr. Selgin? Dr. Chiu will see you now."

The nurse escorted me to a small room and told me to sit down and push up both sleeves of the white turtleneck I wore. Using a series of electrodes terminating in clear plastic suction cups, she connected both of my hands to a machine the size of a toaster oven, with an ovoid central screen surrounded by dials and meters.

Minutes later Dr. Chiu entered, a small man with a goatee. He looked like Dr. Rey in van Gogh's famous portrait. He handed me a rubber-coated tube with a long curled cord connected to the voltaic box. On his command I squeezed the tube as hard as I could with my left hand. Dr. Chiu murmured something and made a note on his clipboard. He had me do the same thing with my right hand, then murmured something else and jotted another note. Then the left again, then the right. Throughout the test Dr. Chiu kept nodding and saying "Ah-ha," "Urm," or "Hmm."

Afterward the doctor did another test with a different machine. This time, instead of suction cups, the device and I were united by a series of long, fine needles, which Dr. Chiu, with gentle gyrating motions, inserted into various muscles of my left hand. It wasn't painful; all I felt was a slight electrical tingle. But the sight of my left hand run through with a dozen needles, like a voodoo doll, distressed me. It took all my self-control for me not to tear the needles out and run screaming from the room.

Finished, Dr. Chiu lowered his clipboard, sat down next to me with his knee touching mine, and spoke of the motor component of the ulnar nerve, fourth-degree damage, the epineurial covering, disruption of something or other and the blood-nerve barrier, and how conductivity was no longer possible.

I didn't have to ask Dr. Chiu what the hell all that meant. Obviously my hand was very fucked up.

Dr. Chiu recommended surgery. He happened to be a microsurgeon. "Of course," he said, "I cannot guarantee anything."

"Of course," I replied.

In high school I was one of the few (four, to be exact) honorary members of the Pthweep Club. Though the origin of the club's weird name escapes me, I still remember the requirements for admission. They were:

a) having the first name Peter
b) a surname starting with *S*
c) brown eyes
d) curly hair
e) artistic inclinations
f) being left-handed

What became of Peter Smith, Peter Sloat, and Peter Scalzo, my fellow Pthweeps, I have no idea; I was never all that close to them. Still, I was glad to belong to a club, especially one that excluded my brother.

Poor George. By then I really had it in for him. It wasn't enough to distinguish myself from him; I wanted him out of the picture entirely. My plan was simple. I would outshine him so thoroughly he would vanish under the glare of my brighter light. I parlayed my drawing skill into a means of winning friends and influencing enemies, doing swift, devastating likenesses of teachers and fellow students that I'd tape to lockers and otherwise disseminate. That left hand of mine could draw like nobody's business. In time I'd train it, like a prize hunting dog — a black Labrador, if you like — to run out and fetch me anything in the form of a rendering. My brother drew too. But I paraded my skill shamelessly, making it known that I, not George, was the artist. To further increase my wattage, I auditioned for and got leads in plays. When George and I both tried out for *West Side Story,* I got cast as Tony, the lead, while George got stuck playing a Shark.

But artistic triumphs weren't enough. I had to best George in all areas (except academics, where, being the bookworm, he outclassed me). If George got a girlfriend, I got a better one. When he got a spiffy car ('65 Barracuda, bronze, stargazing rear window), I bought a spiffier one, an MG convertible. I added wire wheels and painted it bright red.

Was it a coincidence that I, the left-hander, turned out to be the evil, sinister one? Cain to my brother's Abel?

After high school I spent a year driving trucks and moving furniture for Ethan Allen, then did my perfunctory tour of Europe. On returning I went to art school in Brooklyn, where the sooty atmosphere of the drawing studios depressed me. I hated charcoal. My fellow art students thought me arrogant and disturbed. I can't see why, unless it was that time I suspended myself by one arm from a balcony railing at a campus party. The apartment was in a highrise, the balcony on the eleventh floor. I never saw a party clear out so fast. Afterward I claimed that I was drunk. I wasn't; I just longed for attention. The imperative to upstage my twin had mutated into a desire to upstage everyone. Need I point out that the hand with which I clung to my life was my left one?

In February, days before my twenty-fourth birthday, Dr. Chiu operated. I was under the knife for six hours. I awoke in my bed at Cabrini Medical Center to find my prior roommate, an elderly Hispanic with a green eye patch, gone, replaced by a man who looked like the Pillsbury Doughboy, whose name was Gunther, and who'd survived the bombing of Dresden.

Gunther's first words to me were "Don't move it."

"It" was my left hand, which, after I blinked a couple of times and it came into focus, looked in its heavy white wrappings like a beached beluga whale. Gunther asked me if I was left-handed. I nodded. He shook his head and smiled. Gunther had a strange bloated face, as if all the muscles in it had been turned into fat deposits. But then, I was still delirious.

Gunther must have seen that I was queasy. He picked up the hospital menu and recited it to me with his thick German accent.

"Ledz zee now, Beeder," he said. "Vhut zounds gut fuh dinnah? Jicken zalad, zliced beeds, gole zlaw, aw de peas 'n' garots?"

It worked. I lurched over the side of the bed and threw up.

Don't get me wrong. I wasn't obsessed with being left-handed. I wasn't one of those left-handers who goes around claiming Leonardo da Vinci as his ancestor, and Einstein too, the implication being that we left-handers are all born geniuses and renaissance men (in fact, both men were probably ambidextrous). Nor did I take umbrage or solace in having this little something in common with Ben Franklin, Alexander the Great, Harpo Marx, Ringo Starr, Julius Caesar, Ty Cobb, Napoleon, Betty Grable, W. C. Fields, the Boston Strangler, and Jimi Hendrix (Presidents Ford, Reagan, Bush, and Clinton were yet to come).

I wasn't the sort of left-hander who cries "Foul!" whenever he's confronted by a pair of right-handed scissors, or pants with no back pocket on the left side. I didn't lose any sleep over knowing that, because I was left-handed, the writing on my pencil faced away from me when I wrote; or that 99 percent of all boomerangs manufactured in the world were useless if not lethal to me; or that, should I ever have to carry a bicycle, I'd have to do so on my right shoulder, because if I carried it on my left (as I'd be inclined to do), I'd get grease stains all over my clothes; or that, discharged by me, a semiautomatic weapon would tend to blow its hot casings past my left cheek, possibly resulting in second- or third-degree burns. None of these things bothered me very much. Even spiral notebooks caused me little concern, despite the fact that the spirals interfered with my handwriting every time I'd start on a fresh front-sided page.

Not that I wasn't fond of my left hand. I was; I still am. You might say I'm attached to it. It is (after all) the hand that launched a hundred rock-embedded dirtballs at my twin's skull. It's the hand that split open Bobby Mullin's lip after enduring months of faceslappings at the bus stop for admitting that I didn't believe in God. It is the very hand with which I brought myself to my first bewildering orgasm, and with which, a few years later, I would reach deep into my junior high school girlfriend's Levi's and bring her to her first bewildering orgasm. With it I would sketch hundreds of illicit and highly unflattering caricatures, a skill closer to archery than draftsmanship and one requiring tremendous dexterity — an odd choice of words, considering. This hand of mine could draw the sinking *Titanic* like nobody's business (it did a fair *Lusitania,* too).

Soon after Gunther got me to throw up, Dr. Chiu dropped by. He explained that, as he had expected, the nerve had not been "transected," but that a layer of "scar and neuromic tissue" had built up around the affected area, putting pressure on the myelin sheath and "preventing conduction." He said he had done his best to scrape the scar tissue away, but warned me that it might grow back.

"We'll just have to wait and see," he said.

My right-handed twin having taken the straight, narrow path to academe, I, being left-handed, did the opposite, switching schools and interests as often as most people change their oil. After quitting art school, I bummed around. I would have joined the Air Force but for my mortal fear of discipline. Instead, I hitchhiked. On my way nowhere I met George at his undergraduate school, where we got into a fight over a pen he claimed I'd stolen. George collected fountain pens, antique ones. He had at least fifty. The one I took didn't look that expensive; the nib wasn't even gold. Of course, I denied it. He called me a "moocher" and a "libertine" — words I looked up later. I called him a greedy capitalist, or something like that. He said, "Hit the road, shithead," and I did, crossing the dusky campus with tears in my eyes and without saying goodbye, but not before quietly slipping the pen back into my brother's desk drawer.

Then a year at Bard College, on the Hudson River, reading Joyce and spending way too much time doing sit-ups and sunning myself on the quad green, forgetting that my leisure cost me and my folks the then astronomical sum of $8,000 a year. Genius didn't come cheap. When a then twenty-five-year-old Leon Botstein refused to give me a full scholarship, I quit Bard and returned to New York, where I tried my luck in the theater again, and went straight nowhere. A failed foray in Hollywood brought me back, by way of a series of increasingly seedy, low-budget movie jobs, to Connecticut, where I met my future songwriting partner Mark, who taught me how to play guitar and write songs, and with whom I'd go in on a fateful Westchester housesit.

An hour after my brief visit with Dr. Chiu, with my left hand still paralyzed and swaddled in surgical gauze, and my head still groggy from anesthesia, I was discharged from the hospital into the bright light of a winter afternoon. The remnants of snow from a blizzard the week before lay in stained, crusty patches along the sidewalks and gutters, and the low-angled sun blazed off car hoods and windshields. With nowhere to go I wandered the city, feeling the eyes of its myriad windows looking down on and judging me, condemning me, me and my left hand — punished, at last, for our sins. The job that my grandmother and her rice pudding had started years before, God and a black Labrador named Gus had finished. My left-handed days were over. It was time to straighten up and fly right.

Since Mark and I had nowhere else to go, Mr. Hernandez, the manager of the copy shop where we worked, let us sleep on the industrial carpeting next to the hulking Xerox machines. With my left hand out of service, I was reduced to making copies a page at a time, and thus useless as an employee. After a week of this charade Mr. Hernandez said he was sorry, but he'd have to let me go. I couldn't blame him.

Seeing my bandaged left hand, the clerk at unemployment asked me if I was left-handed. I said I was. She said if I couldn't work, I couldn't get unemployment benefits. I asked, What about disability? She said it would be three months before I'd get a check. I said by then I'd be able to work. She said in that case I wasn't qualified for disability, either.

The rehab nurse told me to rub Vaseline Intensive Care lotion into my scar. "You should massage slowly, in circles, like so," she said, looking into my eyes as her fingertips worked the semen-like unguent into my palm and wrist. "You can ask your girlfriend to do this part for you."

"What if I don't have a girlfriend?" I said.

She handed me a ball of yellow-green putty and told me to squeeze it every day. "Like this," she said, showing me.

A month after my surgery I met again with Dr. Chiu, who hooked me up to his machines. The results were gloomy. The nerve showed no signs of renewed life, and already there was evidence of atrophy in the muscles of my left hand. The operation had failed. With luck and practice I might regain 50 to 75 percent of the use of my hand.

"Will I be able to draw again?" I asked.

"That depends," said Dr. Chiu, "on your artistic standards."

I began giving serious thought to my right-handed future, wondering if it was too late for me to go to law school or become an accountant. Maybe I'd go back to moving furniture for Ethan Allen. Or maybe, I thought in one of my more romantic moods, I'd get a job down at the Fulton Fish Market, unloading crates of ice-packed fish from the backs of three A.M. trucks. I pictured myself among fishmongers in plaid coats, warming gloved fingers over an oil-drum fire, Leonard Bernstein's music for *On the Waterfront* swelling in my head.

In March Mark left New York. A country boy by nature, he couldn't stand life in the city. The air infected his sinuses and gave him miserable headaches, and besides, our dream of becoming the next Simon and Garfunkel was ashes, and we both knew it. Even if I could somehow learn to play the guitar again, which was doubtful, it wouldn't matter; I'd lost heart.

I tried drawing with my right hand, but it was like trying to sing with my fingers holding my tongue, or run with my legs tied together. I couldn't be right-handed any more than the earth could spin the other way on its axis. But I couldn't be left-handed, either.

The week after Mark left, walking down the ill-lit and loosely treaded stairs of the Gramercy Park Hotel, where I'd taken a room the size of a closet, I tripped and broke my leg. I spent the next three weeks hobbling around the city, the leg in a cast and my hand and arm still wrapped to my elbow.

One night, still on crutches, I hobbled to the East River, to where, in my wanderings the day of my release from Cabrini, I had located a breach in a chainlink fence. It was still March, and there'd been another big snowstorm. Huge floes floated like the ghosts of ships over the black water. I made my way out to the end of a pier, my crutch tips breaking through the rotted wood every dozen or so yards, to where I stood looking out across the water, at the lights of Brooklyn shattered in inky waves. It wasn't the first time I'd thought of killing myself, but other times I'd done so only in passing, and never with the opportunity so conveniently at hand. As I leaned forward on my crutches, I knew that with an arm and a leg out of whack and winter boots on and the water freezing, even a strong swimmer like me would be done for in a matter of minutes. It was more than tempting; it seemed preordained, a fitting end to a wrong-headed, left-handed life.

My mind flashed a photo of me and my brother, the Selgin boys, topsy-turvy on the front lawn with curly heads touching and big smiles, one of those corny photo ops parents of twins must always insist on, taken in the years before the edict to wipe each other out was issued. I looked up at the clouds sweeping the night sky, pulled back from the brink, had a good cry, and hobbled back to my hotel room.

In the end I decided to sue Miss Leachman. I had no choice. I owed more than $10,000 to Cabrini and Dr. Chiu. The case would drag on for years, with Miss Leachman's lawyers deposing my high school music and art teachers to see if I'd really had any talent. Finally the insurance company settled, but only after the jurors had been sworn in. My lawyer, a woman not that much older than I, urged me to hold out for more. But I wasn't feeling greedy, and said so. I never saw a more disgusted look cross a lawyer's face.

Within two years after my surgery, the surviving muscles in my left hand rallied, taking the place of the ones that had died. With practice I was able to write left-handed again, albeit in a craggy, childlike scrawl that gave way quickly to cramps and that I alone could decipher. Eventually I found myself drawing too, tentatively at first, crude sketches devoid of facility, let alone glibness. But then I realized: facility wasn't everything. In fact, it was very little. Under what had been slick surfaces I uncovered hidden depths.

Twenty-five years have passed since Gruesome Gus's incisors tore into my left wrist. Much has changed since then. I no longer see my left-handedness as a means to prove anything to anyone, myself included . . . Nor do I see it as a way to eclipse my brother, a professor of economics at the University of Georgia, with whom I now get along very well.

I no longer feel blessed or cursed by being left-handed; it's simply the hand that I happen to use. Still, it's been a faithful servant, this left upper limb, and through thick and thin I'm glad I've stuck with it. However much we've both changed, my left hand and I are happily reunited.

And though I now earn my living as a painter and illustrator, my work has nothing in common with what I used to do before. For better or worse, my drawings have turned naive, even primitive. My lack of dexterity has freed me from glibness, which in turn has delivered me from the temptation to show off. For the artist, to master humility is as important as mastering perspective or a graceful line. The hand grasps the instrument, but if we're lucky the heart guides it, not the brain or the ego.

On the ceiling of the Sistine Chapel in Rome, in the central panel of the most famous painting by that other Renaissance lefty, God, floating on a cloud of purple silk, bestows life on the first man, Adam, through the fingertip of his right hand. Adam, however, who has been created in God's image, accepts the gift with his *left* hand. Michelangelo knew what he was doing. According to the Roman poet Isidorus, a secret blood vessel runs directly from the index finger of the left hand to the human heart — the heart, not the brain. God wished to bypass the intellect and launch his spark straight into the heart of man, who reaches out to lend Him a hand. The left one.

It was good enough for Adam, and it's good enough for me.

ALAN SHAPIRO

Why Write?

FROM THE CINCINNATI REVIEW

SOME YEARS AGO, I went to a child psychologist. (If Henny
Youngman had written this opening sentence, he would have
added: "The kid didn't do a thing for me." But I digress.) The
child psychologist I went to had recently tested one of my children
for attention deficit disorder. When the results came back positive,
he called me and my not-yet-ex-wife to suggest that we be tested
too. There may be a genetic component to ADD, he said, and taking the test would not only reveal the extent to which we ourselves
suffered from this condition, but also enable us to better understand our child.

So we took the test. Turns out it's the only test I ever aced. As the
doctor put it, in my case, the results were salient.

"So, I'm ADD," I said. "What does that mean?"

"Well," he said, "according to the test, your ADD manifests itself
in three ways. You have trouble starting tasks. You have trouble
staying on task. And you have trouble finishing tasks."

"That pretty much covers it," I said. "But how do you explain the
fact that I've written a number of books, and even today I spent several hours puzzling over a single sentence in a translation I'm doing of a Greek tragedy?"

He explained that it's not that people with ADD can't concentrate on things they want to do, it's that they lack the ability to concentrate on anything that bores them. People with ADD have no
tolerance for boredom. When I pointed out that I'd been teaching
for over twenty-five years and seldom read a student paper that
didn't make me want to drive an ice pick through my skull just to

relieve the boredom but that I nonetheless returned each and every student paper in a timely fashion (even the ones I bothered to read — just kidding!), my soon-to-be-ex-wife interjected, "But Alan, you can't remember the name of anyone you meet at a party."

"Sweetheart," I said, "that's called a greeting disorder."

"And," she continued, "even if I give you a list of groceries, you come home with the wrong things . . . red peppers instead of tomatoes, bananas instead of squash."

"That's called being a guy," I said.

"And you don't hear five percent of what I tell you."

"That's called marriage."

She wasn't amused.

Sensing the tension, the doctor asked, "So what do you think you want to do about this? How do we proceed?"

"With the ADD or with the marriage?"

Now it was his turn not to be amused. He went on to describe the kinds of medications I could take, but then said he wasn't suggesting I do anything if I didn't think I was a problem to myself: "People who grew up before this condition was named or treated have often found ingenious ways to compensate for their disabilities." Writing, for me, he said, was a prime example of what he called "compensatory behavior."

"Let me get this straight," I said. "I write books in order to make up for my inability to remember the names of the people I meet at a party, or because I come home from the grocery store with a red pepper instead of a tomato?"

"Well, not exactly," he said, but before he could explain exactly what he meant, the hour was up.

I don't know, maybe I was a tad defensive with the psychologist — you think? — and even a little miffed by his reduction of the art I love and have devoted my life to for the better part of almost forty years to a side effect of a neurological condition. At the same time, telling the story over, I can't help but ask myself, "Why do I write?" Is writing a compensation for psychological, emotional, or even neurological deficits? Do we write, as the old saying goes, because we can't *do*? Is art, as Freud believed, a kind of socially acceptable wish fulfillment for asocial infantile desires? A way of finding in imagination what we have lost in life? A sublimation of sexual energy? A way of transmuting our hidden wishes or shameful secrets, our failures and losses and humiliations, into beautiful objects that win us wealth and admiration and all the sexual fulfillment that we put off in order to do the work in the first place? Why else get into the poetry racket? That I could ask this question even in jest, much less attempt to make my way in the world by writing poetry, is yet another manifestation of an abiding suspicion I've had for many years now — that God put me on earth to disprove the stereotype that all Jews make money.

I once asked a very talented student of mine why she wanted to become a writer. "Fame," she said. "I want to be famous." And what did fame mean to her? It meant being able to check into the penthouse suite of a five-star hotel and totally trash the room and then be loved for it. This quintessentially American, celebrity-driven fantasy is just the self-indulgent flip side of an older, time-honored, messianic fantasy of the writer as unacknowledged cultural legislator. Seamus Heaney has written that poetry or great writing of any kind provides a culture with images adequate to its predicament. Who hasn't dreamed of providing everyone with images adequate to their predicament and being loved for it, and maybe even given loads of cash? When we're in our teens and early twenties, maybe we all dream of becoming celebrated shamans of the heart, but that adolescent daydream doesn't begin to explain why we continue writing after the age of twenty-five or thirty, once we realize that the world isn't exactly rushing out to take its marching orders from anything we've written.

I think of my dear friend Tim Dekin, a wonderful poet who died a few years ago at the age of fifty-eight, of pulmonary fibrosis. Tim's second full-length book, *Another Day on Earth,* was published posthumously in 2002 by TriQuarterly Books. Tim and I met at Stanford in 1975. Eventually, we both ended up teaching in the Chicago area. He was a brilliant talker and a very funny man who lost many years of his writing life to alcoholism. He held down a series of demanding, low-paying jobs teaching freshman comp at various universities. After years of struggling unsuccessfully to find a publisher for his poetry, he wrote three very good novels that he likewise couldn't publish. In his last year of life, he returned to his first love, poetry, and finished his magnificent book. Tethered to his oxygen machine, he drove from Chicago to Chapel Hill not long before he died so he and I could go over his new poems and put the manuscript together. My brother had just died, and I had broken up with my wife and was living in a basement apartment. Neither Tim nor I was in very good shape at the time, physically or otherwise.

During that visit, I told Tim a joke that a musician friend of mine had told me about the four stages in a musician's career. The first stage is "Who is Richard Luby?" The second stage is "Get me Richard Luby." The third stage is "Get me a young Richard Luby!" And the fourth stage is "Who is Richard Luby?" Tim laughed at the joke, then added ruefully, "I seemed to have passed from stage one to stage four without ever having passed through stages two and three."

I cherish the memory of those few days with Tim, and I love the image of us in my dreary digs, Tim's poems spread out on the coffee table, Tim puffing on the oxygen tube the way he puffed on the forbidden cigars he still occasionally smoked, leaning over the poems, reading out passages, discussing them, rewriting them, the two of us beset with troubles but working rapturously nonetheless, throughout the day and long into the night. What exactly were we doing? What lack were we trying to fill? What were we compensating for? Whatever it was, fame and fortune had absolutely nothing to do with it.

Which is not to say I don't desire fame and fortune. I do. I do. I'm not above them. In fact, I'm so far beneath them that I'd even happily forget fame if I could have just a little fortune. When I take a good hard look at the life I've chosen, I have to wonder how I've stuck it out as long as I have. For there's a Grand Canyon's worth of difference between the literary life I dreamed of as an adolescent and the life I found once I began to publish and actually live what passes for a literary life.

I remember thinking in my teens and early twenties that if I could only publish a poem in a magazine, any magazine, I'd feel fulfilled and validated and wildly happy. And then I got my first publication. And I was happy for a day or so, until the bill arrived for the printing cost, and then I thought if I could only get a poem into a real journal, into a magazine that pays, I'd feel validated and happy, and when that happened, I began to feel the need to publish in the *Atlantic Monthly* or *The New Yorker,* a magazine that someone other than my fellow writers may have heard of, and eventually, when that happened, I believed that only publishing a book with a reputable press would make me feel as if I'd earned the right to call myself a poet. And then I published a book, and the resounding silence and inattention of the world (it's my books that suffer from attention deficit disorder, not me) made me feel that the only measure of my poetic worth would be to get a book reviewed somewhere by someone I didn't know, someone who wasn't related to me, and when that occurred, and pleased me, and the pleasure passed, I thought that only winning a big book award could quell this anxiety about my literary worth. I didn't realize how preoccupied I was with literary recognition till one day when I overheard my seven-year-old son negotiating with my five-year-old daughter over who got to hold the TV's remote control. He said, "Izzy, if you give me the controller, I'll give you a Pulitzer Prize." Anyway, eventually I did win a big award — not a Pulitzer, alas — and even then I found myself beset with all the same anxieties. I've been at this long enough to know that even if God Himself, the Lord Almighty, hallowed be His name, came down from heaven and gave me a big fat kiss on the back of the brain, I'd probably shrug it off: "What? That's it? For years you don't write, you don't call, and now all I get is a lousy kiss?"

Don't get me wrong. Acclaim of any kind is wonderful, except when it goes to someone else. But even at its best, that sort of "reward" or "recognition" is like cotton candy: it looks ample enough until you put it in your mouth; then it evaporates. All taste and no nourishment.

Then there's the thrill of dealing with editors. By way of illustration, let me tell you a story. In 1976, before I'd published anything, I wrote a long, windy poem called "Fathers and Sons." I sent it to the journal *Quarterly West.* The editor sent the poem back with a note suggesting I rewrite the middle two sections and resubmit it. I knew from watching the editors of *Sequoia,* the Stanford literary journal, that all editors are overworked and underpaid and can't possibly read everything that crosses their desks with keen attention. So I waited six months and sent the poem back unchanged, with a letter thanking the editor for his suggestions, all of which I said I took. I even said that if he didn't accept the poem, I was still in his debt, because his suggestions had made the poem new to me again and more like what I initially envisioned when I started writing it. Within days, I received a letter from the editor accepting the poem and commending me for my professionalism.

At the Bread Loaf Writers' Conference in 1997, I participated in a roundtable discussion. At the time, I was the editor of the University of Chicago's Phoenix Poets Series, and I told that story in order to make the point that writers need to treat what editors tell them with a healthy dose of skepticism. Don't presume editors are smart just because they are editors. They should have to earn their authority by reading what is sent them with intelligence and imagination, and in any case the writers ought always to be the ultimate arbiters of what they do. Editors, I said, are mostly obstacles to get around. I returned to Bread Loaf two years later, and one of the students there stopped to thank me for my advice back in 1997. He said he followed it, and it worked like a charm.

"What do you mean?" I asked. "What advice?"

"Well, I got a poem back from *Boulevard,* and the editor suggested I do a major rewrite. So I waited six months like you said and sent it back with a letter thanking him for his time and help, and he accepted the poem."

The moral of this story isn't that editors are fools, though some are. The moral isn't that you should con your way into print, though if you do, more power to you. Rather, the moral is you needn't listen to everything an editor tells you. The moral is you need to be cynical about publishing in order not to be cynical about writing, in order to protect and preserve the deeply private joy of doing the work itself (I'll say more about that private joy in a moment). I know it's hard, sometimes impossible, to keep the po biz out of the poetry, to keep the anxieties and injustices of trying to publish from contaminating your relationship to what you do. It's hard to find the proper balance between the arrogance we need to keep on writing — the arrogance that assumes we have something worth saying, and we're smart enough to learn what someone's smart enough to teach us — and the humility we also need in order to grow and develop, the humility that knows we cannot nurture and refine our gifts without the help of others, that other people, including editors, can sometimes tell us things we need to hear. Too much arrogance and not enough humility and we close ourselves off from the world; nothing new comes in, and we eventually become imitators of ourselves, turning what at one time were discoveries into mannerisms. Too much humility and not enough arrogance and we lose our center of gravity, finding ourselves at the mercy of everyone else's opinion. Striking the right balance between humility and arrogance is another exhausting and often frustrating aspect of the writing life.

Then there's the frustration that surrounds the work itself, the work we've already done and the work we want to do. The dissatisfactions we often feel toward older work, not to mention the frustrations we often feel about what we're writing now, as well as the anxieties over what we may do next, put me in mind of the old joke about the Jew who's shipwrecked on a desert island. Twenty years later, he's discovered, but before he leaves, he wants to show his saviors the three synagogues he's built: "Over there," he says, "is the synagogue I used to go to. Over there's the synagogue I go to now. And over there, that synagogue, I wouldn't set foot in." I know this is really a joke about class and status and the need to feel superior to something. But I do think the more we refine our abilities, the more embarrassing our older work becomes. That is, if we're truly lucky, we'll despise our early work. If we're lucky, we'll feel as if nearly everything but what we're writing now was written by someone we'd rather not be seen in public with. And if we're lucky, what we're writing now won't compare with what we'll write ten years from now. That's the price we pay for getting better. The problem is, the better we get at writing, the better we get at imagining getting even better. So the discrepancy between the writer one is and the writer one wants to be only widens as one improves. To flourish as an artist requires a tolerance for frustration, inadequacy, and a deepening sense of failure.

And as if that weren't bad enough, let's consider the effect of what we write on those we write about, especially those closest to us. Over the years, I learned the hard way that no one wants to give up narrative control over his or her life. People have a right not to be written about. Yet I violate that right in nearly everything I've written. I've done it in the writing of this essay. My theory's always been that if I only try to tell the truth, if I have no ax to grind and write about others in a spirit of forgiveness, curiosity, and understanding, then no one should be upset by anything I say. Well, so much for theory. Even the most affectionate portrait of a loved one, the most intimate praise (never mind depictions of estrangement or disaffection), can and will offend. In 1996 I published a book of personal essays. My mother called to congratulate me. "Have you heard from anybody about the book?" she asked.

"Only my shrink," I joked. "He's upset that I've gone public with stories I should have only shared with him. He's threatening to sue me, Ma!"

"That's ridiculous," she said, not joking. "If anyone's going to sue you over this book, it's me."

But even if we never write about our families, there's still the often painful fallout on them from the dedication, time, and solitude that the art requires. I don't want to suggest, even for a moment, that artistic success depends on domestic instability, or that there's any correlation between art and suffering. One doesn't have to have a tortured soul to become a writer. Or rather, our souls don't have to be tortured any more than most people's souls are tortured. Catastrophe or self-destructiveness is no prerequisite for the position. Nor need one be a drunk, a womanizer, or a victim of abuse. If bad behavior or bad luck were essential ingredients of a writing life, our detox centers, prisons, and twelve-step programs would be full of writers. All one has to do to be a writer is to write. We're writers only when we're writing. In other words, it's an activity; it's something we do, not something we are. When we're not writing, each of us is just another poor slob trying to get through the day without hurting anyone too much. That said, let's also recognize that many of us live within rather stringent economies of energy, and to do this is not to do that. With jobs, kids, and relationships, it's impossible to balance the competing claims of life and art without slighting one in favor of the other. I should add too that the muse is an especially demanding and jealous mistress, and most of us, when we're not writing, wish we were. It may be that even if I were a shepherd or a proctologist, I'd be just as troubled as I've often been throughout my life, struggling to satisfy both my need to work and my need to love. Maybe, but I doubt it. The fact is, like most writers, I've been and continue to be monomaniacal about putting in my hours at the desk. And that dedication to work has sometimes proven lethal to my loves and friendships.

So the work itself always entails frustration and failure; it can damage our most intimate relationships; its public rewards are illu-

sory at worst, fleeting at best. And if you write poetry, hardly anyone is listening. So why do it?

Elizabeth Bishop provides a possible answer in a famous letter to
Anne Stevenson. Bishop writes that what we want from great art is
the same thing necessary for its creation, and that is a self-forgetful, perfectly useless concentration. We write, Bishop implies, for
the same reason we read or look at paintings or listen to music:
for the total immersion of the experience, the narrowing and
intensification of focus to the right here, right now, the deep joy of
bringing the entire soul to bear upon a single act of concentration.
It is self-forgetful even if you are writing about the self, because you
yourself have disappeared into the pleasure of making; your identity — the incessant, transient, noisy New York Stock Exchange of
desires and commitments, ambitions, hopes, hates, appetites, and
interests — has been obliterated by the rapture of complete atten-
tiveness. In that extended moment, opposites cohere: the mind
feels and the heart thinks, and receptivity's a form of fierce activity.
Quotidian distinctions between mind and body, self and other,
space and time, dissolve.

Athletes know all about this nearly hallucinatory state. They call
it being in the zone. They feel simultaneously out of body and at
one with body. I also think that infants inhabit a rudimentary version of this state of being. When my children were babies, I would
often awaken in the morning to the sound of my son or daughter
babbling happily in the crib. He or she would be talking, but the
meaning of the words were indistinguishable from the sensation of
the sound, and the sound was part and parcel of the mouth that
made the sound, of the hands and fingers that the mouth was suck-
ing as it sang. No matter how sophisticated our poems may be, or
how deadly serious they are about eradicating or exposing the terrible injustices around us, I still think that we are trying — by
means of words, of consciousness — to reawaken that pre-verbal
joy, to repossess, reinhabit what someone else has called the seriousness of a child at play. Bishop says this concentration's useless
because it is its own reward, the mysterious joy of it. It is singing for
the sake of singing. And even if the singing pleases others or consoles them, stirs them to further the cause of justice in the world or
simply brings the parent to the crib with food, warmth, and maybe
a dry diaper, those effects and ramifications are nonetheless inci-
dental to the primal, fundamental urge to sing, to the sheer gaiety

(to borrow a word from Yeats's "Lapis Lazuli") of projecting our
voices out into the ambient air.

Maybe it's because I do have ADD, and have always been a
deeply and often painfully distracted human being, that my best
days are the ones in which I sit down at the desk at nine A.M. and
look up to discover that it's three P.M. and that six hours have
passed in a single moment. It doesn't matter, ultimately, whether
what I've written is any good or not. I always feel renewed and
grateful if the material, whatever it is, induces that self-forgetful,
perfectly useless concentration. While I'm working, I'm only working; nothing else exists. Inside and outside feel perfectly aligned,
and throughout the full range of my faculties and sensibilities I'm
entirely alert, entirely present — and this, for me, too rare experience of being there, wholly there, never fails to exhilarate. While it
lasts, there's no joy like it. And it never lasts long enough or happens often enough to satisfy my yearning for it. Emily Dickinson
describes its passing as a "sumptuous destitution." Wallace Stevens
expresses the desperate desire to prolong this blessed state when
the speaker of "This Solitude of Cataracts" says that he wants to die
in "a permanent realization." The pleasure of that concentration is
addictive, and it's that addiction, I think, that accounts for the rest-
lessness and melancholy many writers feel when they're not writing. It's not, as John Berryman believed, that poets need to suffer
in order to write — that misery produces art — it's rather that that
self-forgetful, perfectly useless concentration makes them happy, is
itself the happiness that may elude them or never come so purely
or reliably in their nonwriting lives.

In February 2001, a month before Tim Dekin died, I flew to Chicago to spend a few last days with him. Tim was bedridden by then,
his breathing labored, his consciousness a little compromised by
lack of oxygen. One afternoon, Reg Gibbons, his good friend and
editor at TriQuarterly Books; Reg's wife, Cornelia Spelman; and I
were sitting around Tim's bed, talking about poetry, as we almost
always did. The subject of *Another Day on Earth*, Tim's forthcoming
book, came up. He had just seen a mockup of the cover, which
consisted of a picture of Tim fly-fishing, one of his great passions
and the subject of many of the poems in the book. Tim was happy
with the cover and hopeful he'd be around when the book came
out in the fall. I don't remember who suggested this, but Reg and I
began to take turns reading from the last poem in the book, a

poem in four sections called "Woodmanship." Tim, by then, was too weak to read aloud. His eyes were closed throughout the reading, while his fingers tapped out the rhythm of the poem on the bed's railing. Though fly-fishing is the occasion of the poem, the subject is really acceptance of mortality, failure, and loss, and the value of joy in all its elusiveness.

The poem is also about writing, the moment of creation, when we forget all else but the task at hand, when preparation and luck coincide, when the burden of the past and the future lifts and exhilaration comes, what Tim calls "Delight being. Joy being . . . My childhood's earliest familiar." The poem itself, he implies, the writing of it, is both the crumbs that lead us as adults back to that childhood paradise and the measure of how far we've traveled from it. When the moment passes and the poem's written, when we rise from the desk to return to the world awaiting us — our tangled loves and commitments — the exhilaration is nearly indistinguishable from "unfathomable loss."

Careerwise, Tim's life was not a happy one. But in his last six years he remarried, had another child, and despite his worsening physical condition, he did his finest writing. His life contradicts the cliché that great art springs from misery. Illness and the terrors of dying certainly inform Tim's rueful, funny, heart-wrenching final poems, but so too do the joys of fatherhood and marriage and the deep pleasure of domestic peace. The poems, in fact, are inconceivable without them. Ill as he was in his last years, Tim had never been so happy — as a writer or as a man.

Early and late, though, Tim's only constant was his work, his poetry, the pleasure of sitting down to write each morning, and those marvelous days when hours would pass in what would feel like seconds. Through all the vagaries of love and loss, addiction, illness and recovery, he took delight in the work, and the delight and the surprise that found him as he wrote these final poems are now our delight and surprise as we read them. It was for that pleasure that he wrote. It was for that self-forgetful, perfectly useless concentration that he kept on writing even when the world paid no attention. He didn't write for fame, however much he may have longed for recognition and suffered keenly for the lack of it. He wrote for the sheer joy of the writing, which, as a writer, was his most durable sustenance. It was less than he deserved, but lucky for us, it was enough to keep him going.

LILY TUCK

Group Grief

FROM THE HUDSON REVIEW

IN THE ELEVATOR going down from the seventeenth floor, everyone is crying. My bereavement support group has just let out. The
Visiting Nurse Service of New York runs two groups: one is for
adults whose parents have died, the other is for adults whose life
partner or spouse has died. My group meets one evening a week
for an hour and a half. It lasts eight weeks and is free. According to
an article in this December's *Harvard Women's Health Watch* news-
letter, I am among the one million Americans who have lost a
spouse this year.

1. Sharing Our Stories

There are seven of us in the group — five women, two men, plus
the bereavement counselor, Sally. Each session has a theme. The
first thing Sally asks us to do is write our spouse's name on a little
stone with a felt marker. I write *Edward*, but the last *d* does not
quite fit on the stone: *Edwar*. Then Sally tells us to shut our eyes,
put our feet flat on the floor (we are sitting) and our hands palms-
up on our thighs, and breathe deeply. I do yoga and I know about
breathing exercises, but instead of making me relax, they make me
anxious — most of the time I can't tell whether I am inhaling or
exhaling — nevertheless I try to inhale deeply through my nose
and exhale through my mouth. Afterward we go around the table
and each one of us has a chance to tell his or her story.

Fred, who is a dapper, chatty, white-haired man in, I guess, his
mid-seventies, and who sits on my right, begins. Fred was married

for fifty-four years, and one of the hardest things for him now, he says, is having to shop and cook for himself. He starts to say that something else is hard, but he starts to cry and cannot go on.

Amy goes next. She is an African American in her late forties, the youngest in the group. She wears large gold hoop earrings, which she touches and twirls nervously. Amy tells how her husband, Johnny, was on dialysis and sick for a long time. She says that although she knew Johnny was going to die, she was not prepared for how she felt after he did. She has panic attacks, she cannot sleep or eat, her heart beats too fast; only her daughter, whom she looks after, keeps her from jumping out of the window.

Next is Florence, an older, heavyset woman, also an African American. Florence has a quiet dignity. She tells how she was cooking supper for her husband the way she always did, only that night it happened to be his favorite meal — fish cakes, sweet potatoes, and green beans — and how her husband, also called Johnny, told her he was just going to run to the corner for a minute and buy a lotto ticket, and then she tells how she waited and waited for him, supper getting cold and getting spoilt, and after an hour and a half had gone by, the telephone rang, and it was a call from Bellevue Hospital saying her husband had been hit by a bicycle and was in the emergency room. Her husband underwent several operations but he never fully recovered. Her husband, who was six foot five inches, a big man, deteriorated horribly, Florence said; he no longer looked or acted like himself, nor was he able to care for himself. After her husband died, Florence, like Amy, could not eat or sleep. Eventually she had to take antidepressants, and although she feels calmer now, the feelings of grief and loss remain.

Sue, a Korean-American woman, starts out by saying how all their lives she and her husband worked hard; how they saved their money in order to give their three children an education; and how this year, finally, their youngest son, who is twenty-three years old, got a job, and Sue and her husband could stop sending him money. Sue and her husband were looking forward to spending the money on themselves, giving themselves some small — small, she repeats the word — pleasures, like ballroom dancing lessons. Sue is a tidy-looking woman with short dark hair. I guess she is in her late fifties or early sixties, about my age. (I am sixty-four.) Then her husband got sick, Sue says. A tumor on his kidney was removed, he had chemotherapy, the cancer did not appear to have spread — Sue speaks matter-of-factly; she and her husband were able to resume the ballroom dancing lessons. After a few months, however, her husband began to have digestion problems (without any sign of embarrassment, Sue describes in detail his bowel movements, or lack of them, and having to administer enemas), and he had to go back to the hospital. A larger tumor was found. This time the tumor was inoperable. Sue says that she too is on antidepressant medication, but yesterday, Sunday, she could not get out of bed all day. Also, her whole body aches. Sue raises her arms in the air and starts to cry.

Robert, a gray-haired man in his fifties, who was married for thirty-one years and whose wife, Marjorie, died four months ago of lung cancer, shakes his head. The only thing he says is that he sometimes thinks that Marjorie never existed.

Teresa is the loose cannon; I don't trust her. The first thing she says is that she suffered from child abuse. She speaks with a thick middle European accent, and she is difficult to understand. Teresa's brown hair is cut short, in bangs, a girlish hairstyle that does not suit her. She frowns when she speaks (maybe she is near-sighted, I don't know). William, Teresa's husband, had a lovely singing voice, she says. He also played the trumpet, but then he got throat cancer. For two years William had to be fed through a tube in his stomach. Teresa shows how she opened the cans of Ensure and poured them into the tube. Twice the tube broke and had to be replaced. One day William could not get out of bed; when he tried, he fell to the floor. He was foaming at the mouth, Teresa says. She called 911, and in her panic she could not remember her street address, whether it was 325 or 235 — she had to look it up in the phone book. By the time the paramedics arrived it was too late. Nevertheless, they spent an hour trying to resuscitate William. To show how hard they tried, Teresa grabs and squeezes the arm of the man sitting next to her, Robert, Marjorie's husband.

My turn, but I cannot speak.

2. *The Journey of Grief*

What shall I do about my wife's clothes? Fred asks right away. He says he does not know whether to keep the clothes or give them away. (Earlier, as we were coming in, Fred seemed cheerful enough: he commented on the cold weather, asked each one of us how our week had been, joked with Sally.) Now his face crumples and he starts to cry. Sally makes soothing noises and tells him that it is probably too soon. She also says it is best to give clothes away to someone one knows. Fred says his wife was very petite, very slender; he does not know anyone who would fit into her clothes. She had a lot of beautiful clothes, he adds. Sue, the Korean-American woman, says that she got rid of all her husband's clothes right away, that she could not bear the sight of them. She asked her children to dispose of them and they did. Now she regrets that she did not keep something, a sweater. Sally tells how someone once told her about finding a candy in one of her husband's pockets and she ate it. The candy was a comfort. (What, I think, if she had found a condom? a woman's phone number? But I don't say anything. Am I the only one who has these dark thoughts?)

One of my problems, I realize, is that I tend to feel superior to other people — smarter and, years ago, probably prettier too — and that has always been my problem. Why can't I act like everyone else? Why can't I just fit into the group? Why must I be so judgmental? I remember how once a writing teacher told me I had an "attitude," and I could never write until I got rid of it. He was probably right. Another time, in another group, we were asked to write down the quality we liked best about ourselves, and everyone wrote down things like loyalty, honesty, a sense of humor, and I, to show off (and to disrupt), wrote: my slender ankles.

Tonight there are only six of us — no Robert.

In the printout we have been given, grief is defined as "the realization that life will no longer be lived in the way we expected. We grieve not only the past history we've shared with our loved one, but also our hopes and dreams for the future." This realization will affect us on a number of different levels: physical, emotional, cognitive, and spiritual. Under the cognitive level it says: "Inability to concentrate, preoccupation with thoughts of your loved one or the days and events leading up to the death."

My husband, Edward, who was seventy-five, died within ten days of when he was diagnosed with cholangiocarcinoma, which is cancer of the gallbladder. When I telephoned the doctor to tell him that Edward had died, even he could not hide his surprise. "Oh, my," he said. A friend, who is also a doctor, said, "Edward might as well have been run over by a truck, it happened so fast." All I can think about now is those last days of his life.

In August, while we were vacationing in our house on an island in Maine, Edward said he had a pain in his chest, on the right side; it hurt him to take a deep breath, cough, or sneeze. Earlier, he had slipped on rocks on the beach while swimming, and we assumed he had broken or cracked a rib, and we also both knew that nothing could be done about that. However, the pain did not go away, it got worse. Mid-August, we went by boat to the neighboring, larger island, where there was a physician's assistant. The PA examined Edward and found nothing amiss. She did, however, suggest that he have blood work done at Penobscot Bay Medical Center, the nearest hospital on the mainland, but with two more weeks of vacation left and houseguests arriving, Edward decided to wait until we returned to the city. By this time, we had discarded the broken-rib theory and had adopted the gallstones theory.

On September 5, home again, Edward had a thorough physical checkup, the first in many years (Edward was the sort of person who shunned both doctors and dentists). The physician, whom Edward liked, found nothing much wrong except when he did an ultrasound of Edward's liver, but even so, he did not seem particularly alarmed. Edward then underwent a number of procedures (a hateful word): a colonoscopy, a CAT scan, an endoscopy, and finally a biopsy of his liver. All this took time. During that time, Edward, who was a lawyer, continued to go to the office, although he went in later and came home earlier than usual. He was tired and his skin had turned yellow. He had lost his appetite and no longer drank alcohol, not even a glass or two of red wine, which he had always enjoyed. In addition, he had trouble sleeping. One night — temporarily, I hoped, I had moved to the guest room — I was woken by Edward opening the front door. "Where have you been?" He had frightened me. "I could not sleep. I went walking around the block," Edward answered. "But it's three o'clock in the morning!" I said. Finally a tentative diagnosis was made (it still was not 100 percent clear where the cancer had originated, also there was a slight possibility that the cancer was lymphoma, which is treatable), and Edward made an appointment to see an oncologist at Memorial Sloan-Kettering Cancer Center.

The appointment was on Friday, September 27. Edward and I went together. By this time, Edward's stomach was very bloated and he was in severe discomfort. After the oncologist, Dr. Carlton (not his real name, and all names but Edward's have been changed), had examined Edward and studied the pathologist's report, he told Edward that in his case, since the cancer had spread so invasively to the liver, neither chemotherapy nor radiation was an option. Edward then asked Dr. Carlton how long he thought he still had to live. Dr. Carlton answered: "Oh, I would say between two to six months" (which makes me think of the article by Dr. Jerome Groopman in *The New Yorker* not too long ago about how ill equipped doctors are at predicting their patients' life expectancy). Edward got dressed and we went home; he died five days later.

Sally hands out paper and crayons and says we are going to do a visualization exercise. Sally tells us to shut our eyes and breathe deeply and try to relax as she reads aloud a description of a bridge. She then asks us to draw that bridge from the place where we are now to the place where we hope to be in the future. I draw a blue line straight across the page, and around the line I draw blue and green tsunamis. Gradually the waves diminish in size and become a tranquil pool — wishful thinking, I think.

Fred says he could not draw anything.

Amy drew a window with rain outside. She says she cannot see beyond that.

Florence says she could not see the bridge. She drew a smudgy black line across the paper.

Sue drew mountains and a little figure at the bottom. She says she cannot picture herself getting to the top. As a matter of fact, she cannot picture any kind of life for herself at all, and she starts to cry.

Perhaps, Sally tells Sue, they should talk privately.

Teresa drew a house and a tree and a figure running away. Ever since she was seven years old, she says, her mother would grab her by the hair and beat her head against a wall. Her mother, Teresa says, wanted to kill her.

I am the only one who drew the damn bridge.

3. *Asking for Help*

Again Fred starts out by talking about his wife's clothes. Again Sally says that it may be too soon to give them away. Maybe, she suggests,

Fred should put the clothes in a box, a first step. Fred says all right. He also says that he feels he is slipping backward. Three months since his wife died, and he seemed to be coping better before. For example, he says, he goes into the kitchen and can't remember what he went in there for. This happens all the time now; he can't concentrate.

Frowning, Teresa says the same thing happens to her. Teresa, I notice, is wearing the same clothes, a plaid suit, she wore last week and the week before. I too, I realize, wear the same thing every day — a long, gray wool cardigan. The cardigan is a small comfort.

No Florence and still no Robert this week.

Amy is going to visit her in-laws for the holidays. Reaching for the box of tissues on the table, she says she is afraid that her mother-in-law is going to disapprove of her grieving and crying all the time.

Fred says he likes to go out so long as he doesn't have to talk about his wife.

I say I feel just the opposite. I want to talk about Edward when I go out. I don't want to hear people talk about trivia or laugh or tell jokes. I want them to honor my grief, I say dramatically. I am not fine, I add, and I am not going to "have a nice day."

Sally hands out a sheet with a list of the dos and don'ts of what you say to a grieving person. Some of the don'ts are:

"I know you will be okay . . ."

"At least you have your children . . ."

"It's God's will . . ."

"Time heals all wounds . . ."

Wiping her eyes with the tissue, Amy says that on the day of her husband's funeral, her brother came up to her and said: Amy, I don't want you to be lonely — when are you going to find someone else? We agree that was the dumbest thing in the world he could say.

Apropos of nothing, Teresa tells about a dream she had in which her husband asked her to write a letter to his mother, who died a long time ago. She tells the group that her husband fled the Communists and went to Siberia, where his father and his three brothers were killed, and also that he never saw his mother again.

Sally asks her how she feels about the dream.

Teresa says the dream frightened her.

I do not tell the group that last night I again dreamt about Edward. In my dream, I am walking somewhere and I am going to throw away a garlic clove (this summer, in Maine, I was given a garlic clove, red garlic, by a friend who grew it in his garden, and I have the clove in my kitchen now, only in the dream the garlic clove is larger and far heavier; inexplicably, it is the size of a rabbit) and Edward is with me. When we stop walking, he kisses me. The kiss is hard to describe: it is passionate but not sexual, our mouths are pressed together. Afterward, in the dream, Edward tells me to write him a letter — a one-page letter, he specifies. In the morning, first thing, I write:

> Dear Edward,
>   I wish we could have had more time together. I wish we could have driven through Tuscany and Umbria together. I wish we could have gone to Burma, the way we had talked about, and watched as the "dawn comes up like thunder outer China 'crost the Bay!" I wish we could have gone to Paris again and had dinner at the Voltaire, the restaurant we liked so much, and drunk a lot of good wine and eaten white asparagus to start with and veal kidneys cooked in a mustard sauce and fraises des bois for dessert; I wish we could have walked hand in hand around the reservoir in Central Park just one more time. I love you very much. I don't think I knew how much I loved you until you died. I miss you more than I can ever say or write, you gave me a marvelous life.
>
>   Lily

4. Taking Care of Ourselves

I went away Christmas week and missed this session (only two people came to it, Fred and Florence). Over the holidays, my daughter-in-law gave me *A Grief Observed* by C. S. Lewis. (Earlier, someone had given me *When Things Fall Apart: Heart Advice for Difficult Times* by Pema Chödrön, a Buddhist nun. I tried to read it but nothing she said stayed with me — that my grief can also be my source of wisdom sounds good but is too abstract and not practical.) In *A Grief Observed*, Lewis begins by writing: "No one ever told me that grief felt so like fear. I am not afraid, but the sensation is like being afraid."

And speaking of being afraid, normally I am afraid to fly. This time, as I flew to California for the holidays, I almost wished for turbulence or for worse — what did I care? To make matters still worse, last year Edward and I had also spent the holidays in California, and I would be at the same hotel we had stayed in together, and that, more than anything else, made me afraid. "At first," C. S. Lewis also writes, "I was afraid of going to places where H. [his wife] and I were happy — our favourite pub, our favourite wood. But I decided to do it at once — like sending a pilot up again as soon as possible after he's had a crash. Unexpectedly, it makes no difference. Her absence is no more emphatic in those places than anywhere else. It's not local at all . . . Her absence is like the sky, spread over everything."

5. Using Rituals to Heal Our Grief

Tonight there are only four of us: Teresa, Fred, Florence, and myself. Hard to believe but true, once more Fred speaks about his wife's clothes. This time, however, he says that he feels much better about the clothes because, urged by his sons, he has made up his mind to give the clothes away. Sally nods her approval.

Teresa says that she has thirteen cases of Ensure (everyone understands her to say "booze") and does not know what to do with them. There are various tentative suggestions before it becomes clear what the cases in fact contain.

Florence says she stayed home alone for Christmas. For the first time since her husband died, she cooked herself a proper dinner (Florence was the one cooking dinner when her husband went out to buy a lotto ticket and was run over by a bicycle). She describes how she stuffed a chicken, bought cranberry sauce, and cooked string beans. Everyone agrees that cooking is a therapeutic activity.

Sally begins by listing certain rituals that could be helpful: lighting a candle, planting a tree — not so easy in the city — going to a homeless shelter to help out, giving money to charity, wearing the spouse's ring or making it into another piece of jewelry.

I say that, to me, rituals smack of superstition and I am superstitious enough as it is.

Fred says he is taking care of his wife's hibiscus plants, and for him that is like a ritual.

I say, "What if the plants should die?"

"The plants have never done better," Fred answers me.

Edward and I were married six weeks after we met, we were so certain of each other. Afterward we took our combined children, six teenagers, to Europe on our honeymoon. In a rented Volkswagen bus, we drove from Paris to Venice. During those two weeks, the children made it clear how much they disliked us — one of us — and each other. Whenever Edward and I looked back on that time, we would marvel at our naive optimism and laugh out loud.

Next Sally says that we are going to do a visualization exercise. She reads from a piece she calls "The Wise Guide." (I understand her to say "Wise Guy.") In the piece, we are walking through a pretty wood, gentle breezes are blowing, birds are chirping. Then we get to a moss-covered clearing where there is a fire burning and the Wise Guide is waiting for us. We sit down next to the Wise Guide and we are allowed to ask him a question. After he answers it he gives us a present that we can take back home with us.

Tonight everyone strikes me as particularly stupid and uninteresting, and Teresa, I have decided unkindly, is certifiably mad. To make matters worse, the Wise Guide in the story makes me think of a hunchbacked dwarf with a long white beard in a fairy tale. We are supposed to draw what comes to mind. I don't draw anything. Nevertheless, the question that comes to my mind, the one I would ask the Wise Guide, is:

"Where is Edward?"

6. *Spirituality for Healing Grief*

There are six of us — Robert, Sally tells us, wrote her a letter saying he was not coming back, but he did not state a reason. I keep thinking about his wife, Marjorie, and his saying that sometimes he thought Marjorie never existed. I too am afraid, not that I will think Edward never existed, but that his memory will fade. Already, it has a bit. The physical part I remember best about Edward is his head, a big heavy head, and his hair, thick curly blondish-white hair. Edward had a wonderful leonine look, with robust legs. Like C. S. Lewis writing about his wife, I fear that "slowly, quietly, like snow-flakes — like the small flakes that come when it is going to snow all night — little flakes of me, my impressions, my selections, are settling down on the image of her. The real shape will be quite hidden in the end. Ten minutes — ten seconds of the real H. would correct all this. And yet, even if those ten seconds were allowed me, one second later the little flakes would begin to fall again. The rough, sharp, cleansing tang of her otherness is gone. What pitiable cant to say, 'She will live forever in my memory!' *Live?* That is exactly what she won't do."

We begin with another visualization exercise. After handing out the paper and crayons, Sally reads a piece describing how one can put all one's anxieties and troubles into a box and send the box — there could be several boxes — across a smooth surface. We are to draw what we see. I am reminded of the Isaac Bashevis Singer story about how if everyone was told to put all his troubles inside a sack and put the sack in the center of the room and then everyone could choose any sack to take away, how everyone would choose his own sack of troubles. Familiarity breeds what? acceptance? resignation? more familiarity?

I see a bomb exploding in the box I draw in my head.

Sally asks me what I felt when she read, and I say I did not feel anything. In spite of myself, I go on to tell her that I feel infantilized by these stories (why can't I just keep quiet? why must I sound so angry?) and that my grief is being trivialized by having to draw pictures. I compare this to our way of thinking about 9/11 (with a big nod to Joan Didion) — why must we feel okay? Sally looks both hurt and pleased — pleased that I have spoken out. She says she worried about me and about my body language. *Body language!* (I hate Sally all of a sudden, and I hate her clothes — a clown outfit — at each session she has worn the same odd-looking overalls that require suspenders.) And what, I think, if I were to slap or kick her? Would she still consider that body language? Unruffled, Sally goes on to say that drawing can bring one in touch with some other level of feeling. I say I feel very much in touch with my feelings — too much, in fact. Sally then says that counseling is not like therapy. Counseling is meant to be educational and to leave one with more positive feelings.

Turning on me and sounding smug, Fred asks: What is it that you are looking for?

I say I don't know. Something more. Words of comfort. Words of wisdom.

Fred says, Wisdom does not exist. Only experience.

Fuck you, Fred, I want to tell him.

Florence says that she has tried the ritual of lighting a candle in front of a picture of her husband and speaking to him for fifteen minutes each day. She says that this has made her feel better.

Sue says that all of a sudden, she does not know why, she feels a bit better too. During the holidays, her children and friends gave her many gifts, more gifts than she had ever received in her life, and for the first time she realized how loved she was. Her daughter who had always appeared cold is now very affectionate. She feels she must go on for her children's sake. She has made a plan for her life. No more tears, she says; she has to be strong. Not looking at me — no one but Teresa, who is frowning, looks at me — Sue says that everyone has to find their own way to deal with their grief.

Sally says that since the theme of this session is spirituality, does anyone have anything to say about that?

Florence says that her sister keeps calling and telling her to read the Bible, but her sister, she says, has a husband.

Afraid of offending again, I don't say how a few friends, who are religious, have sent me cards saying that they have arranged for special Masses to be said for Edward's soul. Likewise, a Buddhist priest friend wrote that he asked his brother monks in a faraway monastery in India to pray for Edward. For some reason, instead of comforting me, this irritates me. Neither Edward nor I was particularly religious. To me, although I know better and I know that prayers cannot hurt, this feels like an intrusion and as if those people have in some way appropriated Edward's soul and had no business doing it.

Teresa says she goes to church to pray, but also because it is quiet there. Then, again, she goes off on a tangent, this time about her neighbor who, Teresa says, has lost five family members, beginning with her husband, who had a heart attack last year, and a daughter who died of colon cancer. (I look over at Sally — why doesn't she stop Teresa's crazy rant? Instead, Sally is nodding encouragement at Teresa.) The neighbor drinks, Teresa continues. The neighbor is seventy-six and she began drinking when she was thirteen. She smokes, too, Teresa says. Teresa and her husband tried to help the neighbor, they gave her money, bought her groceries, but the neighbor was not grateful (who can blame her?). Teresa says she's tried to get the neighbor to come to church with her, but the neighbor refuses to.

Amy says that for her daughter's sake she has to be careful and she no longer drinks. She starts to fiddle with her gold hoop earrings. She also says that all the things that once made her happy, like Christmas and parties, make her unhappy now.

Sally says, Your life has changed.

Florence says a friend asked her to a wedding next month. The friend insists that Florence go to the wedding, but Florence does not want to go. She won't have an escort, she says, and who, she asks, would dance with her?

A week or so before he died, Edward, who loved to dance, took me in his arms and we did a brief little fox trot down the hall of the apartment.

7. *Creating Your Own Inner Sanctuary*

Yes! Fred starts in on how, this week, he chose some of his wife's best clothes, some of the clothes he says were custom made, and offered them to his neighbor, and as a result he feels that he has made progress and is coping better.

Shaking her head, Amy says she still feels lonely. She says that at night she sleeps in her daughter's bed instead of in her own and Johnny's bed.

Sally says that grief is a very isolating experience. One can be in a room full of people and still feel alone.

Sue says that she has always slept in her and her husband's bed, and in fact, after her husband died — in that bed — she did not change the sheets for a week. She could still smell him, she says, and there were urine stains on the sheets.

I don't say that I, too, sleep in our bed, and that while Edward was alive I used to change the sheets on the bed once a week, on Tuesday. Now the sheets don't get dirty, and only one side of the bed is slept on and the other stays fresh and clean. Sometimes two or three weeks go by before I bother to change the sheets on the bed.

Sally then asks if there is something someone wants to talk about.

Remorse and regret, I suggest.

I say I regret that I was not more tender or affectionate with Edward during the last few weeks of his life. Part of the reason for this, I say, was that I wanted to put on a brave face, I wanted to protect Edward from my own fear and grief. Also I did not want him to have to worry about me. As a result, I acted too much like an efficient nurse: Did you take your meds? Did you have a bowel movement? Did you drink enough water? I never once said: Edward, I love you.

Florence says she knows just what I mean. Two days before her husband, Johnny, died, he told her that he was tired, and although she knew perfectly well what he meant, that he was tired of living, she pretended not to, and she acted as if what he meant was that he was tired of the hospital routine, of the procedures. She said that she and her husband had always understood each other and they had never played games with each other; and this time she did play a game by pretending not to understand what he had meant by "tired," and she deeply regrets that, and that she did not confront him honestly.

Amy says that her husband was the affectionate one. He was the one to rub her back and tell her how much he loved her or how she meant the whole world to him, while she never told him how much she loved him. She hopes and prays that he knows now.

Again Teresa tells how her husband tried to get out of bed and how instead he fell and began to foam at the mouth. I cannot look at her as she speaks. Teresa says she regrets that she did not know how ill William must have been and that she did not take him to the hospital. The paramedics, when they finally arrived, told her it would not have made a difference.

One time, a week or so before Edward died and while I was helping him get dressed, buttoning his shirt, Edward said he was not afraid to die. He was afraid of being a burden and of losing his dignity. He also told me, "I don't know what I would do without you," which is when I could have said "I love you."

(During this session we never mention creating your own inner sanctuary — whatever that is.)

8. Remembering and Honoring

This week, for this our final session, we were asked to bring photos of our loved ones.

Fred has made a collage of his wife when she was young. His wife is surprisingly beautiful and fashionable — she looks like a young Katharine Hepburn — and everyone remarks on it. "She looks like a movie star," says Florence. We all agree. I show my photo of Edward taken in Bermuda this past summer, where we went as a family (seventeen of us, including six grandchildren and one more on the way) to celebrate his seventy-fifth birthday. In the photo, Edward looks strong and healthy; there is absolutely no sign in his face that he will be dead in less than three months. Florence hands around a framed picture of Johnny. A big man, Johnny is wearing his security guard uniform. He is smiling, laughing almost. Sue has brought two photos of her husband: before and after he got sick, to show the difference, she explains. In the first, her husband is standing between his two sons-in-law, who are much taller and not Asian. He has his arms around his sons-in-law's shoulders and he is smiling. In the second photo, he is sitting in a chair in what looks like his underwear, his bony knees jutting out. His family stands behind him. Bald and skeletal, he looks like someone in a prison camp. Teresa has brought a bunch of photos: William playing the trumpet; William with his brother (one of the brothers, she says, who died in Siberia); William and Teresa all dressed up in evening clothes — Teresa's hair is done up in a beehive — at a formal dinner, an older woman standing behind them, her hands resting possessively on both their shoulders (Teresa's mother!).

Amy has the flu and could not come, Sally says.

Sally then takes out the "bridge" drawings we did in an earlier session and hands them back to us. Do we perceive ourselves on the bridge differently now? she asks.

Sue says that she does. She sees herself climbing a little way up the mountain. She says that the group has helped her. In fact, she says she is doing pretty well. She sounds almost cheerful and she laughs, embarrassed at herself. What has helped? she asks, and answers her own question: a combination of family, her job, her own efforts to keep busy. It is true, today, when she was walking to work, she remembered something her husband had said to her and she started to cry. Fortunately she was wearing a hat and no one could see her tears, but she is determined to be strong. She also says that she wants to survive. (Funny how people, even if you expect them to, surprise you. At the beginning of our group counseling I felt certain that Sue was by far the most vulnerable among us, I even thought she might commit suicide, yet now she appears to be the strongest and the one who is handling her grief and bereavement with the most aplomb and equanimity.)

I say that the tsunamis' waves are still huge but there are not as many of them.

Fred, who did not draw a bridge, says he has a surprise. He sounds pleased. What kind of surprise? Sally asks. Fred says that against the advice of everyone — his friends, his sons — he put a notice in D'Agostino, the grocery store, saying that he was looking for a roommate. And guess what? he asks us, smiling. The roommate he found is a woman! Sue giggles. No, Fred says, it is not like that. He has a big two-bedroom apartment, and the woman is a teacher and she is serious. Fred says he knows he is taking a risk, but it will do him good because he has gotten into the habit, as he puts it, of "going native," of wandering around his apartment in his underwear. Now he will have to get dressed. For the first time, Fred looks happy (he has not mentioned his wife's clothes once).

All of a sudden, I like Fred a lot.

Even though she is still on medication, Florence says, she is grateful to the group. It has helped her, she says, to know that we all feel the same.

Teresa starts on another story about someone she knows who has lost her entire family, but this time I do not even try to listen.

As a parting gift, I have brought everyone in the group a copy of Auden's poem "Funeral Blues." I say that although it is not a cheerful poem, it is the poem that captures best how I feel. Sally asks me to read it out loud. When I get to the lines "He was my North, my South, my East and West, / my working week and Sunday rest," my voice breaks and I think I will not be able to read on. When I finish, I look at Florence, who is sitting next to me. Tears are streaming down her face.

The night before Edward died, I asked my son and Edward's son, my stepson, to spend the night with me in the apartment, since I had not gotten much sleep the night before and I was afraid I would not be able to manage Edward alone — I was afraid he would try to get out of bed and fall, he had become so weak. We each sat with Edward in two-hour shifts, and at about four o'clock in the morning, when it was my turn, I walked into our bedroom and found both my son and stepson, dressed in only their boxer

shorts, sitting next to Edward's bed, talking softly about Carly Simon and the songs Edward liked to listen to. Edward was asleep.

Sally then hands out a sheet with a list of our names and telephone numbers. She says that we could have a reunion at some
later date if we wanted to. We all say yes, we want to. (I want to,
too.) All of a sudden, I know that I will miss everyone (except for
Teresa).

Florence and I hug, I shake Fred's hand and wish him luck.
When Sue and I say goodbye, she smiles and tells me to call her: I
work in the city, she says, and I say that I will. I wave to Teresa, and
Sally promises me that she will stay in touch.

Before we leave, we each take back our stones with our spouses'
names written on them. I am surprised at how little the stone is —
I had remembered it as being a lot bigger. Also, I had fantasized
about picking up my stone and hurling it through the room's
plate-glass window and having the stone fall seventeen stories to
the street below — what then? Instead, I slip the stone into my
purse — *Edwar.*

SCOTT TUROW

Missing Bellow

FROM THE ATLANTIC MONTHLY

I NEVER MET SAUL BELLOW. Billions who walk the planet —
Bantu tribesmen and Brazilian rose farmers and factory workers in
Guangdong Province — could say the same thing if they had an inkling who Saul Bellow was, and so could millions of the late novelist's admirers who relished his work but never really imagined that
their paths might cross his. But in my case this nonevent occurred
by choice. Over the decades I had a glancing, minimal relationship
with Bellow, awkward and comic in some of its dimensions, but I
ultimately opted not to seek the great man out, a decision whose
complex meanings seem to have come into focus for me since Bellow's death, in April of this year.

When I first began reading Bellow's work, in 1966, as a freshman at Amherst College, it was as if a hand had reached up
and dragged me into the pages. My ambition was to be a novelist,
and I read all contemporary fiction intently, a detective looking
for clues. But Bellow overpowered me in a way no other writer
had. I remember hiking through the snow with missionary determination in November of 1969 to get a copy of the *Atlantic* —
where Bellow's only novel published during my college years,
Mr. Sammler's Planet, was first serialized — the day it reached the
stands.

To say merely that I read and reread all of Bellow does not come
close to portraying my fixation. I studied Bellow like Scripture, reflecting on every word, sometimes picking out a favorite paragraph and musing on it for an hour, even sometimes running my
fingertips across the words as if they were in Braille. How did he do

that? I always wondered. How did he manage to pipe the sound of an entire human chorus through his powerful voice? How could he sing the scales, as it were, in different pitches, with an effect of such eloquence and comedy? One of the most insistent messages in Bellow's gloriously varied rhetorical style — which effectively fused the argot of Chicago tough guys with the high-flown oratory of a professor, often in the same sentence — is that the power of ideas reaches into and enriches everyday life, a lesson of unique timeliness for someone in the middle of a college education.

With a fan's typical ardor, I collected gossip and trivia about Bellow, and cross-examined anyone I found who knew him. It was a quest: I just had to understand everything I could about this man.

In retrospect I see other motives for my fierce attachment to Bellow's work besides a deep literary appreciation. Saul Bellow was not merely the Great American Novelist of my formative years, the usual straw-poll winner when critics were asked to name our leading living author, but also, like me, a Chicagoan and a Jew. The astonishing commercial success of *Herzog*, which was published in 1964 and spent forty-two weeks on the *New York Times* bestseller list (it also garnered a fistful of literary prizes, including the National Book Award), made Bellow the intellectual prince of my celebrity-starved hometown, where national success in the arts almost always comes only to those who have abandoned America's shoulder-chipped Second City. And that titanic civic pride was magnified intensely in Chicago's large Jewish community, where Bellow had come of age and where many people could claim, with justification, to know the models for various Bellow characters.

But not even Bellow's local fame fully accounted for my attraction. Saul Bellow, it turns out, grew up in the same Humboldt Park neighborhood as my father. They were rough age peers (Bellow was three years older), with striking congruences in their biographies. Both were the children of immigrants. My father as a young boy was known as David Turowetsky, and Bellow was Solomon rather than Saul. Each was the baby of the family, and both were sometimes scorned by their difficult fathers. My dad lost his mother at the age of four; Bellow's high school years were haunted by the lingering illness of Liza Bellow, who died only a month after her son graduated from Tuley High.

That high school, Tuley, was the same one my father attended.

Because my grandfather did not want his motherless son on the streets, he pushed my dad into summer school, which led him to graduate from Tuley at the age of fifteen, in January of 1934, only one year after Bellow. (In those years the Chicago public schools allowed grade-schoolers to start in January, and winter graduation classes at Tuley were nearly as large as those in June.)

This is not to suggest that my father and Saul Bellow were good friends. According to my dad's closest pal in those years, Irving Pesock, my father and he had only limited interaction with Bellow's circle — the self-styled "intelligentsia," as Pesock refers to them, who wrote for the *Tuley Review*. I remember my father mentioning occasionally that in high school he had known Sydney J. Harris, one of Bellow's dearest chums, who went on to local renown as a columnist for the *Chicago Daily News*. Most likely, given the evidence, my father and Bellow enjoyed the marginal acquaintance that comes from the brushing of shoulders in the cafeteria and the gym that would be routine in a school of roughly 1,200 — the kind of contact that gives one the right to declare later in life, "Oh, yeah, I knew that guy in high school." I remember excited talk in my house about *Herzog*. But I cannot establish at this point that my father even connected the world-famous novelist with Solomon Bellow.

That hardly mattered to me, because while either man was alive, I drew no conscious connection between Bellow and my father. I was enough of a Bellow aficionado that I sometimes surprised my friend Jim Atlas, the author of the most acclaimed Bellow biography, with the minutiae I had scraped up — details of love affairs, favored restaurants, his course of study in school — yet I somehow avoided recognizing that Bellow and my father had grown up blocks from each other and walked the halls of the same school at the same time.

One of my favorite psychological maxims, which I attribute to the psychoanalyst Myron Gunther, is "Every adolescent needs an adult to help him grow up, and it can't be a parent." My father was an excellent physician whose rough charm many people savored. But he was a tough dad. Like many men of his generation, he was mystified by his emotions; they controlled him, but not in ways he could anticipate or name. Toward me I felt some clotted yearning. Having lost his mother at such an early age, my father needed a great deal from my mother, and inevitably treated his children as rivals at times. He was an obstetrician-gynecologist. While that may signify more mother issues (as my psychiatrist aunt once pointed out), to his son the principal meaning was that he worked constantly. I had little time with my father and was hungry for his approval, which was seldom expressed. More often I was subjected to sharp sarcasm at the evidence of any shortcomings.

As a result, by the time I was seventeen I had concluded that I did not want to grow up to be my father. I spurned the idea of medical school — his hope for me — and instead, in a clever strategy of divide and conquer, absorbed my mother's ambition to be a novelist. It was a calling more in tune with my rapturous fantasy life and my endless love affair with narrative of every kind, whether in comics, TV, movies, or books. But having rejected my father's example, I still faced the question of how to become a man.

Thus enter Saul Bellow. As a boy who wanted to be a novelist, I couldn't have found a better idol than Bellow, who cast his enormous shadow over the world I came from. Bellow was a writer, a wild success, and a genius. In a few words, he was just the guy I wanted to be. Or was he perhaps the man I wished my father was? Or both? This kind of self-analysis can be a trap when it tries to become too precise. Suffice it to say that to me Saul Bellow was a very big deal. He was the articulate voice of my father's often opaque sensibility, and an interpreter of my father's world in the very terms, literary ones, I hoped to make my own: How could I not have been hooked, especially by *Seize the Day*, which I was assigned as a college freshman? The novella centers on poor Tommy Wilhelm's doomed struggle to win approval from his unforgiving doctor father. I see all that now. But I recognized none of it then.

In September of 1970 I arrived as a writing fellow in the vaunted Stegner program at Stanford, and ended up spending the next five years there, two as a fellow and three as a lecturer in the creative writing program. In the Advanced Fiction Writing seminar, where fellows and graduate students read and discussed one another's work, I spoke of Bellow constantly. My passion was not widely shared. The workshop's most sophisticated thinkers about fiction — Chuck Kinder, Bill Kittredge, Raymond Carver — were drawn to a cooler, more minimal style. And Wallace Stegner, who today has his own coterie of those who regard him as the best novelist of his era, resented Bellow, seeing him as the designee of what Stegner called "the *Partisan Review* crowd" — the Jewish intellectuals who dominated the literary world and who had treated Wally with far more indifference than he deserved.

By then there was an unruly literary mob that wanted to knock Bellow off his throne. Published at the dawn of the era of political correctness, *Mr. Sammler's Planet* had shocked many readers, particularly in its portrayal of a regal black pickpocket whom Artur Sammler detects at work on the Riverside bus in Manhattan. The pickpocket, aware that he has been identified, follows Sammler home one day, forces the elderly one-eyed man against the wall in the vestibule of his apartment building, and then in warning exposes his flaccid penis, "a large tan-and-purple uncircumcised thing — a tube, a snake . . . suggesting the fleshly mobility of an elephant's trunk." I give Bellow credit for his perspicacity in recognizing the lethal admixture of crime and sexuality that was already being adopted as an underground ideal of black masculinity, but it always seemed to me that the scene was fundamentally wrong — just not something that would happen that way. It opened Bellow and his book to the first real fusillades aimed at his world view. There is no more damaging charge against a novelist, especially a realist like Bellow, than the claim that he has got life wrong — especially when he can be characterized as a bigot, as Bellow was.

On balance, though, I thought *Sammler* was magnificent, a stunning coming to terms with a world in which humankind was capable of both landing on the moon and perpetrating the Holocaust, and I was delighted when in early March of 1971 he — and I, in a way — were vindicated by his again winning the National Book Award. I was so pleased by this triumph that after several days of mental preparation I dared to write Bellow a congratulatory note. (Was it significant that my father was then enduring the first of his traumas over what was soon to become the hobgoblin of all obstetricians' lives: a medical-malpractice lawsuit?) I did not keep a copy of the brief letter I sent, but I considered what I would write for so long, and my involvement with Bellow and his work was so charged, that I still remember the critical line. "Despite your reputation for putative solemnity," I wrote, "I know you have a warm Jewish heart." Because of that, I said, I believed he might appreciate knowing how much his books meant to a humble graduate student in California.

Leigh Bienen today is a writer of short fiction and a lawyer and lecturer at Northwestern's law school, but years ago, before she was established in either career, she had been hired by Bellow after the publication of *Herzog* to help him deal with the torrent of mail the novel had brought him. This outpouring was invited not simply because *Herzog* had garnered a large bestseller's audience but also because it was an epistolary novel, made up of Moses Herzog's urgent communications "to the newspapers, to people in public life, to friends and relatives and at last to the dead, his obscure dead, and finally the famous dead." I had taken it for granted that Bellow would spend the rest of his life receiving letters from people who, like Moses, felt inclined to toss off a few passionate lines — contentious and quarrelsome, or adoring, but always impelled by the kind of boiling emotions to which Herzog regularly gave vent. This expectation both gave me permission to write and assured me of no response. I knew that my message would be a teaspoon in the ocean of congratulatory mail that Bellow was likely to receive, having survived his usurpers.

Yet the next month, as I remember it, a blue air-mail envelope from the Committee on Social Thought at the University of Chicago arrived at my Palo Alto apartment. The one-page note was handwritten in a style, as one might expect of those who had the same teachers in penmanship, that, I now see, closely resembles my old man's.

"Sometimes I fear 'the warm Jewish heart' may be misleading," Bellow wrote, "i.e. that it does not give or receive the *real* facts. Which seem always worse and worse. But then it must *in itself* be a good thing." Epigrammatic and musing, the few lines were essential Bellow, especially the brief meditation about the "*real* facts," a preoccupation that was typical of his characters from Henderson the Rain King through Sammler and Herzog, all struggling to discern the true position of humankind in a universe made ever more chaotic by unruly human feelings. Leigh Bienen says that when she worked for Bellow it was not his habit to answer all fan mail, and generally his correspondence was typed. So something in my note must have moved him to dash off his quick reply — probably my choice of words about a "warm Jewish heart." In retrospect, of

course, I wonder if I don't have my father to thank for Bellow's response: Did Bellow recognize the last name my father had taken by
high school?

In the summer of 1975 I left Stanford, and academic life, to enter
Harvard Law School. It would require an essay longer than this
one to fully explain that decision. But I was fascinated by the law
and dreamed (stupidly, my lawyer friends told me) of both practicing and continuing to write.

A year later, on October 21, 1976, Saul Bellow won the Nobel
Prize in literature. By then my own literary career, largely stalled to
that point, had made a surprising advance: I was then putting the
finishing touches on *One L,* a memoir of my first year at Harvard,
which had been commissioned by Ned Chase for G. P. Putnam's
Sons. Even so, I was excited when a Stanford friend, Mike Rogers,
called to ask me to interview Bellow for *Rolling Stone.* Mike, who
had enjoyed great success as a novelist and short story writer, had
also become a magazine editor, and subsequently remained in the
publishing world for many years. At that point Mike and his boss,
Jann Wenner, had decided that the journal of American pop culture should include an interview with America's latest high-culture
hero. And Mike knew no one better informed about Bellow than I
was.

I started with a letter to Bellow's address at the Committee on
Social Thought, which, unlike my fan letter, drew nothing in the
way of a response.

Then a second request. And a third. Eventually I resorted to
phone calls to Bellow's office, leaving unanswered messages with
secretaries. Finally I went for the nuke of 1970s telecommunica-
tions: the person-to-person call. I would dash out of class to a pay
phone in the basement of Austin Hall and tell the operator I
wanted to speak to Saul Bellow. He was never available. But one
day at lunchtime, when, I suppose, the secretaries were out, a surprisingly weak hello came from the other end after many rings.

Somehow I knew the gentle voice was Bellow's. I gave him no
chance to speak, bursting forth. I can't recall exactly what I said,
but I'm sure it's best summarized as "Please please please please
please please please please." How many interviews, I asked,
could he possibly grant to someone who had not only read all his

books but read each dozens of times? If I was not exactly Boswell, wasn't I the best he could hope for in speaking to the American masses in the popular press? This assumed a fact, as I was learning to say, that was not in evidence — namely, that Bellow had any interest in being understood by that audience on any terms other than the ones he had established in his books.

One of my favorite moments in *Herzog* comes when Moses Herzog has a fender-bender on Lake Shore Drive, in Chicago. The police officers who arrive at the scene are, in the parlance of the mid-1960s, "two big Negro cops." Revered and famous though Professor Herzog is, the cops examine his license and address him as "Moses." " 'There it was,' Herzog thinks, 'that note of deadly familiarity that you heard only when immunity was lost.' " It is a lovely little illustration of the mutability of power and the tyranny of petty bureaucrats (and a potent vignette about racial payback, since these middle-aged black cops have been relegated to traffic patrol).

Now, as I beseeched Bellow, and he began his demurrers, the operator suddenly broke in. "Wait a minute," she said harshly, "wait a minute." We had yet to establish that I had reached the proper person, as the call's terms required. And so she addressed the Nobel laureate just like the cops on Lake Shore Drive, albeit in a drilling Dorchester accent. "Wait a minute," she said again. "Is this Saul?"

How could he deny it? He had no more wish to continue this conversation than to use sandpaper as a face towel, but in a tinier voice than the one in which he had answered the phone, he submitted to petty authority. Yes, he reluctantly admitted, he was in fact the wanted man.

The operator left us, and our conversation lasted no more than another minute. I begged, and Bellow said no several times. He was polite, even kindly. He did not disparage *Rolling Stone,* or even me. He was, he said, just not interested in being interviewed yet again. He sounded beleaguered by the attention that had come with the Nobel. We hung up. It was, as it turned out, the only conversation I had with Saul Bellow in my life.

Bellow's magic did not work on everyone. As I pressed friends and relatives to read his books over the years, they often had a common complaint: nothing happens. This is a fair observation about Bellow's novels, whose plots can usually be summarized as follows: a guy wanders around. Bellow's protagonists think, they fulminate, they suffer, their brains speed them through life like meteors, but outside events provide only occasional propulsion. The action of these novels is for the most part routine. We read Bellow to find out about ideas, values, nuanced reflection — not what happens next.

As the years had worn on, as I slunk from adolescence to young adulthood, as I accepted the fact that I was not Saul Bellow, I had begun to think differently about the mission of fiction, or at least my own writing. Storytelling in particular seemed to have been neglected in American realism, of which Bellow was the champ. Realist writers were committed to representing the middle range of experience, the mundane daily existence that virtually all of us endure most of the time. "What happens next?" was not a question the archrealists wanted their readers to ask, because the answer was assumed: "What happened the day before." Melodrama, coincidence, extreme events, were not, therefore, the proper centerpieces of fiction, and the plots of Bellow novels like *Dangling Man, The Victim,* and *Seize the Day* were clearly not intended to increase a reader's heart rate. But I was spending my days as a prosecutor in Chicago, living in a world animated by a constant struggle with the transgression of norms. And I was repeatedly struck by the spell that came over a courtroom when the critical witness in a criminal case took the stand to offer his account of how evil had happened. There was a lesson there to me. Our lives may be ensnared in a web of dailiness, but our imaginations are not. There is something essential in our fascination with crime and the law's struggle to impose reason on impulses that have proved ungovernable for some. Of such reflections was my first published novel, *Presumed Innocent,* born.

When *Presumed Innocent* appeared, in 1987, it changed my life. I went from being a prosecutor cadging moments to write on the commuter train to the author of a novel that was both at the top of the *New York Times* bestseller list and hailed on the front page of the *Times Book Review.* More than one person pointed out to me that Saul Bellow was no longer the only hot literary gun in town, which I regarded as laughable. I put few contemporary writers in Saul Bellow's league, and I certainly would never make such a claim for myself. I was sure that Bellow would condemn *Presumed Innocent* for what it was confessedly meant to be: a work committed to the tropes of popular fiction with a plot whose events were anything but routine.

Nonetheless, the novel made me a local celebrity, with the attendant duties. Late in 1991 I signed a form letter from Chicago's largest literacy organization, asking hundreds of authors across the country to donate books for a fundraising auction. I did not even know who was on the mailing list, and I was therefore astonished when, in January of 1992, I found a note from Saul Bellow in my law office in-box. He had scratched his home address at the top of the page, commented on American illiteracy rates, and promised to send a book to the auction. Then he added, "I read your first novel with admiration and pleasure. The new one I haven't caught up with yet."

"The new one" was my second novel, *The Burden of Proof,* which had also been reviewed on the front page of the *Times Book Review,* albeit sourly. Nonetheless, the book had prolonged my fifteen minutes, landing me on the cover of *Time,* and had remained number 1 on the *Times* bestseller list for eleven straight weeks in the summer of 1990.

I wrote back to Bellow at home, and enclosed a copy of *Burden,* telling him how thrilled I was to know that my work had come to his attention. I realize in retrospect that when a Nobel Prize winner bothers to send you a handwritten response to a form letter, and takes the trouble to give you his home address, he's not trying to remain remote. The logical thing would have been to propose lunch or a cup of coffee, and deliver my second novel in person. But Bellow for me was a figure steeped in symbolism, and I suppose I could not bring myself to think of his realm and mine converging in real life.

I was excited nevertheless to send him the book. Although I had occasionally imitated authors I admired, I had never tried to write like Bellow. But some of his diction and, more, his irony have stuck to me forever, in the way the lessons of youth always do. The internal chats of Sandy Stern, the protagonist of *The Burden of Proof,* palely echo several Bellow characters — something I had been aware of when I wrote, and which others had occasionally commented on. I hoped Bellow would recognize the homage and be flattered.

Thus I hardly got what I expected when Bellow sent a typed letter to my home eleven months later. He apologized for not acknowledging my gift earlier, which he blamed on "a succession of stunning deaths." One of those certainly was that of Allan Bloom, the author of *The Closing of the American Mind,* with whom Bellow had taught for more than a decade at the University of Chicago, and who had passed away the month before. Then Bellow continued,

> I think I told you how much I admired *Presumed Innocent.* Of course your first book was particularly attractive. I have always succumbed happily to the terrible weight of criminality, investigation, and prosecution — especially on our own Chicago turf. *The Burden of Proof* could not match the attractions of its predecessor. I always hate to write critical letters and avoid them. I especially hate getting them myself. Because of my advanced age, there always seems to be an element of speaking de haut en bas. I shun that kind of thing and I would be terribly sorry to be seen by a colleague as anything but a fellow writer. I preferred your first book to your second, it's as simple as that. Now I shall look forward to the third. I apologize for what may appear to be impoliteness and send my best wishes.

Thirteen years later, I still don't know exactly what to make of this letter. It goes without saying that a simple thank-you note, especially nearly a year late, would have sufficed. I did not request or need this candid putdown, and I have never quite understood why Bellow would say he avoided critical letters and then drop this one in the mail. Nonetheless, if I were more secure, I might have recognized this blast from the mountaintop as entrée to a personal relationship founded on my acknowledgment that, whatever the whirling of literary fashion, Bellow was the master — ground I will always willingly concede. After all, I didn't like Bellow's novels equally either.

But at that point I heard his message as unambiguously harsh. It did not help, of course, that this response out of the blue was the kind of gratuitous knock my father had regularly delivered when I was least suspecting. Reading the letter was a blow to the noggin, as Bellow might put it. Who looks a gift horse in the mouth like that? "De haut en bas" indeed. What was French for "jerk"?

I decided then that I was finished with Saul Bellow. I never wrote back, never sent the third novel he claimed to look forward to, never communicated again.

A year later Bellow was gone — wooed away by John Silber, the president of Boston University. Chicagoans were stunned when Bellow's intention to leave the University of Chicago was announced, in the spring of 1993, but I imagine the deaths that Bellow complained of in his letter to me had made Chicago seem a haunted place.

About a year later, the summer after Bellow took up his duties at BU, a prominent cultural journalist from Germany arrived to interview me in connection with the German publication of my third novel, *Pleading Guilty.*

"I met Saul Bellow last night," my German visitor told me when our meeting began. I assumed that he had used his journey to Chicago also to interview Bellow, who was still turning up in the city now and then. But no, the encounter had been purely fortuitous. The German had gone into the Berghoff, a fabled Chicago eatery, and there in line in front of him, also alone, was Saul Bellow. The reporter recognized him, and they had a pleasant conversation. The Berghoff stands directly behind the Federal Building, where I had worked as an assistant U.S. attorney for eight years, and I had probably eaten a hundred meals in the place. The irony of this European's wandering in once and meeting Chicago's most celebrated literary citizen gave me a pang. Should I perhaps reconsider, I wondered, and seek out Bellow while he was around? But again I decided no. The memory of his letter remained fresh, and coming of age in the literary world I had learned more than once that some authors are better read than met.

Now and then in subsequent years I encountered friends of Bellow's whom I'd amuse with the tales of our near midair collisions. Several offered to arrange a meeting. I suppose that if I'd bumped into Bellow in the Berghoff, as the German reporter had, I would have been thrilled, but I was unwilling to initiate a meeting, feeling that I would somehow be a supplicant. This was a psychodrama of my own authorship. But it remained imperative to me to say I didn't need that.

And so Bellow's passing was an occasion for mourning. The door was closed. My father, too, has been gone for several years, and I experienced again a bit of that startling absence. Reading the obits that mentioned that Bellow had attended Tuley, the mental crossing gates finally lifted and I realized that my relationship, such as it was, was with two men, not one — a harmonic that undoubtedly complicated my few personal dealings with Bellow, but which, I also realized, dramatically heightened my stake in his books and my appreciation of them. Lying in my Amherst dorm rooms, Bellow's novels seizing me by force, I felt as if I were somehow reading the secret story of my own life. And I suppose I was.

MARJORIE WILLIAMS

A Matter of Life and Death

FROM VANITY FAIR

THE BEAST FIRST SHOWED its face benignly, in the late June
warmth of a California swimming pool, and it would take me more
than a year to know it for what it was. Willie and I were lolling happily in the sunny shallow end of my in-laws' pool when he — then
only seven — said, "Mommy, you're getting thinner."

It was true, I realized with some pleasure. Those intractable ten
or fifteen pounds that had settled in over the course of two preg-
nancies — hadn't they seemed, lately, to be melting away? I had
never gained enough weight to think about trying very hard to lose
it, except for sporadic, failed commitments to the health club. But
I'd carried — for so many years I hardly noticed it — an unpleasant sensation of being more cushiony than I wanted to be. And
now, without trying, I'd lost at least five pounds, perhaps even
eight.

I suppose I fell into the smug assumption that I had magically restored the lucky metabolism of my twenties and thirties, when it
had been easy for me to carry between 110 and 120 pounds on a
frame of five feet six inches. True, in the months before Willie's
observation, I'd been working harder, and more happily, than I
had in years — burning more fuel through later nights and busier
days. I'd also been smoking, an old habit I'd fallen into again two
years earlier, bouncing back and forth between quitting and suc-
cumbing, working up to something like eight cigarettes a day.

Of course Willie noticed it first, I now think: children major in
the study of their mothers, and Willie has the elder child's umbilical awareness of me. But how is it that I didn't even question a

weight loss striking enough for a child to speak up about? I was too happy enjoying this unexpected gift to question it even briefly: the American woman's yearning for thinness is so deeply a part of me that it never crossed my mind that a weight loss could herald something other than good fortune.

As it happened, I took up running about a month later, in concert with quitting smoking for good. By the end of the summer I was running about four miles a day, at least five days a week. And with all that exercise I found I could eat pretty much anything I wanted without worrying about my weight. So more weight melted away, and the steady weight loss that might have warned me something was going badly wrong disguised itself instead as the reward for all those pounding steps I was taking through the chill of early fall, the sting of winter, the beauty of spring's beginning. I went from around 126 pounds, in the spring of 2000, to about 109 a year later.

Somewhere in there my period became irregular — first it was late, then it stopped altogether. Well, I'd heard of this: women who exercise heavily sometimes do become amenorrheic. I discussed it with my gynecologist in January, and he agreed it was no real cause for alarm. He checked my hormone levels and found I definitely hadn't hit perimenopause, but what I most remember about that visit is the amazed approval with which he commented on the good shape I was in.

Around that time — I can't pinpoint exactly when — I began to have hot flashes, almost unnoticeable at first, gradually increasing in intensity. Well, I said to myself, I must be perimenopausal after all; a gynecologist friend told me that hormone levels can fluctuate so much that the test my doctor had done wasn't necessarily the last word on the subject.

Then one day in April I was lying on my back, talking idly on the telephone (strangely, I don't remember to whom), and running my hand up and down my now deliciously scrawny stomach. And just like that I felt it: a mass, about the size of a small apricot, on the lower right side of my abdomen. My mind swung sharply into focus: Have I ever felt this thing before, this lump? Well, who knows, maybe this is a part of my anatomy I was just never aware of before — I had always had a little layer of fat between my skin and the mysteries of the innards. Maybe there was some part of the intestine that felt that way, and I had just never been thin enough to notice it before.

You know how you've always wondered about it: Would you notice if you had a sudden lump? Would you be sensible enough to do something about it? How would your mind react? For all of us, those wonderings have a luxuriantly melodramatic quality. Because surely that isn't really how it works; you don't just stumble onto the fact that you have a lethal cancer while you're gabbing on the phone like a teenager. Surely you can't have a death sentence so close to the surface, just resting there, without your being in some other way aware of it.

I thought about calling my doctor, but then remembered that I had a full checkup scheduled in about three weeks anyway; I would bring it up then. In the intervening weeks I often reached down to find this odd bump: sometimes it wasn't there, and at other times it was. Once, I even thought it had moved — could I possibly be feeling it three inches up and two inches to the left, nearly underneath my belly button? Surely not. This must be just another sign that I was imagining things.

Checkup day came. I had been seeing the same doctor for at least a decade. I'd chosen him casually, foolishly, at a time in my life when having a general practitioner didn't seem like a very important decision. For most of the past decade almost all my health-care issues had taken me to the office of my obstetrician, the man who delivered my two babies. To him I felt infinitely bonded. And because he had tested my health so diligently — and appropriately for a mother who had her first baby at thirty-five — I hadn't really seen the need, for years, for a general checkup.

So this doctor I was seeing now had never had to see me through anything serious. But he had always handled what little I brought to him with sympathy and dispatch; I had a mild liking for him.

To begin the checkup, he ushered me into his office, fully clothed, to talk. I told him about all of it: the stopped periods, the hot flashes, the fact that I could intermittently feel a mass in my belly. But I also told him what seemed most true to me: that overall I felt healthier than I'd been in years.

Right off the bat, Dr. Generalist advised me to press the matter of hot flashes, and of the vanished period, with my gynecologist.

No Hormones Handled Here. Then he ushered me into his examining room next door, with the standard instruction to dress in a flimsy robe while he stepped out of the room. He inspected me in all the typical ways, then told me to get back in my clothes and step back into his office. I had to remind him that I had reported a strange lump in my abdomen. So he had me lie back down, and felt all around that area. No mass. He got me to feel there too; it was one of those times when I couldn't feel it.

"I would think," he said, "that what you're feeling is stool that's moving through your bowel. What you're feeling is a loop of intestine or something where the stool is stuck for a while. That's why sometimes it's there and sometimes it's not. The bad things don't come and go; the bad things only come and stay." He could send me off for a lot of tests, he said, but there really wasn't any point in going to that trouble and expense, because I was so obviously a perfectly healthy patient. He repeated all the same information in a letter mailed to me the following week after my blood tests came back: healthy healthy healthy.

Looking back, I know I was uneasy even after I got this clean bill of health. Sometimes I sensed what seemed like a flicker of movement in my belly, and got the oddest feeling that I might be pregnant. (At one point, I even bought a home pregnancy test and furtively took it into a stall in the ladies' room in the little mall that housed the pharmacy.) Every now and then, the mass in my abdomen actually stuck out when I lay on my back; once, I looked down to see my stomach distinctly tilted — high on the right side, much lower on the left. I was at some pains never to point this out to my husband, Tim.

Finally, on the last Friday night in June 2001, I had a huge hot flash while my husband was tickling my back, in bed. Suddenly I was drenched; I could feel that his fingers could no longer slide easily along the skin of my back. He turned to me, astonished: "What *is* this?" he asked. "You're *covered* in sweat."

It was as if someone had at last given me permission to notice fully what was happening inside me. I made an appointment with my gynecologist — the earliest one I could get was the next week, on Thursday, July 5 — and began deliberately noticing how overwhelming the hot flashes had gotten. Now that I was paying close attention, I realized they were coming fifteen or twenty times a day, sweeping over and through me and leaving me sheathed in a layer of sweat. They came when I ran, making my joyous morning run a tedious slog that must be gotten through; they came when I sat still. They exceeded anything that had been described to me as the gradual coming of menopause. This was more like walking into a wall. On both Monday and Tuesday of that week, I remember, I stopped about two miles into my morning run, simply stopped, despite the freshness of the morning and the beauty of the path I usually cut through the gardened streets of Takoma Park. Any runner knows the feeling of having to push past the body's observation that it might be more fun to walk slowly home and pop open a beer (just keep putting one foot in front of the other), but this was something different, like an override system I could no longer ignore. It said: Stop. It said: This is a body that can no longer afford to run.

My gynecologist's office is way, way out in the long exurban belt stretching westward from D.C. Pat was running late that afternoon, so it was probably after five when he finally called me into his office. I told him about the hot flashes, and about the lump I was feeling in my abdomen. "Yup, you're in menopause," he said somewhat brusquely. "We can start giving you hormones, but first let's check out that lump you say you're feeling."

We went into the examining room, where he keeps his ultrasound equipment. He'd given me dozens of quick exams with it over my childbearing years. I hopped up on the table, and he slapped on some of the chilly goo they apply to your belly, to make the ultrasound mouse slide over your skin, and almost immediately he stopped. "There," he said. "Yeah, there's something here." He looked at it a bit more, very briefly, then started snapping off his gloves. His face looked as neutral as he could possibly make it, which alarmed me instantly. "Just so you know," he said quickly, "it's probably fibroids. I'm not thinking cancer, but I am thinking surgery. So get dressed and come on back to my office, and I'll explain."

We sat back down on opposite sides of his desk. But before we talked, he called out to his receptionist, who was just packing up for the evening. "Before you go," he said, "I need you to book her an ultrasound and a CT scan. Tomorrow, if possible."

I told Pat he was scaring me. What was all this speed about if he wasn't thinking cancer?

"Well," he said, "I'm pretty sure it's not — I'll explain why in a minute — but I hate to have something like this hanging over a weekend. I want to know for sure what we're dealing with."

He went on to explain that he'd seen what looked like a fairly large growth on my ovary, but that it didn't look like ovarian cancer; its consistency was different. (Here, he drew me a picture on the back of a piece of scrap paper.) He explained that fibroids can sometimes be removed with surgery but that very often they grew back, even worse than before. His own typical recommendation, for a woman who was done having babies, he said, was a hysterectomy.

"Does this have anything to do with my hot flashes?" I asked.

"No, not a thing, in all probability. You just happen to be starting menopause, too."

I felt on the verge of tears. When I left, I sat in the car to collect myself, boggling at the thought of losing my uterus at the age of forty-three. I didn't even call my husband on my cell phone. I just wanted to calm down and get home and then seek the sanctuary of his sympathy.

The next morning, Pat's office called to say they had scored a formal ultrasound examination at three in the afternoon, in a D.C. radiology practice I'd visited from time to time before. When I got there, Pat's nurse told me, they would give me an appointment — probably early the next week — to come back for a CT scan.

I told my husband I didn't need him to come to the sonogram: it would probably only give a clearer picture of what Pat's ultrasound had already told us, I assumed. There's nothing painful or difficult about a sonogram, and I didn't want to haul Tim out of work twice; I knew I'd want him with me for the CT scan later.

That was a bad decision.

I remember waiting endlessly at the desk for the receptionist to finish a peckish, convoluted phone conversation with the manager of the garage downstairs, about why she'd been billed wrong for that month's parking. She talked on and on ("Yes, I *know* that's what I owe for each month, but I already paid you for both June and July"), with zero self-consciousness about keeping a patient standing there at the desk. There was a sign that instructed one to sign in and then take a seat, but, of course, I needed to talk to her about scheduling the CT scan after the sonogram. She kept flicking her hand at me and trying to shoo me toward a chair, then pointing at the sign. I just waited.

Finally I told her why I was standing there: "Um, CAT scan . . . The doctor's office told me . . . as soon as possible . . ."

"What are you?" she said. A puzzled silence. "I mean, what *kind* are you?"

"Well, um, they're looking at something in my pelvis —"

"Oh, body," she said, her scowl regathering. "We are really, really booked on bodies." She started to flip through her appointment book. I stood there trying to radiate as palatable a combination of charm and distress as I could manage. "Well, I'll talk to the doctor," she finally mumbled. "Ask me again when your sonogram's done. We might be able to do Monday morning, eleven o'clock."

When my father was under treatment for cancer, which put him in and out of various hospitals for five years, I used to roll my eyes at the way he ingratiated himself with all the staff. You could walk into intensive care and he'd be there, his face wan against the pillow, but with his usual charming, modest smile ready for everyone. He would introduce his nurse and tell you where she was born, and how her sister wrote romance novels, and that her brother was on a track-and-field scholarship at the State University of New York.

Part and parcel, I thought, of his lifelong campaign to be loved by everyone he met. He had always put more energy into captivating strangers than anyone else I knew.

But I learned right away, when I went for this very first test, how wrong I'd been. As a patient, you come to feel that you need everyone — from the chairman of the oncology service at a major cancer center down to the least-paid clerk in the admissions department — to like you. Some of them may have the power to save your life. Others have the power to make you comfortable in the middle of the night, or to steer away from you the nurse-in-training who is still just learning to insert IVs, or to squeeze you in for a test you might otherwise wait days for.

I was discovering this truth on my back, while the ultrasound technician guided her wand through the chilly gel she had squeezed onto my belly. She was a friendly young woman with a

Spanish accent of some kind, and her job was to get an accurate picture of what was going on in my pelvis while divulging the least information possible to the anxious patient. My job was to find out as much as I could, as quickly as I could.

So there I am: "Gosh, Friday afternoon . . . Have you had a long week? . . . How long have you been working in ultrasound? . . . Oh! Is that my ovary there, really? . . . Ah, so you're taking pictures now . . . Uh-huh . . . Gee, that must be the growth my gynecologist was talking about."

Under this onslaught of niceness, the technician begins to think aloud a bit. Yes, she is seeing a growth. But usually fibroids, which grow from the outside of the uterus, move in concert with it: poke the uterus and the growth will move too. This growth seemed to be independent of the uterus.

Is it a mild chill I'm feeling, or a mild thrill? I am still reeling at the thought that I might have a hysterectomy at forty-three; perhaps I am thinking it would at least be fun to have something more interesting than a fibroid?

But if there is a tinge of that interest, it vanishes when she speaks again: "Huh. Here's another one." And another. Suddenly we are seeing three strange round plants that yield to a mild shove, but don't behave like anything she's ever seen before. She is doubly skeptical now about the fibroid theory. My gynecologist had examined me in detail the previous January, so much of what we're looking at has to have grown within six months. Fibroids, she says, don't grow nearly that fast.

I am surprised that she is so forthcoming, but soon see that it is of little use to me: she is looking at something she's never seen before. She summons the doctor — the chief radiologist in the practice — who in turn summons a younger colleague she is training. They all crowd around the machine in fascination.

Again we do the poking-the-uterus exercise. We try the transvaginal sonography wand. Their mystification has begun to make me seriously frightened. I begin to question the doctor very directly. She is quite kind. She really can't say what she's seeing, she tells me.

It almost seems an afterthought — the indulgence of a hunch — when the doctor turns to the technician and says, "Try moving up, yes, to the navel or so." I can still remember the feel of the equipment casually gliding up toward my navel, and then a sudden, palpable tension in the air. For, immediately, another large growth — one even bigger than the three below — looms into view.

This is the moment when I know for certain that I have cancer. Without anyone's even looking very hard, this exam has been turning up mysterious blobs in every quarter. I go very still as the doctor begins directing the technician to turn here, look there. Her voice has dropped almost to a whisper, and I don't want to distract her with my anxious questions: I can hold them long enough for her to find out what I need to know.

But then I hear one of them mumble to the other, "You see there? There is some ascites . . . ," and I feel panic wash through me. Along with my sisters, I nursed my mother through her death from a liver illness, and I know that ascites is the fluid that collects around the liver when it is badly diseased.

"Are you finding something on my liver too?" I croak.

"Yes, something, we're not sure what," says the doctor, pressing a sympathetic hand to my shoulder. And then suddenly I'm aware that they've made a decision to stop this exam. What's the point in finding more? They've found out enough to know that they need the more subtle diagnostic view of a CT scan.

"Is there a case to be made against my freaking out now?" I ask.

Well, yes, replies the doctor. There's a lot we don't know; there's a lot we need to find out; it could be a great range of different things, some of which would be better than others.

"But then let me ask you this way," I press. "Do you know of anything other than cancer that could give rise to the number of growths we just saw? Could it be anything benign?"

"Well, no," she says. "Not that I'm aware of. But we'll be sure to work you in Monday morning for a CT scan, and then we'll know a lot more. I'm going to call your doctor now, and then I assume you'd like to talk to him after me?"

She shows me to a private office to wait; she will let me know when I should pick up the phone there. In the meantime, I choose a free phone line and dial my husband's cell phone. I have caught him somewhere on the street. There is a huge noise behind him; he can barely hear me.

"I need you —" I begin, barely in control of my voice. "I need you to get in a cab and come to the Foxhall medical building."

This is what he says: "Okay." He doesn't say, "What's wrong?" He doesn't ask, "What did the test show?" It is my first glimpse of the miraculous generosity that will help me get through everything that is about to happen. He can tell how tenuous my control is; he can tell that I need him; he has agreed without speech to hold the anxiety of knowing nothing more for the twenty minutes it will take him to get here.

After this, I talk briefly with my gynecologist on the phone. Pat's first words are "What time's your CT scan? I'm going to cancel all my Monday-morning appointments and come to your scan." I have never heard of a doctor coming to a CAT scan before this. It foretells the huge seams of good fortune that will run through the black rock of the next three years. There is nothing like having a doctor who really cares about you — who can speed up the inhuman pace of medical time, which usually leaves patients begging to hear their test results, waiting too many days for an appointment, at a loss until the conveyor belt brings along the next hurried intervention. Pat is one of the doctors who are willing to break the rules: Here is my cell phone number — call me anytime this weekend. We will figure out together what to do on Monday.

Somehow, my husband and I stagger through the weekend. Every hour or so one of us steals away to a computer to re- or misdiagnose for the fourteenth time. The truth is that we know for sure I have some kind of cancer, and that any cancer that has metastasized is bad, and that that is all we will know for a few more days.

Finally, Monday comes. After the CT scan, Pat takes me directly to the hospital to get prodded by his favorite surgeon, whom I'll call Dr. Goodguy. ("The surgeon I'd take my own family to," Pat says.) In the examining room, Dr. Goodguy frowns over my films, palpates my abdomen, interviews me, and schedules me for both an MRI that afternoon and a biopsy two days later. I think to ask how big all these growths are. *Several oranges and even one grapefruit,* Dr. Goodguy says, my first inkling that citrus metaphor is essential to cancer treatment.

Being a patient requires that you master the Zen of living in hos-

pital time, tuning out as much as possible while also demanding a
constant vigilance, because some people really will screw up your
treatment if you're not paying strict attention. When I go for my
MRI, the technician — a lovely, smiling man with a very uncertain
command of English — seems very vague about what, exactly, he's
supposed to be examining. I insist that he call Dr. Goodguy's office.

Pat and Dr. Goodguy have been scratching their heads. What
could possibly grow so fast, and so widely? Probably — maybe —
lymphoma. They keep telling me this, which would be the good
news, because lymphomas are increasingly treatable. My gynecologist friend, Laura, has told me the same thing over the weekend.
My psychotherapist nods at the wisdom of this off-the-cuff prognosis. I find myself on the point of hysterical laughter. How many
more people, I wonder, are going to tell me, Congratulations!
You've got lymphoma!!

By Thursday afternoon this is no longer funny. I've had a biopsy
the previous day, and Dr. Goodguy calls about three P.M. He has a
Very Serious Doctor Voice on, and jumps right in: "Well, this isn't
good. It's not lymphoma. Your pathology report shows that your
tumor is consistent with hepatoma, which is, uh, which is liver cancer." Already I am struggling: Does "consistent with" mean they
think that but they don't really know it? No, those are just scientific
weasel words they use in pathology reports. (A pathologist, I will
learn, would look at your nose and report that it is consistent with
a breathing apparatus.)

I know this diagnosis is very, very bad. Liver cancer is one of the
possibilities I researched in my compulsive tours of the Internet
over the weekend, so I already know it's one of the worst things you
can have. Still, I say to the doctor, "Well, how bad is that?"

"I won't avoid it. It's very serious."

"And it would presumably be bad news that it's already created
other tumors around my body?"

"Yes. Yes, that is a bad sign."

A lovely man, who's doing a hard job with a patient he just met
three days before. There are at least five large metastases of the
cancer in my pelvis and abdomen, and the mother ship — a tumor
the size of a navel orange — straddles the channel where the major blood vessels run into and out of the liver. Tumors so wide-

spread automatically "stage" my cancer at IV(b). There is no V, and there is no (c).

When I hang up the phone, I call Tim and tell him. We make it as clinical a conversation as possible, because otherwise there will be so much feeling it might stand in the way of acting. He is on his way home, right away.

I call my friend Liz and tell her. I tell her some of the statistics — that, as I read the data, I may be dead by Christmas. Liz almost always says the perfect thing, from the heart, and now she says the two things I most need to hear. The first is "I want you to know that, whatever happens, I will be with you the whole way."

The second is "And you know that all of us — but this is my promise — we will all work to keep you alive in your children's minds." Now tears are pouring down my cheeks, and they feel good.

The drama of discovery and diagnosis happened so long ago, and has been followed by so many drastic plot twists, that it feels to me like ancient history. But I've noticed that almost everyone I talk to is very curious to know those details. Whenever the whim of disease takes me into the view of a new doctor or nurse, we fall into the standard, boring rhythm of summarizing history and condition (when diagnosed; at what stage; what treatments have been administered since, with what results). If the person I'm talking to is young and relatively inexperienced, I may find myself more schooled in this procedure even than she or he is. But there always comes a moment when their professionalism suddenly drops, their clipboards drift to their sides, and they say, "Uhn, how — do you mind if I ask you how you happened to find out you had cancer?" I realize at these times that they are asking as fellow humans, not too much younger than I am, and their fascination is the same as everyone else's: Could this happen to me? How would I know? What would that feel like?

We have all indulged this curiosity, haven't we? What would I do if I suddenly found I had a short time to live . . . What would it be like to sit in a doctor's office and hear a death sentence? I had entertained those fantasies just like the next person. So when it actually happened, I felt weirdly like an actor in a melodrama. I had — and still sometimes have — the feeling that I was doing, or had

done, something faintly self-dramatizing, something a bit too at-
tention-getting. (I was raised by people who had a horror of melodrama, but that's another part of the story.)

In two months I will mark the finish of year 3 B.T. — my third
year of Borrowed Time (or, as I think of it on my best days, Bonus
Time). When I was diagnosed with stage IV(b) liver cancer in early
July of 2001, every doctor was at great pains to make clear to me
that this was a death sentence. Unless you find liver cancer early
enough to have a surgeon cut out the primary tumor before it
spreads, you have little chance of parole. The five-year survival rate
for those who can't have surgery is less than 1 percent; my cancer
had spread so widely that I was facing a prognosis somewhere between three and six months. I was forty-three; my children were
five and eight.

Liver cancer is so untreatable because chemotherapy has little
effect. There are other, localized treatments that can slow the
growth of the main tumor, or tumors, in the liver. (They pump
chemo through an artery directly into the tumors and block the
exits; they ablate them with radio-frequency waves; they freeze
them; or they install localized chemo pumps to blast them.) But if
the cancer has spread, the medical textbooks say, there is no therapy that can stop it, or even slow it down much. Chemo has about a
25 to 30 percent chance of having any impact, and even then it will
almost always be a small and transient one: a slight and temporary
shrinkage, a short pause in the cancer's growth, a check on further
metastases that can add to the patient's pain.

But for some reasons I know and others I don't, my body — with
the help of six hospitals, dozens of drugs, a teeming multitude of
smart doctors and nurses, and a heroically stubborn husband —
has mounted a miraculous resistance. As seriously fucked cancer
patients go, I am an astonishingly healthy woman.

I live at least two different lives. In the background, usually, is the
knowledge that, for all my good fortune so far, I will still die of this
disease. This is where I wage the physical fight, which is, to say the
least, a deeply unpleasant process. And beyond the concrete chal-
lenges of needles and mouth sores and barf basins and barium, it
has thrown me on a roller coaster that sometimes clatters up a hill,
giving me a more hopeful, more distant view than I'd expected,

and at other times plunges faster and farther than I think I can endure. Even when you know the plunge is coming — it's in the nature of a roller coaster, after all, and you know that you disembark on the bottom and not the top — even then, it comes with some element of fresh despair.

I've hated roller coasters all my life.

But in the foreground is regular existence: love the kids, buy them new shoes, enjoy their burgeoning wit, get some writing done, plan vacations with Tim, have coffee with my friends. Having found myself faced with that old bull-session question (What would you do if you found out you had a year to live?), I learned that a woman with children has the privilege or duty of bypassing the existential. What you do, if you have little kids, is lead as normal a life as possible, only with more pancakes.

This is the realm of life in which I make intensely practical decisions — almost, these three years on, without thinking about it. When we bought a new car last fall, I chose it, bargained for it, and paid for it with the last of an old retirement account my father had left me. And then I registered it only in my husband's name — because who needs the hassles over title if he decides to sell it later? When an old crown at the back of my lower right jaw began to disintegrate last summer, I looked at my dentist, whose fastidiousness I have relied on for almost twenty years, and said, Jeff, look: I'm doing okay right now, but I've got every reason to think it would be foolish to sink four thousand dollars into, um, infrastructure at this point. Is there anything sort of half-assed and inexpensive we could do, just to get by?

Sometimes I feel immortal: whatever happens to me now, I've earned the knowledge some people never gain, that my span is finite, and I still have the chance to rise, and rise, to life's generosity. But at other times I feel trapped, cursed by my specific awareness of the guillotine blade poised above my neck. At those times I resent you — or the seven other people at dinner with me, or my husband, deep in sleep beside me — for the fact that you may never even catch sight of the blade assigned to you.

Sometimes I simply feel horror, that most elementary thing. The irreducible fear, for me, is the fantasy that I will by some mistake be imprisoned in my body after dying. As a child I never enjoyed a minute of any campfire stories of the buried-alive genre. And even without that unwelcome and vivid fear in my mind, I can't find any way around the horror of being left alone down there in the dark, picked apart by processes about which I'm a little bit squeamish even when they're just fertilizing my daylilies. Intellectually, I know it won't matter to me in the slightest. But my most primal fear is that somehow my consciousness will be carelessly left behind among my remains.

But, of course, I am already being killed, by one of nature's most common blunders. And these blunt fears are easily deconstructed as a form of denial: if I'm stuck alive in my coffin, well, that will in some sense override the final fact of my death, no? I can see these dread-filled fantasies as the wishes they are: that I really can stay in this body I love, that my consciousness really will run on past my death, that I won't just . . . die.

There are a million lesser fears. The largest category concerns my children, and weighs both the trivial and the serious. I fear that my Alice will never really learn to wear tights. (You'd think, from watching my husband try to help her into them on the rare occasion when he's asked, that he'd been asked to perform a breech birth of twin colts at the peak of a blizzard.) That no one will ever really brush her fine, long hair all the way through, and that she will display a perpetual bird's nest at the back of her neck. (And — what? People will say her slatternly mother should have drummed better Hair Care into her family's minds before selfishly dying of cancer?) That no one will ever put up curtains in my dining room, the way I've been meaning to for the last three years.

Deeper: Who will talk to my darling girl when she gets her period? Will my son sustain that sweet enthusiasm he seems to beam most often at me? There are days I can't look at them — literally, not a single time — without wondering what it will do to them to grow up without a mother. What if they can't remember what I was like? What if they remember, and grieve, all the time?

What if they don't?

But even this obvious stuff, the dread and sorrow, make up a falsely simple picture. Sometimes, early on, death was a great dark lozenge that sat bittersweet on my tongue for hours at a time, and I savored the things I'd avoid forever. I'll never have to pay taxes, I thought, or go to the Department of Motor Vehicles. I won't have to see my children through the worst parts of adolescence. I won't have to be human, in fact, with all the error and loss and love and inadequacy that come with the job.

I won't have to get old.

It says a lot about the power of denial that I could so automatically seek (and find!) the silver lining that might come with dying of cancer in my forties. For good and ill, I no longer think that way. The passage of time has brought me the unlikely ability to work, simultaneously, at facing my death and loving my life.

Often it is lonely work. And I have nothing happy to impart about the likelihood that I will have to take chemotherapy for the rest of my life — nothing, except that I should be so lucky. But I am now, after a long struggle, surprisingly happy in the crooked, sturdy little shelter I've built in the wastes of Cancerland. Here, my family has lovingly adapted to our awful tumble in fortune. And here, I nurture a garden of eleven or twelve different varieties of hope, including the cramped, faint, strangely apologetic hope that, having already done the impossible, I will somehow attain the unattainable cure.

Our first stop, after I received my diagnosis, was the office of my GP, the one who missed all the signs and symptoms of my disease. We were not feeling especially confident in his skills, but we thought he might have ideas about treatment, and could at least perform the service of doing a full set of blood tests.

As we were driving over to Dr. Generalist, Tim turned to me at a stoplight and said, "I just want you to know: I'm going to be a total prick." What he meant by this was that there was no log he wouldn't roll, no connection he wouldn't tap, no pull he wouldn't use. Tim, a fellow journalist, is a man who would rather swallow gravel than use a job title to get a good table at a restaurant. But within an hour of hearing the bad news, he had scored me an appointment early the next Monday at Memorial Sloan-Kettering Cancer Center, in New York City, one of the country's most eminent cancer-treatment centers. Tim had done this by the simple expedient of calling Harold Varmus, president and chief executive officer of MSKCC, with whom we'd formed a warm but very tangential friendship when Harold was in Washington running the National Institutes of Health during the Clinton administration.

These are the kinds of appointments, I was to learn, that some people wait weeks or even months for. I say that not in the spirit of a boast, only as a reminder that in this way, as in most others, medicine is unfair — rationed in fundamentally irrational ways. But when your own time comes, you will pull pretty much every string available to get what you need.

By the next morning — it was still only the day after my diagnosis — I had a noon appointment with the topmost GI oncologist available at Johns Hopkins University Medical Center, which is in Baltimore, a little less than an hour from our house. This conquest of the appointment book was the doing of another friend, one of my bosses. We also got an appointment at the National Cancer Institute for later the following week.

So I had all the appointments I needed, and a husband who did yeoman legwork running from place to place getting copies of MRIs and CT scans and pathologists' reports and blood tests. If speed was needed in my case, I was well on my way to a record pace.

Just one problem: all this moving and shaking, driving to Baltimore and flying to New York, took us to the very same brick wall. In strode the doctor (usually trailing a retinue of students) to meet me, ask me a little about the onset of my disease. Out he went with my films under his arm, to look at them in privacy. In he came, quietly, his pace slowed and his face grim. He said some version of what the oncologist at Hopkins had said: "I couldn't believe — I just told my colleague, 'There is no way she looks sick enough to have this degree of disease. Someone blew this diagnosis.' Then I looked at this MRI."

It fell to the man at Hopkins to be the first to tell us just how bad my situation was. But they all said more or less the same thing. The Hopkins doc did it while focusing intently on the shape of his cuticles, turning his fingers in and then splaying them forward like a bride showing off her new rock. Another did it while holding my hand and looking sweetly into my face. "My dear," this one said, "you're in desperate trouble." One did it in the midst of a completely impenetrable lecture on the chemistry of chemotherapy. One did it with a look of panic on his face.

What it boiled down to was: We have nothing to do for you. You can't have surgery, because there's so much disease outside the liver. You're not a good candidate for any of the newer interventional strategies, and we can't do radiation, because we'd destroy too much viable liver tissue. All we can do is chemotherapy, and to be honest, we really don't expect much in the way of results.

The first time we heard this lecture, at Hopkins, we stepped blinking into the sunshine of a hot July day. "I need to take a walk," I told my husband, and we set off in the direction of Baltimore's Fell's Point neighborhood. Before long, I wanted to sit and talk. The only place we could find to sit was the concrete staircase of a public library. We sat there to absorb what we'd just heard.

"Maybe," said Tim, "the doctors at Sloan-Kettering will have something different to say."

"I doubt it," I said, out of the certainty of my Internet travels and the doctor's unambiguous pessimism. This pretty much set the pattern Tim and I would follow for the coming months: he took care of the hope, and I took care of getting ready to die.

The days fractured into lurching, indelible moments and odd details that stuck. The way the Sloan-Kettering waiting room — lush with Rockefeller-funded orchids and a plashing water sculpture — had nice rows of seats whose armrests were attached with Velcro so you could tear them away when you needed to sit and sob in your husband's arms. The black-and-white bumper sticker on the glass door of an East Side coffee shop we stopped into while killing time before an appointment: THIS IS REALLY HAPPENING, it said, in what felt like a message nailed there just for my eyes.

For the first ten days or so, I had a necessary composure. I got to and through all those appointments. I went to my desk and put together a filing system for all the names and information that were flooding into our life. I knew I wanted to keep it together while we decided what we were going to tell the children.

But after our discouraging visit to Sloan-Kettering, I could feel the waters at the dam getting close to overflowing. We decided to stay in New York an extra night or two to take advantage of the hospital's offer of a PET scan, which might identify new tumors, or spot the regression of old ones, more quickly than a CT scan.

As we sat in that plush waiting room making this decision, it came to me that I couldn't bear to continue staying with the old friends who had put us up the night before. They were contemporaries of my parents' and very dear to me, but I couldn't face talking to anyone about this latest news, or having to be in the least bit socially adept.

Tim, who knows me so well, put his arm around me and said, "Let's not think about money. Where do you want to go?" I brightened for a moment. There might not be any treatments out there that would work for me, but, by God, New York had some fine hotels. "Mmmm . . . the Peninsula?" So off we went to the land of high thread counts and long baths, with a TV screen just above the taps.

It's amazing how you can distract yourself in the midst of such a dramatic experience — because you can't believe such awful news twenty-four hours a day. So I surrendered to the pleasures of a great hotel for about a day. I had my hair washed and blow-dried, and received a pedicure in the Peninsula salon. (I still remember sitting there staring, staring at all the colors of polish I could pick from. It took on the crazy proportions of an important decision: a docile sort of peach? a very feminine light pink, which might acknowledge surrender? Hell, no: I chose a violent red, brighter than fire engines, bright as lollipops.)

Then, feeling beautiful, I actually danced around the room when Tim was out, my CD headphones blasting Carly Simon in my ears. When I was done, I looked out the window of our room on the eighth floor, down all those hard surfaces to the tarmac of Fifth Avenue, and wondered what it would feel like just to jump. Would it be better or worse than what I was stepping into?

That night, finally, the dam broke. I was lying in bed with Tim when I realized it was all true: I was dying. Soon I would be dead. No one else would be in it with me.

I would be the one on the bed, and when the hospice nurse stopped by, my dearest loves would retreat to the hallway and swap impressions — separated from me already. Even while still alive, I would leave their party. I lay under those wonderful sheets and felt cold to the bone. I began to cry, loud, then louder. I shouted my terror. I sobbed with my entire rib cage. Tim held me while I heaved it out this way, a titanic purging. I was so loud that I wondered why no one called the police to say there was a woman getting murdered across the hall. It felt good to let go, but that feeling was little. It was dwarfed by the recognition I had just allowed in.

*

We have come to think of my cancer not just as a disease but also as a locale. Cancerland is the place where at least one of us is often depressed: it is as if my husband and I hand the job back and forth without comment, the way most couples deal with child-minding or being the Saturday chauffeur.

I try to remember that I'm one of the luckiest cancer patients in America, by dint of good medical insurance, great contacts who gained me access to the best of the best among doctors, an amazing support system of friends and family, and the brains and drive to be a smart and demanding medical consumer, which is one of the very hardest things I've ever done. I'm quite sure that if I were among the forty-three million of my fellow Americans who have no health insurance — let alone really good insurance — I'd be dead already. As it is, I never see a hospital bill that hasn't already been paid. And there is no copayment on the many medications I've taken. Which is fortunate: one of them — the Neupogen with which I inject myself every day for a week after chemo to boost my bone marrow's production of white cells — costs about $20,000 a year.

For me, time is the only currency that truly counts anymore. I have weathered days of chemo-induced wretchedness and pain without a whimper, only to come unglued when some little glitch suddenly turns up to meddle with the way I had planned to use some unit of time: that this half-hour, and the contents I had planned to pour into it, are now lost to me forever seems an insupportable unfairness. Because of course any old unit of time can suddenly morph into a bloated metaphor for the rest of your time on earth, for how little you may have and how little you may control it.

Most of the time, for the past three years, even my good days have given me energy to do only one Big Thing: lunch with a friend, writing a column, a movie with the kids. Choose, choose, choose. I find myself on the phone with someone I'd love to see, and then I look at my calendar and find that, realistically, my next episode of unscheduled Free Play is five weeks off, on the far side of my next treatment, and even then there will really be a total of only about seven hours I can assign before the treatment after that. I am forced to admit that, in this cramped context, I don't actually want to spend two of these hours with the person I'm talking to. These forced choices make up one of the biggest losses of sickness.

But on the other side of this coin is a gift. I think cancer brings to most people a new freedom to act on the understanding that their time is important. My editor at the *Washington Post* told me, when I first got sick, that after his mother recovered from cancer, his parents literally never went anywhere they didn't want to. If you have ever told yourself, breezily, that life is too short to spend any of it with your childhood neighbor's annoying husband, those words now take on the gleeful raiment of simple fact. The knowledge that time's expenditure is important, that it is up to you, is one of the headiest freedoms you will ever feel.

Some of my choices surprise me. One afternoon — a blowy day in early spring, the first day when the sun actually seemed to outpower the wind — I ducked a meeting people were counting on me to come to, and I didn't lie or apologize for my reasons, because the most pressing thing I could possibly do that afternoon was plant something purple in that little spot next to the garden gate, the one I'd been thinking about for two years.

Time, I now understand, used to be a shallow concept to me. There was the time you occupied, sometimes anxiously, in the present (a deadline in three hours, a dentist's appointment for which you were ten minutes late), and there was your inarticulate sense of time's grander passage, and the way it changes with age.

Now time has levels and levels of meaning. For example, I have clung for a year and a half to a friend's observation that young children experience time in a different way from adults. Since a month can seem an eternity to a child, then every month I manage to live might later teem with meaning and memory for my children. This totem is all I need during times when my pockets are otherwise empty of wisdom or strength.

Since I was diagnosed, I have had an eternity of time — at least six times as much as I was supposed to have — and sometimes I think that all of that time has been gilded with my knowledge of its value. At other moments, I think sadly of how much of the past three years has been wasted by the boredom and exhaustion and enforced stillness of treatment.

Not long after my diagnosis, in the pleasant offices of one of my new doctors, a liver specialist, we finally had the obligatory conversation about how I could have gotten this cancer. "You've got no cirrhosis," he said wonderingly, ticking off the potential causes on his fingers. "You've got no hepatitis. It's wild that you look so healthy."

So how do you think I got it? I asked.

"Lady," he said, "you got hit by lightning."

My biggest fear in those early days was that death would snatch me right away. An oncologist at Sloan-Kettering had mentioned, parenthetically, that the tumor in my vena cava could give birth at any time to a blood clot, causing a fast death by way of pulmonary embolism. The tumor was too close to the heart for them to consider installing a filter that would prevent this. It would be "rational," he said, in answer to our questions, to make it a policy for me not to drive anywhere with the children in the car.

I knew, too, that the disease outside my liver had grown with incredible speed. Only a couple of weeks after diagnosis, I began having symptoms — including stomach pain bad enough to hospitalize me for two days. After watching my father's five-year battle with cancer, I was aware that a cascade of side effects could begin at any time, some of them fatal.

I wasn't ready, I said to friends. Not in the way I could be ready in, oh, three or four months. Perhaps I was kidding myself in imagining that I could compose myself if only I had a little time. But I think not entirely. I had watched my parents die three years earlier, seven weeks apart — my mother, ironically, of liver disease, and my father of an invasive cancer of unknown origin. I had a pretty good idea, I thought, of what was coming.

But from almost the first instant, my terror and grief were tinged with an odd relief. I was so lucky, I thought, that this was happening to me as late as forty-three, not in my thirties or my twenties. If I died soon, there would be some things I'd regret not having done, and I would feel fathomless anguish at leaving my children so young. But I had a powerful sense that, for my own part, I had had every chance to flourish. I had a loving marriage. I'd known the sweet, rock-breaking, irreplaceable labor of parenthood, and would leave two marvelous beings in my place. I had known rapture, and adventure, and rest. I knew what it was to love my work. I had deep, hard-won friendships, and diverse, widespread friendships of less intensity.

I was surrounded by love.

All this knowledge brought a certain calm. I knew intuitively that I would have felt more panicked, more frantic, in the years when I was still growing into my adulthood. For I had had the chance to become the person it was in me to be. Nor did I waste any time wondering why. Why me? It was obvious that this was no more or less than a piece of horrible bad luck. Until then my life had been, in the big ways, one long run of good luck. Only a moral idiot could feel entitled, in the midst of such a life, to a complete exemption from bad fortune.

So now my death — as a given — dominated my relationships with all of those close to me: with my two dear, dear older sisters, to whom I was doubly bonded by the shared ordeal of helping my mother die; and with my stepmother, a contemporary of mine, who had seen my father through his five ferocious years of survival. With my best friends, who spoiled and cosseted and fed and sat with me, rounding up great brigades of clucking acquaintances to bring us dinners, saying just the right thing, and never turning aside my need to talk — especially my need to talk about when, not if. My friend Liz even went out to look over the local residential hospice, to help me work through my practical concerns about whether, with children so young, I was entitled to die at home.

Above all, of course, death saturated my life with my children — Willie, then eight, and Alice, then five. I don't think death (as opposed to illness) dominated their view of me, but it certainly barged its cackling way into my heart and mind during even the simplest of family interchanges. After talking to friends and reading several books, Tim and I had decided to handle the matter openly with them. We told them that I had cancer, and what kind. We told them about chemotherapy, and how it would make me seem even sicker than I looked then. We emphasized that they couldn't catch cancer and had nothing to do with causing it.

Beyond that, we would answer with honesty any question they asked, but wouldn't step ahead of them in forcing their knowledge of just how bad things were. When the timing of my death revealed itself, then we would have to tell them. Above all, I wanted to spare them the loss of their childhood to a constant vigilance: if they knew we would talk to them honestly, they wouldn't have to put all their energy into figuring out at every turn what new distress was agitating the air around them. Neither of them, at first, chose to ask the $64,000 question. But I couldn't lay eyes on them without seeing them swallowed by the shadow of devastation to come.

Notice, though, that I don't include my husband among those to whom my death was an imminent fact. From the moment of diagnosis, Tim rolled up his sleeves and went to work. In this way, we divided the work of assimilating our nightmare: I addressed myself to death; he held a practical insistence on life. It was the best possible thing he could have done for me, although it often separated us at the time. It could make me crazy, lying awake on the left side of the bed, wanting to talk about death, while Tim lay awake on the right side, trying to figure out the next five moves he had to make to keep me alive, and then, beyond that, to find the magic bullet in which I did not believe.

But I never thought of refusing treatment. For one thing, it was obvious that I owed my children any shot at reprieve, no matter how improbable. Also, my doctors said that even the slim prospect of mitigation was worth a try. And so, Tim and I drifted into a tacit, provisional agreement to act as if . . . as if, while I began chemotherapy, I were in some genuine suspense about the outcome.

Yet it made me furious anytime someone tried to cheer me up by reciting the happy tale of a sister-in-law's cousin who had liver cancer but now he's eighty and he hasn't been troubled by it in forty years. I wanted to scream, *Don't you know how sick I am?* I knew how narcissistic and self-dramatizing this sounded. Still, it enraged me when anyone said, *Aaanh, what do doctors know? They don't know everything.* I was working so hard to accept my death; I felt abandoned, evaded, when someone insisted that I would live.

That was a deeper anger than the irritation I felt at the people — some of them important figures in my life — who had memorably inappropriate reactions. I can't count the times I've been asked what psychological affliction made me invite this cancer. My favorite *New Yorker* cartoon, now taped above my desk, shows two ducks talking in a pond. One of them is telling the other, "Maybe you should ask yourself why you're inviting all this duck hunting into your life right now."

One woman sent me a card to "congratulate" me on my "cancer journey," and quoted Joseph Campbell to the effect that in order to achieve the life you deserved, you had to give up the life you had planned. Screw you, I thought. *You* give up the life *you* had planned.

Common wisdom insists, in answer to the awkward feelings that always accompany sickness and death, that there's really no wrong thing to say. This is entirely false. Around the same time I started treatment, my friend Mike revealed to all his friends that he had been dealing for some years with Parkinson's disease. We began a competition, by e-mail, to see who could compile the most appalling reactions.

I found my best ones in hospitals, among doctors and nurses who seemed unacquainted with — or terrified of — fear and death, who were constantly holding up the garlic of their difference from me, to ward me off even as they pretended to minister to me. There was the nurse who hissed at me, with inexplicable ire, "You have a very bad disease, you know." There was the nurse's aide at Georgetown University Hospital who trudged into my room one morning, heaved a great sigh, and said, "I tell you, I hate working the oncology floor. It's so depressing." Her aunt had died of cancer, she said, and, "boy, is that an awful disease."

At least her oddball gloom was right out there on the surface. Perhaps worst of all was the nurse in the chemo-infusion ward, with whom I fell into conversation to while away my seventh hour of chemotherapy on a gray day in late December. We talked idly about vacations we'd like to take someday. "Oh, well," she said, putting down my chart and stretching kittenishly on her way out the door, "I have all the time in the world."

I had bought deeply into the pessimism of the doctors treating me. We think our culture lauds the stubborn survivor, the one who says, "I will beat this cancer," and then promptly wins the Tour de France. But the truth is that there is a staggering vulnerability in asserting one's right to hope. Even most of the doctors who have from time to time promoted my optimism tend to wash their hands of it as soon as some procedure or potion fails to pan out. So I have carried what hope I have as a furtive prize.

This attitude was driven, too, by what I brought to the fight. I grew up in a house where there was a premium on being wised up to impending disapproval or disappointment, and there was punishment by contempt for any blatant display of innocence or hopeful desire. It was all too easy for me to feel shamed in the blast of medicine's certainty. If I carried hope from the start, I did it in secret, hiding it like an illegitimate child of a century past. I hid it even from myself.

It is in my personality, anyway, to linger on the dark side, sniffing under every rock, determined to know the worst that may happen. Not to be caught by surprise. I was raised in a family full of lies — a rich, entertaining, well-elaborated fivesome that flashed with competition and triangles and changing alliances. If your sister was becoming anorexic, no one mentioned it. When your father's ubiquitous assistant came along on family vacations year after year, and sat at picnics with him thigh to thigh, no one named the strangeness of it. That my parents divided me and my sisters up between themselves and schooled us in scorn for the other team — that was certainly never acknowledged. But it married me for life to the inconvenient argument, the longing to know what was real.

Hence, even when my prospects for recovery or remission have looked best, there has always been one face of my being that was turned toward the likelihood of death — keeping in touch with it, convinced that denying it any entry would weaken me in ways I couldn't afford. Forced into a corner, I'll choose truth over hope any day.

I worried, of course, that I was dooming myself. Americans are so steeped in the message that we are what we think, and that a positive attitude can banish disease. (You'd be amazed how many people need to believe that only losers die of cancer.) Was my realism going to shoot down any possibility of help? Superstitiously, I wondered.

But it turns out that hope is a more supple blessing than I had imagined. From the start, even as my brain was wrestling with death, my body enacted some innate hope that I have learned is simply a part of my being. Chemotherapy would knock me into a passive misery for days. And then — depending on which formula I was taking at the time — a day would come when I would wake up feeling energetic and happy and very much like a normal person. Whether the bad time I had just had lasted five days or five weeks, some inner voice eventually said — and still says — *Never mind.* Today is a ravishing day, and I will put on a short skirt and high heels and see how much of the future I can inhale.

*

Three weeks after my diagnosis, on the morning of my first chemo-therapy, my liver specialist dictated notes that closed with this frag-mentary, misspelled sentence: "It is to be hoped . . . , unlikel that we will get a second chance."

Two chemo cycles later, I had a CT scan that showed dramatic shrinkage in all my tumors — shrinkage by as much as half. Dr. Liver actually hugged me, and hinted that it was not impossible I might be a "complete responder." The first thing you learn when you get cancer is that the disease you've always thought of as ninety or one hundred precise conditions is in fact hundreds of different diseases, which shade into each other all along the spectrum. And I turned out to have some mysterious fluke, a bit of biological filigree in the makeup of my tumors, that rendered them far better targets than I'd had any right to expect.

I went right out and bought four bottles of champagne and in-vited our eight dearest friends to the house for a party. It was a beautiful September night and we all ate pizza on the front porch. The kids were thrilled by the energy of it all, without quite under-standing it. (After all, I still had cancer, didn't I? And they hadn't known how firmly I had felt sealed in my coffin before now.) It was as if a door far across a dark room had opened a small crack, ad-mitting brilliant light from a hallway: it was still a long, long shot, I knew, but now at least I had something to drive toward. A possible opening, where before there had been none.

I became a professional patient. And all my doctors learned my name.

Biographical Notes

LAURIE ABRAHAM is a freelance writer and senior editor at *Elle* magazine and the author of *Mama Might Be Better Off Dead: The Failure of Health Care in Urban America*. Formerly the features editor at *Mirabella*, she has written for publications such as *New York*, the *New York Times Magazine*, and *Mother Jones*. Her work is also included in the original essay collections *The Bitch in the House* and *Maybe Baby*. She lives in Brooklyn, New York, with her husband and two daughters.

POE BALLANTINE writes: I'm an average guy who used to wander around a lot in a suicidal daze, but now I've finally settled in Chadron, Nebraska, in a slump-roofed house across from the railroad tracks, where a wife and child and a seven-day-a-week job cleaning floors at the local Safeway have cured me for the while of my malaise. I would recite the names of my books here, but my eyes glaze over when I see others do it. Buy me buy me. Are we nothing but a parade of piffling harlots and T-bone steaks? I would also like once again to give heartfelt thanks to the editorial staff at the *Sun*, Sy Safransky and Andrew Snee especially, whose bafflingly persistent efforts occasionally provide the illusion that I know what I'm doing.

EMILY BERNARD is an associate professor in the English department and teaches in the ALANA U.S. Ethnic Studies Program at the University of Vermont. She is the editor of *Remember Me to Harlem: The Letters of Langston Hughes and Carl Van Vechten* and *Some of My Best Friends: Writers on Interracial Friendships*. She dedicates this essay to her amazing Honors 195 students (Sarah, Lauren, Emily, Ben, Nate, Tyler, David, Stephanie, Colin, Hazel, Eric) and to Lizzie.

KEN CHEN hails from the Bay Area, where he attended the University of California at Berkeley. In addition to being one of the original contributors to *Arts & Letters Daily,* a popular cultural Web site, he also founded *Satellite: The Berkeley Magazine of News and Culture.* His work, available at www.kenchen.org, has been published in the *Boston Review of Books, Pleiades, h2so4, Radical Society, IndieWire, Reverse Shot,* and *Bridge.* He has been a finalist for the following prizes: the Barrow Street Press book contest, the Anthony Hecht Poetry Prize, the Diner poetry contest, the Me Three Literary Criticism Award, and the Lili Fabilli and Eric Hoffer Essay Prize. A recent graduate of Yale Law School, he now works for a law firm in New York. He would like to thank *Mānoa*'s managing editor, Pat Matsueda, for her patient and helpful edits, as well as Beth Hillman and Sarah Karmazin.

TOI DERRICOTTE, a professor of English at the University of Pittsburgh, has published four books of poems: *The Empress of the Death House, Natural Birth, Captivity,* and *Tender* (winner of the 1998 Paterson Poetry Prize). Her memoir, *The Black Notebooks,* was named a New York Times Notable Book of the Year. She is the recipient of a Guggenheim fellowship, two fellowships in poetry from the National Endowment for the Arts, and two Pushcart Prizes. She is the cofounder of Cave Canem, the workshop/retreat for African-American poets.

JOSEPH EPSTEIN is the author of eighteen books, among them *Snobbery: The American Version, Friendship: An Exposé,* and *Alexis de Tocqueville.* A new book of his essays, *In a Cardboard Belt,* will be published by Houghton Mifflin in 2007.

EUGENE GOODHEART was born in Brooklyn, New York, in 1931. He was educated at Columbia College (B.A. '53), the University of Virginia (M.A. '54), and again at Columbia (Ph.D. '61). His teaching résumé shows a restless effort to find a congenial academic home: Bard College, the University of Chicago, Mount Holyoke College, MIT, Boston University, and for eighteen years, until retirement in 2001, Brandeis University. He has also been a visitor at Wesleyan University, Columbia, and Wellesley College. He is the author of ten books of literary and cultural criticism, among them *Culture and the Radical Conscience, The Skeptic Disposition,* and *The Reign of Ideology.* During the past decade or so he has become addicted to the writing of personal essays, a number of which went into the making of a memoir, *Confessions of a Secular Jew.* He hesitated about writing "Whistling in the Dark," knowing that mortality would be a hard act to follow.

ADAM GOPNIK has been on the editorial staff of *The New Yorker* since 1987 and is the author of the essay collection *Paris to the Moon* and an adventure story for children, *The King in the Window.* He has received three National Magazine Awards for essays and criticism and the George Polk Award for magazine reporting. His new book, *Through the Children's Gate: A Home in New York,* about Manhattan life in the new millennium, will be published in fall 2006.

KIM DANA KUPPERMAN was born and raised in Manhattan. She now lives in Gettysburg, Pennsylvania, where she works as the managing editor of the *Gettysburg Review.* Her work has appeared in *Alaska Quarterly Review,* the *Baltimore Review, Brevity,* the *Cimarron Review,* the *Eclectic Literary Forum, Hotel Amerika, ISLE,* the *Louisville Review,* the *Maine Scholar,* and *River Teeth.* In 1996 she was honored with the first-place award in the Elie Wiesel Prize in Ethics essay contest. In 2003 she was the recipient of the Robert J. DeMott Prose Prize from the journal *Quarter After Eight.*

MICHELE MORANO is the author of the essay collection *Grammar Lessons: Travel Stories from Spain,* which will be published in spring 2007. Her essays have appeared in the *Georgia Review, Missouri Review, Fourth Genre,* and *Under the Sun,* as well as on Chicago Public Radio. She has been awarded grants and fellowships from the Rona Jaffe Foundation, the Illinois Arts Council, and the American Association of University Women. She lives and teaches in Chicago.

SUSAN ORLEAN has been a staff writer for *The New Yorker* since 1992. In addition, she has contributed to *Vogue, Outside, Rolling Stone,* and the *New York Times Magazine.* Her books include *The Orchid Thief, The Bullfighter Checks Her Makeup, Saturday Night,* and *My Kind of Place.* In 2004 she was a fellow at the Nieman Foundation for Journalism at Harvard University. She is currently at work on a biography of Rin Tin Tin.

SAM PICKERING teaches English at the University of Connecticut. His most recent book is *Indian Summer,* a collection of familiar essays, published in 2005. In press at the University of South Carolina is *Edinburgh Days,* an account of a semester he spent as a fellow at the Institute for Advanced Studies in the Humanities in Scotland.

ROBERT POLITO was born in Boston and now lives in New York City and New Paltz, New York. He is the author of *Savage Art: A Biography of Jim Thompson, A Reader's Guide to James Merrill's "The Changing Light at Sandover,"* and *Doubles,* among other books. He also edited *The Selected Poems of Kenneth Fearing, Crime Novels: American Noir of the 1930s and 40s,* and *Crime Novels: American Noir of the 1950s.* He writes regularly for *Bookforum* and directs the graduate writing program at the New School.

DAVID RIEFF is a contributing writer to the *New York Times Magazine.* He is the author of seven books, most recently *Slaughterhouse: Bosnia and the Failure of the West, A Bed for the Night: Humanitarianism in Crisis,* and *At the Point of a Gun: Democratic Dreams and Armed Intervention.* A contributing editor to the *New Republic* and contributing writer for the *Los Angeles Times,* he also writes for many other newspapers and magazines in the United States and western Europe. He lives in New York City.

OLIVER SACKS was born in London in 1933 and educated in London, Oxford, and California. He has received numerous honors for his writings, which include *Awakenings, The Man Who Mistook His Wife for a Hat,* and *An Anthropologist on Mars.* His most recent books are *Uncle Tungsten: Memories of a Chemical Boyhood* and *Oaxaca Journal.* Dr. Sacks practices neurology in New York City, and he is a fellow of both the American Academy of Arts and Letters and the American Academy of Arts and Sciences. He is an honorary board member of the National Aphasia Association, which promotes public awareness and resources for this condition. The association's Web site is www.aphasia.org.

PETER SELGIN's stories and essays have appeared in dozens of magazines, including *Glimmer Train, Missouri Review,* the *Sun, Alaska Quarterly Review, Descant, Northwest Review, North Dakota Quarterly,* and in the anthologies *Our Roots Are Deep in Passion* and *Writing Fiction.* His book *Life Goes to the Movies* was a finalist for the James Jones First Novel fellowship, and his short story collection, *Nothing but Water,* was shortlisted for the Iowa Fiction Award. His children's book, *S.S.* Gigantic *Across the Atlantic,* was a Scholastic Book Club selection and won the Lemme Award for best children's book in 2000. As a playwright, Selgin has won the Mill Mountain Theatre new plays competition and the Charlotte Repertory Theatre Festival competition. His drama *A God in the House,* based on Dr. Jack Kevorkian and his suicide machine, was staged at the Eugene O'Neill National Playwrights Conference. His paintings have been featured in *The New Yorker, Gourmet,* the *Wall Street Journal,* and on *Good Morning America* and NPR's *Weekend Edition.* He lives in the Bronx, New York, where he is coeditor of the journal *Alimentum: The Literature of Food.*

ALAN SHAPIRO, a newly elected fellow of the American Academy of Arts and Sciences, has published eight books of poems, including *The Dead Alive and Busy* (winner of the 2001 Kingsley Tufts Award), *Song and Dance,* and, most recently, *Tantalus in Love.* He has published several books of prose, including *The Last Happy Occasion,* a finalist for the 1996 National Book Critics Circle Award, and *Vigil.* Shapiro is a recipient of two awards from the National Endowment for the Arts, a fellowship from the Guggenheim Foundation, the O. B. Hardison Jr. Poetry Prize from the Folger Shakespeare Library, the Sarah Teasdale Award from Wellesley College, and an award in literature from the American Academy of Arts and Letters. He teaches at the University of North Carolina, Chapel Hill, where he lives with his wife, Callie Warner, and their three children.

LILY TUCK was born in France and lives in New York City. She is the author of four novels: *Interviewing Matisse, or The Woman Who Died Standing Up; The Woman Who Walked on Water; Siam, or The Woman Who Shot a Man* (a 2000 PEN/Faulkner Award finalist); and *The News from Paraguay* (winner of the 2004 National Book Award). Her collection of short stories is *Limbo and Other Places I Have Lived.*

SCOTT TUROW is the author of seven best-selling novels, from *Presumed Innocent* (1987) through *Ordinary Heroes* (2005), and of two nonfiction books, *One L* (1977) and *Ultimate Punishment* (1997). His piece on Saul Bellow is one of a number of essays he has occasionally contributed to magazines, including *The New Yorker,* the *New York Times Magazine,* and *Vanity Fair,* and to the opinion pages of several leading newspapers. He lives with his family outside Chicago and continues to practice law there with Sonnenschein, Nath & Rosenthal.

MARJORIE WILLIAMS was born in Princeton, New Jersey, in 1958 and died in Washington, D.C., in 2005. At the time she was diagnosed with liver cancer, Williams was writing a weekly op-ed column for the *Washington Post;* frequent political profiles for *Vanity Fair,* where she was a contributing editor; and regular book reviews for *Slate.* "A Matter of Life and Death" was assembled after Williams's death from portions of an unfinished memoir. A longer version of the essay can be found under the title "Hit by Lightning," in *The Woman at the Washington Zoo: Writings on Politics, Family, and Fate,* which won PEN's Martha Albrand Award for first nonfiction book.

Notable Essays of 2005

SELECTED BY ROBERT ATWAN

JOHN BIGUENET
Antediluvian. *Granta,* Winter.

SVEN BIRKERTS
A Weekend at Montauk. *Virginia Quarterly Review,* Winter.

EULA BISS
The Pain Scale. *Seneca Review,* Spring.

LYNN Z. BLOOM
(Im)Patient. *Prose Studies,* April/ August.

LOUISE A. BLUM
Killing My Father's Cat. *Cream City Review,* Fall.

CAT BOHANNON
Shipwreck. *Georgia Review,* Spring.

JOE BONOMO
Caught. *River Teeth,* Spring.

WILLIAM BRADLEY
The Bald and the Beautiful. *Bellevue Literary Review,* Spring.

JENNIFER BRICE
On Keeping House. *Iron Horse Literary Review,* vol. 6, no. 2.

REBECCA BROCK
You Can't Even Remember What I'm Trying to Forget. *Threepenny Review,* Winter.

FLEDA BROWN
I Am Sick of School. *Iowa Review,* Spring.

FRANKLIN BURROUGHS
Deceptions of the Thrush. *Sewanee Review,* Fall.

JANET BURROWAY
Six Months On: What I Have Learned about Grief. *New Letters,* vol. 71, no. 2.

IAN BURUMA
Uncaptive Minds. *New York Times Magazine,* February 20.

FREDERICK BUSCH
Don't Watch the News. *Harper's Magazine,* November.

ROBERT OLEN BUTLER
Boot Camp. *Five Points,* vol. 9, no. 1.

TERRY CAESAR
English in Japan. *Salmagundi,* Spring/Summer.

BILL CAPOSSERE
Man in the Moon. *Colorado Review,* Fall.

DAVID CARKEET
Mountain Boy Meets Plato. *River Styx,* no. 71.

KELLY GREY CARLISLE
Physical Evidence. *River Teeth,* Fall.

MICHAEL CHABON
Hypocrisy and the Art of Parenting. *Details,* December.

KAREN CHASE
Learning to Shoot. *Southwest Review,* vol. 90, no. 1.

ALISON CLEMENT
They Always Call You "Miss." *The Sun,* March.

DIANE COMER
In the Drawer of Sharp Things. *North American Review,* January/ February.

REBECCA COOK
Inside Herman Inside Irene. *Northwest Review,* vol. 43, no. 3.

LISA COUTURIER
The Hopes of Snakes. *Orion,* January/February.

MARILYN J. CURRY
On Not Being Photographed by Diane Arbus. *New York Stories,* Spring.

RENÉE E. D'AOUST
Graham Crackers. *Mid-American Review,* vol. 26, no. 1.

NICHOLAS DELBANCO
In Defense of Quotation. *Fugue,* Winter.

DANIEL HARRIS
  Whining. *Salmagundi,* Fall/Winter.
KATHY HAYES
  Jump. *Louisville Review,* Fall.
DAVE HICKEY
  Welcome to Dreamsville. *Vanity Fair,*
  August.
OSCAR HIJUELOS
  Lunch at the Biltmore. *The New
  Yorker,* January 17.
EDWARD HOAGLAND
  The Glue Is Gone. *American Scholar,*
  Winter.
MARK HOLDEN
  Red Queen. *Chattahoochee Review,*
  Summer.
T. E. HOLT
  Delirium Tremens. *Tin House,* Fall.
LAZ HOULIGAN
  A Modest Proposal for Our Time.
  Ruminator, January/February.
HENRY HUGHES
  Lisa's Treatment. *Northwest Review,*
  vol. 43, no. 1.
WILLIAM HUHN
  Call of the Child. *Seems,* no. 38.

JUDITH JONES
  A Ripe Old Age. *Vogue,* August.

STEFAN KIESBYE
  Behind the Candy Factory. *Strange
  Fruit,* December.
DAVID KIRBY
  Like a Twin-Engine Bomber. *Mid-
  American Review,* vol. 26, no. 1.
WALTER KIRN
  Lost in the Meritocracy. *Atlantic
  Monthly,* January/February.
WILLIAM KITTREDGE
  Flyway. *Flyway,* Winter.
WILLIAM KLOEFKORN
  Walking with the Dog to Dover.
  Virginia Quarterly Review, Summer.

WAYNE KOESTENBAUM
  Perspicuous Consumption. *Artforum,*
  March.
TED KOOSER
  A Thanksgiving Surprise. *Country
  Living,* November.
ERIC KOTILA
  A Language Like Granite. *Nordic
  Reach,* vol. 12, no. 18.
LEONARD KRIEGEL
  Boy on the Pony: Encounters with
  the Socialism of Fools.
  Hotel Amerika, Fall.
CATHERINE KUDLICK
  The Blind Man's Harley: White
  Canes and Gender Identity in
  America. *Signs,* Winter.

ROBERT LACY
  Sing a Song of Sonny. *Sewanee
  Review,* Spring.
NATON LESLIE
  Roadside Attractions. *Under the Sun,*
  Summer.
DORIS LESSING
  The Death of a Chair. *Granta,*
  Summer.
JONATHAN LETHEM
  The Beards. *The New Yorker,*
  February 28.
PHILIP LEVINE
  A Day in May: Los Angeles, 1960.
  Georgia Review, Spring.
SARA LEVINE
  The Essayist Is Sorry for Your Loss.
  Puerto del Sol, Summer.
E. J. LEVY
  Home Is Where the Heart Aches.
  Missouri Review, vol. 28, no. 2.
CYNTHIA LEWIS
  Going Plastic in Costa Rica. *Antioch
  Review,* Winter.
MICHAEL LEWIS
  Wading Toward Home. *New York
  Times Magazine,* October 9.

WILLARD SPIEGELMAN
  Dallas On (and Off) My Mind.
    Parnassus, vol. 28, nos. 1 and 2.
BRIAN JAY STANLEY
  The Finite Experience of Infinite
    Life. *Hudson Review*, Spring.
JOHN STATTMANN
  Trial by Trash. *Post Road*, no. 11.
DONNA STEINER
  The Loupe. *Shenandoah*, Spring/
    Summer.
DEBORAH STONE
  Hungry for Air. *Boston Review*,
    February/March.
LAURIE STONE
  Five Scars. *Literary Review*, Spring.
MARK STRAND
  An Inside Story. *Story Quarterly*,
    no. 41.
ANDREW SULLIVAN
  The End of Gay Culture. *New
    Republic*, October 24.
FELICIA C. SULLIVAN
  Night Work. *Mississippi Review*, Fall.

BARRY TARGAN
  Little Art. *Sewanee Review*, Fall.
ALEX TAYLOR
  Unclean Acres. *River Teeth*, Spring.
JOHN THORN
  The Color of Sport. *Woodstock Times*,
    February 3.
ERIC TRETHEWEY
  The Coat. *Bayou*, no. 44.
NANCE VAN WINCKEL
  The Godchild and the Doll.
    Massachusetts Review, Winter.

WILLIAM VESTERMAN
  Plum Time in Neverneverland: The
    Divine Comedy of P. G.
    Wodehouse, *Raritan*, Summer.

GAIL WALDSTEIN
  Singing in the Ear Canal. *Iowa
    Review*, Winter.
GARRY WALLACE
  The Scent of Russian Olive. *Owen
    Wister Review*, 2005.
NATALIE WEXLER
  Perfect. *Gettysburg Review*, Summer.
ANGELA WHEELOCK
  Nesting in a Season of Light.
    Bellevue Literary Review, Spring.
EDMUND WHITE
  My Women. *The New Yorker*, June
    13/20.
VICKY WICKS
  A Boneyard Reverie. *South Dakota
    Review*, Spring/Summer.
JASON WILSON
  Wash Thoroughly Without a
    Swimsuit. *Washington Post
    Magazine*, March 6.
IRA WOOD
  Instead Of. *Ploughshares*, Spring.
SAINT JAMES HARRIS WOOD
  Captive Audience: Confessions of a
    Book Junkie. *The Sun*, August.

LEE ZACHARIAS
  A Stone's Weight. *Shenandoah*,
    Spring/Summer.
GENIE ZEIGER
  Before. *Upstreet*, no. 1.

Notable Special Issues of 2005

Creative Nonfiction, "Writing It Short:
  The Best of Brevity," ed. Lee
  Gutkind, no. 27.
Fourth Genre, "Travel in Nonfiction,"
  ed. Michael Steinberg and David
  Cooper, Fall.

Georgia Review, "Special Focus:
  Creatures," ed. T. R. Hummer,
  Fall.
Hobart, "The Travel Issue," ed. Aaron
  Burch, no. 5 (Summer).
Isotope, "Voices from the Ice:

Antarctica," ed. Christopher Cokinos, Fall/Winter.

Michigan Quarterly Review, "The Documentary Imagination," ed. Tom Fricke and Keith Taylor, Fall.

New Letters, "New American Essays," ed. Conger Beasley Jr. and Robert Stewart, vol. 72, no. 1.

New Literary History, "Essays Probing the Boundaries of the Human in Science and Science Fiction," ed. Ralph Cohen, Spring.

Northwest Review, "Essays and More Essays," ed. John Witte, vol. 41, no. 3.

Oxford American, "Southern Food Issue," ed. Marc Smirnoff and John T. Edge, Spring.

Parnassus, "Travel and Place," ed. Herbert Leibowitz and Ben Downing, vol. 28, nos. 1 and 2.

Seneca Review, "New Lyric Essayists," ed. Deborah Tall and John D'Agata, Spring.

Speakeasy, "New Orleans: Before and After," ed. Bart Schneider, Winter.

Sport Literate, "Retrospective Reflections," ed. William Meiners, vol. 4, no. 4.

Tin House, "Work," ed. Win McCormack, Fall.

Virginia Quarterly Review, "Walt Whitman and *Leaves of Grass* at 150," ed. Ted Genoways, vol. 81, no. 2.

Witness, "Childhood in America," ed. Peter Stine, no. 19 (Spring).

Yale Journal of Criticism, ed. Sean McCann and Michael Szalay, "Countercultural Capital: Essays on the Sixties from Some Who Weren't There," Fall.

THE B·E·S·T AMERICAN SERIES®

Introducing our newest addition to the BEST AMERICAN *series*

THE BEST AMERICAN COMICS 2006. Harvey Pekar, guest editor, Anne Elizabeth Moore, series editor. This newcomer to the best-selling series — the first Best American annual dedicated to the finest in graphic storytelling and literary comics — includes stories culled from graphic novels, pamphlet comics, newspapers, magazines, mini-comics, and the Web. Edited by the subject of the Oscar-nominated film *American Splendor*, Harvey Pekar, the collection features pieces by Robert Crumb, Chris Ware, Kim Deitch, Jaime Hernandez, Alison Bechdel, Joe Sacco, Lilli Carré, and Lynda Barry, among others.

ISBN-10: 0-618-71874-5 / ISBN-13: 978-0-618-71874-0 $22.00 POB

Alongside our perennial favorites

THE BEST AMERICAN SHORT STORIES® 2006. Ann Patchett, guest editor, Katrina Kenison, series editor. This year's most beloved short fiction anthology is edited by Ann Patchett, author of *Bel Canto*, a 2002 PEN/Faulkner Award winner and a National Book Critics Circle Award finalist. The collection features stories by Tobias Wolff, Donna Tartt, Thomas McGuane, Mary Gaitskill, Nathan Englander, and others. "Story for story, readers can't beat the *Best American Short Stories* series" (*Chicago Tribune*).

ISBN-10: 0-618-54351-1 / ISBN-13: 978-0-618-54351-9 $28.00 CL
ISBN-10: 0-618-54352-X / ISBN-13: 978-0-618-54352-6 $14.00 PA

THE BEST AMERICAN NONREQUIRED READING 2006. Edited by Dave Eggers, introduction by Matt Groening. This "enticing . . . funny, and wrenching" (*Cleveland Plain Dealer*) collection highlights a bold mix of fiction, nonfiction, screenplays, alternative comics, and more from publications large, small, and online. With an introduction by Matt Groening, creator of *The Simpsons* and *Futurama*, this volume features writing from *The Onion, The Daily Show, This American Life*, Judy Budnitz, Joe Sacco, and others.

ISBN-10: 0-618-57050-0 / ISBN-13: 978-0-618-57050-8 $28.00 CL
ISBN-10: 0-618-57051-9 / ISBN-13: 978-0-618-57051-5 $14.00 PA

THE BEST AMERICAN ESSAYS® 2006. Lauren Slater, guest editor, Robert Atwan, series editor. Since 1986, *The Best American Essays* has annually gathered outstanding nonfiction writing, establishing itself as the premier anthology of its kind. Edited by the best-selling author of *Prozac Diary*, Lauren Slater, this year's "delightful collection" (*Miami Herald*) highlights provocative, lively writing by Adam Gopnik, Scott Turow, Marjorie Williams, Poe Ballantine, and others.

ISBN-10: 0-618-70531-7 / ISBN-13: 978-0-618-70531-3 $28.00 CL
ISBN-10: 0-618-70529-5 / ISBN-13: 978-0-618-70529-0 $14.00 PA

THE BEST AMERICAN MYSTERY STORIES™ 2006. Scott Turow, guest editor, Otto Penzler, series editor. This perennially popular anthology is sure to appeal to mystery fans of every variety. The 2006 volume, edited by Scott Turow, author of the critically acclaimed *Ordinary Heroes* and *Presumed Innocent*, features both mystery veterans and new talents, offering stories by Elmore Leonard, Ed McBain, James Lee Burke, Joyce Carol Oates, Walter Mosley, and others.

ISBN-10: 0-618-51746-4 / ISBN-13: 978-0-618-51746-6 $28.00 CL
ISBN-10: 0-618-51747-2 / ISBN-13: 978-0-618-51747-3 $14.00 PA

THE B·E·S·T AMERICAN SERIES®

THE BEST AMERICAN SPORTS WRITING™ 2006. Michael Lewis, guest editor, Glenn Stout, series editor. "An ongoing centerpiece for all sports collections" (*Booklist*), this series stands in high regard for its extraordinary sports writing and top-notch editors. This year's guest editor, Michael Lewis, the acclaimed author of the bestseller *Moneyball*, brings together pieces by Gary Smith, Pat Jordan, Paul Solotaroff, Linda Robertson, L. Jon Wertheim, and others.

ISBN-10: 0-618-47021-2 / ISBN-13: 978-0-618-47021-1 $28.00 CL
ISBN-10: 0-618-47022-0 / ISBN-13: 978-0-618-47022-8 $14.00 PA

THE BEST AMERICAN TRAVEL WRITING 2006. Tim Cahill, guest editor, Jason Wilson, series editor. Tim Cahill is the founding editor of *Outside* magazine and a frequent contributor to *National Geographic Adventure*. This year's collection captures the traveler's wandering spirit and ever-present quest for adventure. Giving new life to armchair journeys are Alain de Botton, Pico Iyer, David Sedaris, Gary Shteyngart, George Saunders, and others.

ISBN-10: 0-618-58212-6 / ISBN-13: 978-0-618-58212-9 $28.00 CL
ISBN-10: 0-618-58215-0 / ISBN-13: 978-0-618-58215-0 $14.00 PA

THE BEST AMERICAN SCIENCE AND NATURE WRITING 2006. Brian Greene, guest editor, Tim Folger, series editor. Brian Greene, the best-selling author of *The Elegant Universe* and the first physicist to edit this prestigious series, offers a fresh take on the year's best science and nature writing. Featuring such authors as John Horgan, Daniel C. Dennett, and Dennis Overbye, among others, this collection "surprises us into caring about subjects we had not thought to examine" (*Cleveland Plain Dealer*).

ISBN-10: 0-618-72221-1 / ISBN-13: 978-0-618-72221-1 $28.00 CL
ISBN-10: 0-618-72222-X / ISBN-13: 978-0-618-72222-8 $14.00 PA

THE BEST AMERICAN SPIRITUAL WRITING 2006. Edited by Philip Zaleski, introduction by Peter J. Gomes. Featuring an introduction by Peter J. Gomes, a best-selling author, respected minister, and the Plummer Professor of Christian Morals at Harvard University, this year's edition of this "excellent annual" (*America*) gathers pieces from diverse faiths and denominations and includes writing by Michael Chabon, Malcolm Gladwell, Mary Gordon, John Updike, and others.

ISBN-10: 0-618-58644-X / ISBN-13: 978-0-618-58644-8 $28.00 CL
ISBN-10: 0-618-58645-8 / ISBN-13: 978-0-618-58645-5 $14.00 PA

THE BEST AMERICAN GOLD GIFT BOX 2006. Boxed in rich gold metallic, this set includes *The Best American Short Stories 2006*, *The Best American Mystery Stories 2006*, and *The Best American Sports Writing 2006*.

ISBN-10: 0-618-80126-X / ISBN-13: 978-0-618-80126-8 $40.00 PA

THE BEST AMERICAN SILVER GIFT BOX 2006. Packaged in a lavish silver metallic box, this set features *The Best American Short Stories 2006*, *The Best American Travel Writing 2006*, and *The Best American Spiritual Writing 2006*.

ISBN-10: 0-618-80127-8 / ISBN-13: 978-0-618-80127-5 $40.00 PA

 HOUGHTON MIFFLIN COMPANY www.houghtonmifflinbooks.com